RUSSIA'S RESPONSE TO SANCTIONS

In the first in-depth analysis of the effects of sanctions on the Russian political economy, Richard Connolly details the Western sanctions targeting the energy, defense and financial sectors and the Russian response. He explores how Western sanctions have caused Russian officials to formulate rapid policy responses to enable the country to adapt to its new circumstances. The sanctions and the Russian response have caused the state's role in the Russian economy to grow stronger and led its policymakers to accelerate efforts to shift Russia's foreign economic relations away from the West and toward Asia. Connolly analyzes how the political economy in Russia and the nature of the country's integration with the global economy have been fundamentally reshaped. He demonstrates that a new system of political economy is emerging in Russia and how it is crucial to understanding Russia's future trajectory.

Richard Connolly is director of the Centre for Russian, European and Eurasian Studies (CREES) at the University of Birmingham. His research and teaching are principally concerned with the political economy of Russia.

Russia's Response to Sanctions

*How Western Economic Statecraft is Reshaping
Political Economy in Russia*

RICHARD CONNOLLY

University of Birmingham

CAMBRIDGE
UNIVERSITY PRESS

CAMBRIDGE
UNIVERSITY PRESS

University Printing House, Cambridge CB2 8BS, United Kingdom

One Liberty Plaza, 20th Floor, New York, NY 10006, USA

477 Williamstown Road, Port Melbourne, VIC 3207, Australia

314-321, 3rd Floor, Plot 3, Splendor Forum, Jasola District Centre, New Delhi - 110025, India

79 Anson Road, #06-04/06, Singapore 079906

Cambridge University Press is part of the University of Cambridge.

It furthers the University's mission by disseminating knowledge in the pursuit of
education, learning and research at the highest international levels of excellence.

www.cambridge.org
Information on this title: www.cambridge.org/9781108400114
DOI: 10.1017/9781108227346

First published 2018
First paperback edition 2019

A catalogue record for this publication is available from the British Library

Library of Congress Cataloging in Publication data
Names: Connolly, Richard, 1979- author.
Title: Russia's response to sanctions : how Western economic statecraft is reshaping political
economy in Russia / Richard Connolly, University of Birmingham.
Description: Cambridge, United Kingdom; New York, NY: Cambridge University
Press, 2018. | Includes index.
Identifiers: LCCN 2018009856 | ISBN 9781108415026 (hardback) | ISBN 9781108400114 (pbk.)
Subjects: LCSH: Economic sanctions–Russia (Federation) |
Russia (Federation)–Economic policy. | Russia (Federation)–Economic conditions. |
Russia (Federation)–Foreign economic relations.
Classification: LCC HF1558.2 .C66 2018 | DDC 330.947–dc23
LC record available at https://lccn.loc.gov/2018009856

ISBN 978-1-108-41502-6 Hardback
ISBN 978-1-108-40011-4 Paperback

For Lucy, Freya and George

Contents

Figures

Tables

Acknowledgments

I would like to thank the large number of people who have helped me write this book – and to absolve them of responsibility for its shortcomings.

First, I would like to thank Mike Bradshaw, who first put the idea of studying the impact of sanctions on the Russian economy to me in the summer of 2014. Together, we applied for funding to support what would have been a detailed examination of how sanctions affected the oil industry. Our proposal was unsuccessful, but the idea to carry out an in-depth study of the impact of sanctions remained with me and provided the germ of the idea that eventually became this book.

I would also like to thank my colleagues at the Centre for Russian, European and Eurasian Studies (CREES), and in particular the extended CREES community that meets annually at the CREES conference in Windsor Great Park, for discussions that have helped form some of the ideas presented in this book. I am especially grateful to Derek Averre and Kasia Wolczuk, who in 2015 invited me to contribute to a special issue of *Europe–Asia Studies* that examined the conflict in Ukraine. The work undertaken in writing my contribution to this collection of essays helped develop my thinking on how sanctions were affecting Russia. I am also grateful to the University of Birmingham for granting me study leave which enabled me to make progress with drafting.

Soon after sanctions were put in place, I was appointed Associate Fellow on the Russia and Eurasia Programme at Chatham House. This afforded me the opportunity to share conversations with a great deal of scholars, policymakers, and other people with an interest in Russia. I am grateful to James Nixey, the head of the programme, and to L'ubica Pollakova, its manager, for involving me in the work that takes place on the program. Papers that I authored or coauthored (with Philip Hanson) on topics related to sanctions over the course of 2015 and 2016 were especially helpful in sharpening ideas that are contained within this book. Thanks are also due to Andrew Monaghan, now at Oxford, who was a constant source of succor and light relief before, during, and after the book was written. As editor of the Russia Studies series for the NATO Defence College, he has also supported my work on Russia's attempts to build a more secure economy.

Since 2014, I have also been fortunate to make more than a dozen trips to Russia due to my position as Visiting Professor of Public Policy at the Russian Academy for the National Economy in Moscow. I would like to thank all those involved, including Robin Lewis and Vladimir Mau, for making this possible.

While researching this book, I was also privileged to be involved in a crossnational project coordinated by Tor Bukkwold of the Norwegian Defence Research Establishment (FFI), entitled "Russia's Defence Industry as a Driver of Economic Modernization." This enabled me to learn from a number of subject matter experts from across Europe, including: Tor, Cecilie Stenstad, and Una Hakvåg at FFI; Susan Oxenstierna and Tomas Malmlöf at the Swedish Defence Research Agency (FOI); Stuart Young from Cranfield University; and Ruslan Pukhov, Konstantin Makienko, and Maxim Shapovalenko from the Centre for the Analysis of Strategic Technologies (CAST) in Moscow. I am especially grateful to Maxim, who provided invaluable information as well as his time and an apple from his garden. Working alongside these people helped dramatically improve my understanding of the Russian defense industry, which in turn made the writing of Chapter 5 so much easier. For this, I am extremely grateful.

I have also benefited from conversations and correspondence with Sir Rodric Braithwaite, Rhod McKenzie, Carolina Vendil Pallin, Elizabeth Teague, Kyle Wilson, and Stephen Wegren.

Several people read one or more draft chapters. Their informed comments helped me avoid making more errors than would otherwise have been the case and enabled me to make a clearer and more informed argument. Nazrin Mehdiyeva gave insightful feedback on an earlier draft of the energy chapter, while Stephen Fortescue helped with comments on several chapters, as well as with interesting articles on Australian flora and fauna that, while having nothing at all to do with sanctions, provided a welcome diversion from writing.

Three people in particular deserve special thanks, both for their help in writing this book and for their intellectual support and friendship over the past decade: Julian Cooper, Philip Hanson, and Silvana Malle. I feel extremely privileged to have benefited from discussions with all three over many years, as well as from their comments on draft chapters of the book. They have served as a source of inspiration and invaluable support throughout my academic career. I hope that this book goes some way to meeting the high standards set by all three over their careers.

Naturally, all remaining errors – whether of fact or interpretation – remain mine alone.

Last, but by no means least, thanks – and apologies – are due to my wife, Lucy, and my two children, Freya and George, for putting up with a husband and father who was often absent during the final months of the book being written.

Introduction

Russia is isolated with its economy in tatters.
Barack Obama (*Moscow Times* 2015)

After Russia's annexation of Crimea in March 2014 and its subsequent involvement in the conflict in eastern Ukraine, economic sanctions became the primary – though by no means the only – instrument of statecraft used by the West to exert pressure on Russia to modify its foreign policy. Initially, sanctions were aimed at selected individuals in and around the Russian foreign policy elite. But as the conflict in eastern Ukraine intensified over the summer of 2014, the scope of sanctions was extended to encompass three of the most important sectors in the Russian economy. While some observers may have questioned whether sanctions represented a sufficiently robust response to Russia's actions, it was clear that their imposition was no trivial matter. This was the first time in the post-Cold War era that such wide-ranging sanctions had been imposed on a country as large and strategically important as Russia. As a permanent member of the United Nations Security Council, and possessing among the largest and most potentially destructive armed forces in the world, Russia carried more political and military importance than any other country that had been subjected to sanctions regimes in the post-Cold War period. In economic terms, it was also much more important than the likes of Iran, Iraq, or Yugoslavia. Measured by purchasing power parity (PPP), in 2014 its economy was the sixth largest in the world. It was also the world's largest exporter of hydrocarbons and second-largest exporter of armaments.

That Russia found itself under sanctions came as a great source of disappointment to those in that country and the rest of the world who had hoped that it would continue on its journey toward becoming a dynamic

1

and globally integrated economic power. After all, its transformation after the disintegration of the Soviet Union was certainly impressive, even if not quite as complete as some might have hoped. Thirty years before sanctions were imposed, Russia, as part of the larger Soviet Union, was part of a centrally planned economic system that was only weakly integrated with the nonsocialist part of the global economy. Three decades on, however, things were much different. Economic reform in the 1990s put the foundations of a market economy in place. Economic activity in Russia was no longer directed and coordinated by the state, but was instead based on the decentralized decisions of millions of independent enterprises and households.

Russia had also become a much more closely integrated member of the global economy. In 2012, it joined the World Trade Organization (WTO). Large multinational companies (MNCs) were active in Russia, investing in a wide range of sectors of the economy. Indeed, in 2013 a United Nations report ranked Russia as the third most attractive country in the world for foreign investment, behind only the United States and China. The weight of Russian firms was felt abroad, too. Russia's large energy and mining companies had a presence across the world, and Russian banks and nonfinancial enterprises borrowed huge sums on global capital markets. To be sure, progress was uneven. For many observers, the state retained an excessively strong presence in the domestic economy, while property rights and the wider institutional environment were considered to be too weak to support sustained growth and modernization. And Russia remained overly dependent on the production and export of natural resources. Nevertheless, it is fair to say that Russia in 2014 was a freer and more open economy than at any other time in its modern history.

The events of 2014 threatened to reverse this trajectory. Western powers' use of economic instruments of statecraft was in many ways predictable. Outright military confrontation was always likely to be eschewed, given Russia's considerable military power. This reduced policymakers' options. Perhaps most importantly, both the United States and the EU had developed an established track record of using sanctions to achieve foreign policy objectives. The post-Cold War period saw an exponential increase in the use of sanctions, signaling both an evolution in the nature of modern interstate conflict and a preference for using their economic strength as an instrument of statecraft. Russia's reintegration with the global economy meant that it was more vulnerable to the imposition of economic sanctions than ever before. Its energy companies tapped the global economy for technology and capital; its defense industry imported components from

Western sources; and its banks relied heavily on foreign capital. Exposure and vulnerability were the flipside of a freer and more globalized economy.

Sanctions appeared to exert an almost immediate effect. In the winter of 2014–2015, a sense of panic swept over Russia. Serendipitously – for Western policymakers, at least – the price of oil, Russia's primary source of export revenue, plunged. This caused a sharp depreciation of the currency and a surge in inflation. Interest rates rose, along with the budget deficit, and official foreign currency reserves dwindled. It was at this point that US President Barack Obama declared that Russia's economy lay "in tatters" (*Moscow Times* 2015). He was not the only one to hold this opinion. British Prime Minister David Cameron stated that sanctions were the reason for Russia's poor economic performance (Wintour 2014). For those hoping that inflicting economic pain on Russia might yield political results, these reports of economic distress in early 2015 made for satisfying reading.

This, however, proved to be the low point for the Russian economy. Although a protracted recession gripped Russia over 2015–2016, most indicators signaled a slow return to normality. The ruble stabilized, the rate of inflation declined, and Russia's foreign currency reserves began to rise again. By 2017, the World Bank had been persuaded that the effects of sanctions had "worn off." Perhaps more importantly, those sectors of the economy targeted by sanctions – energy, defense, and finance – were functioning in a relatively normal fashion. Russia posted post-Soviet record-high oil production figures. The defense industry simultaneously provided large quantities of weaponry to the domestic armed forces as part of a military modernization program while maintaining its position as the world's second-largest arms exporter. And the financial sector continued to supply capital to Russian borrowers. Evidently, these sectors were not in tatters; instead, they appeared to have adapted to the new environment. It is this process of adaptation that is the subject of this book.

PURPOSES OF THE BOOK

This book is intended to answer three primary research questions. First, what impact did Western sanctions have on political economy in Russia in the three-year period after they were put in place? My thesis is that while sanctions caused some initial disruption, the impact on targeted sectors quickly subsided. Second, what was the Russian authorities' strategic response to sanctions, and how did this mediate their impact? My thesis here is that the Russian authorities were able to utilize a range of tools and resources – many of which were readily available due to the specific characteristics of Russia's system of political economy – to cushion the targeted sectors from the worst effects of sanctions. Third, in what way did sanctions and the Russian strategic response to sanctions reshape both the structure of Russia's domestic political economy and its place in the wider global economy? My thesis is that sanctions and the Russian response resulted in a clear shift toward greater reliance on domestic resources – or Russification – on the one hand, and toward a more pluridirectional foreign economic policy that emphasizes closer relations with non-Western countries on the other. This process is, at the time of writing, far from complete. Obstacles to developing alternative trading partners and sources of external capital were encountered between 2014 and 2017, and new ones will no doubt emerge in the future. But the direction of travel is clear.

The book is intended to make a contribution to two strands of scholarship. First and foremost, this book is intended to support a more precise understanding of how sanctions affected political economy in Russia after 2014. In this respect, the book is intended to appeal to those with an academic or practical interest both in contemporary Russian political economy and in Russia's place in the world. The book is intended to serve as the first in-depth, monograph-length study of how sanctions affected Russia. The focus is not on whether the objectives of the sender states were achieved, but instead on how much economic pain was inflicted on Russia and how policymakers adjusted to this threat. This is important from both a scholarly and a practical point of view. In terms of scholarship, there exist very few attempts at conceptualizing the modern Russian economy, let alone at using this conceptualization as a starting point for understanding the impact of sanctions. It is hoped that this book will go some way toward filling this gap. From a practical point of view, I hope that the book will help those with an interest in understanding Russia to do so with the aid of a balanced and evidence-based account of the nature of the contemporary Russian political economy. Policymakers and other public figures prone to making hyperbolic statements about the state of the Russian economy today, and then using those statements as a basis for formulating policy and attitudes toward the country, often appear to do so without the aid of even a rudimentary understanding of Russia and its economy. It is my hope that this book will at least offer an alternative to much of the ignorance that characterizes the public understanding of Russia at the time of writing.

The book is also intended to make a contribution to the wider field of political science and international relations that is concerned with understanding the impact of sanctions on targeted countries. As I show in Chapter 1, a large proportion of the literature that is devoted to examining the phenomenon of sanctions does so without much in the way of book-length analysis of the impact on and responses of target countries. This, I argue, is unfortunate, not least because it is difficult to take seriously the conclusions of studies that are invariably based on only superficial analyses of how target countries are affected by sanctions. Again, this weakness in the existing literature is of both intellectual and practical importance. Intellectually, some of the excellent work in the development of academic theory ought to be supported by robust empirical analysis. In this respect, there is clearly an important role to be played by language-based Area Studies scholars in providing theoretically informed analyses of how sanctions have affected countries from across the world. This need not and ought not to be the preserve of large-N, quantitative studies, or comparative works based on short case studies. In practical terms, understanding the dynamics of sanctions in target countries is as important as ever due to the increasing frequency with which sanctions have been employed over the past three decades. While sanctions have always been a tool of statecraft used by countries, the end of the Cold War coincided with a growing number of countries, led by the United States and the EU, using sanctions in the pursuit of their policy objectives. This led one prominent scholar in the field of sanctions to describe the post-Cold War period as the "golden era of economic statecraft" (Drezner 2015, p. 755). For some observers, this era is not nearly golden enough: A recent study by Robert Blackwill and Jennifer Harris (2016) argued that sanctions and other instruments of economic statecraft were not used enough, and that the United States should consider how to use sanctions more frequently and effectively in the future. As a result, understanding the dynamics of how sanctions affect targeted countries is more important than ever.

THE STRUCTURE OF THE BOOK

The principal purpose of the book is to examine how sanctions affected the political economy of Russia. In order to do this in as rigorous and systematic a fashion as possible, the book is organized as follows. In Chapter 1, the existing scholarship concerned with the study of sanctions is briefly surveyed. It is argued that there is a relative paucity of literature dealing with the impact of sanctions on the domestic political economy of target countries. A straightforward framework for analyzing how sanctions might affect a target country's political economy is outlined. In Chapter 2, the nature of Russia's system of political economy in its form at the outset of sanctions in 2014 is presented. Here, I argue that the Russian state has played an important role in coordinating the flow of natural resource revenues to other parts of the economy. This system benefited some sectors, but also constrained the development of others. The precise nature of the sanctions imposed by Western countries on Russia is laid out in Chapter 3. This is followed by a broad outline of the Russian strategic response to sanctions, which is presented as comprising three main components: the securitization of economic policy in those areas of the economy targeted by sanctions; the Russification of technology and capital in targeted sectors; and the parallel diversification of Russia's foreign economic relations beyond its traditional partners in the West, especially Europe. Chapters 4–6 focus on each of the three sectors targeted by Western sanctions: energy, defense-industrial production, and finance. In each chapter, I show the trajectory of development in each sector prior to the imposition of sanctions. This is followed by an analysis of what sanctions were put in place, how the Russian authorities responded to them, and what influence these sanctions exerted over the functioning and performance of each respective sector. In each case, I show how the three-pronged strategic response of securitization, Russification, and foreign economic diversification played out after 2014. The different threads of the argument are brought together in the conclusion, where I consider what we can learn from the Russian experience with sanctions after 2014, and what it might mean for the country's future political and economic development.

WHAT THE BOOK DOES NOT ADDRESS

It is important to be clear as to what this book is *not* about. First, the focus of the book is on how the response of the Russian state mediated the impact of sectoral sanctions in the three sectors directly targeted by Western sanctions. The decision to focus on sectoral sanctions was taken because, from a methodological perspective, it is more feasible to examine developments within key sectors of the Russian economy, where data and reports are readily available, than it is to examine how asset freezes or travel bans have affected the decision-making of individual elite political actors. In the latter case, data availability and access to key targeted individuals represents an obvious obstacle to any meaningful examination of the impact of how sanctions might have affected individuals in target countries. Neither is the book intended to deliver a quantitative estimate – such as "lost" GDP or tax revenues – of the dollar or ruble impact of sanctions. Quite apart from the numerous methodological difficulties in arriving at such an estimate, especially in the context of the sharp decline in oil prices that took place at around the same time the sanctions were put in place, a quantitative estimate of "losses" tells us nothing about the nature of the policy response or the qualitative changes that take place when a country responds to sanctions.

Second, because this book is intended to show how specific systems of political economy in target countries can adjust to sanctions to reduce their intended impact, Russia's so-called countersanctions in the agricultural sector are not considered either. This is because, in the case of counter-sanctions, Russia was acting as the "sender" country rather than as the "target." As a result, the dynamics of adjustment do not apply in precisely the same way. Thus, to maintain a consistent and coherent approach to the subject matter, the analysis is limited to Russian efforts taken in response to Western sanctions, even though many of the same concerns and motivations that were evident in Russia's response in the financial, defense-industrial and energy sectors – such as concerns for economic security and sovereignty, a commitment to import substitution, and preference for greater diversity in foreign economic relations – were also evident in Russia's own countersanctions regime (Wegren, Nilssen, and Elvestad 2016; Wegren, Nikulin, and Trotsuk, 2017). And because the focus of the book is on the target country, I do not seek to estimate the quantitative economic cost – in the form of foregone trade or investment, for example – to sender countries.

Third, because I am principally concerned with assessing how sanctions affected the dynamics of Russia's system of political economy, I do not seek to analyze whether sanctions achieved the other objectives that sender countries may have had when they were put in place. As such, whether sanctions sent a strong enough "signal" to domestic audiences of the United States or EU, or what the impact of sanctions was on third countries in "signaling" the intent of the United States and EU to uphold the "rules-based international order," are beyond the scope of the analysis. Nor do I seek to make any claims about the efficacy of Western sanctions. As I argue in subsequent chapters, the imposition of a significant economic and political cost on the target country is a necessary, although not sufficient, condition for sanctions to "work," in so far as they were designed to bring about a modification of Russia's foreign policy. As such, any cost assessment of efficacy must be preceded by an assessment of impact. Given the above, it may come as no surprise that I do not seek to deliver a verdict on the normative desirability of sanctions, either. Whether the West was "right" or "wrong" in imposing sanctions is analytically distinct from understanding the dynamics of sanctions within the target country. This book is concerned only with the latter.

1

Sanctions and Political Economy

INTRODUCTION

Before examining how Western sanctions affected political economy in Russia after 2014, it is first necessary to consider the different scholarly approaches to analyzing sanctions. A significant body of scholarship is devoted to understanding what motivates countries to impose sanctions in the first place and whether and under what conditions sanctions succeed in achieving the objectives of those countries that impose them, as well as to assessing how sanctions affect political economy in those countries that are targeted by sanctions. In this chapter, I summarize some of the key findings from the extant literature on sanctions, identify several gaps in the scholarship, and develop a framework for analyzing how sanctions affected political economy in Russia after the imposition of sanctions in 2014.

UNDERSTANDING SANCTIONS

There exists a wide body of academic literature concerned with assessing the motives underpinning the use of sanctions, how sanctions might be expected to impact the target country, and whether sanctions are an effective foreign policy instrument for sender countries. Before outlining the main findings of the scholarship concerned with assessing the impact and effectiveness of sanctions, it is worth briefly noting that in the terminology of the sanctions literature a country imposing sanctions is described as a "sender," while a country that is the object of sanctions is described as a "target." In this book, the term "sender" refers to a wide range of countries, led by the United States and the countries of the European

Union (EU). For much of the book, the shorthand term "the West" is used to described these sender countries, even though "the West" includes countries such as Japan, Australia, and New Zealand. Clearly this is an unsatisfactory term. However, the alternatives are no better. "The Euro-Atlantic alliance," for instance, is also inappropriate in the context of sanctions, given that several countries that imposed sanctions are neither European nor situated anywhere near the Atlantic Ocean. Thus, despite its obvious deficiencies, the shorthand label "West" is often assigned to the US- and EU-led political alliance of countries that imposed sanctions on Russia in the aftermath of its annexation of Crimea in March 2014.

Before examining the main findings from the literature dealing with sanctions, it is worth emphasizing the distinction between the impact of sanctions and their effectiveness. "The impact of sanctions" refers to the observable changes in the political and economic landscape of the target country caused by sanctions. This might include a shortage of goods, a scarcity of capital, or a decline in gross domestic product (GDP). Impact might also encompass a redistribution of political power within the target country that may be a direct result of sanctions. "Effectiveness," on the other hand, refers to whether sanctions perform the functions they are intended to perform by the sender(s). This may include sending a signal to either the sender's domestic audience or the government or population of the target. Where ambitions are higher, sanctions may be considered to be effective if they play a significant role in modifying the domestic or foreign policy of the target state.

It is important to emphasize that it does not necessarily follow that impact leads to effectiveness. A target country that suffers a reduction in the availability of goods or capital, or which experiences a reduction in GDP as a direct result of sanctions, may be said to have been impacted by sanctions. But the target government may not be prompted to modify the policy that caused sanctions to be imposed in the first place. The sources of effectiveness vary across cases. For instance, there may be an asymmetry in the importance attached to the policy issue that is causing conflict between sender and target. If the issue is of central or indeed existential importance to the target country but is only of marginal importance to the sender, sanctions may prove ineffective even if they exert an observable impact. It is probably fair to state that impact is a necessary but by no means sufficient condition for sanctions to be effective. Conversely, it is much less likely that sanctions might be effective without generating an impact.

The Motivations Underlying Sanctions

A useful way to consider the multiple motives or objectives underpinning the use of sanctions is to start by considering two of the numerous definitions of sanctions that are available. David Baldwin, one of the foremost scholars of the sanctions literature, includes sanctions within the realm of economic statecraft (Baldwin 1985). Statecraft, according to Baldwin, refers to "the instruments used by policy makers in their attempts to exercise power, i.e. to get others to do what they would not otherwise do" (ibid, p. 9). Economic statecraft, he argues, "refers to influence attempts relying primarily on resources which have a reasonable semblance of a market price in terms of money" (ibid, p. 13). This includes a range of measures, including asset freezes, trade embargoes, financial restrictions, and other economic sanctions. By this definition, sanctions are essentially economic instruments used by senders to help influence targets.[1]

Elsewhere, Risa Brooks provides a broader definition (Brooks 2002). According to this author, "sanctions involve the imposition of punitive measures on a target state, measures which seek to limit the state's access to resources or cultural and social engagement, and limit movements of its nationals in order to elicit a change in the target's policies" that is consistent with the preferences of the sender (ibid, p. 6). The definition is broader because it includes limiting the target's access to cultural and social engagement. As such, banning a target's athletes from a sporting event or preventing its scholars from attending conferences are classified as sanctions. Bans on individuals from target states entering sender countries are also included.

According to these two definitions, the instruments of sanctions or economic statecraft can vary. Sanctions may be focused on preventing the flow of goods, services, or capital, or they may include prohibitions on travel. But they share in common a clear objective: to induce the leaders of a target state to change their policies. In this respect, sanctions are political acts that utilize economic instruments to either effect a change in the domestic or foreign policy of the target state, or undermine and weaken the authority and effectiveness of its government. Thus, the use of sanctions is based "on the assumption that there exists either a direct or an indirect relationship between economic activity and political behavior, and

---

[1] Targets usually include states or organizations and individuals located within states. They may, however, also include nonstate actors.

that the authority and behavior of a regime rests partly on economic foundations" (Economides and Wilson 2001, p. 142). This means that sanctions – using the expanded range of instruments proposed by Brooks – are essentially "a non-military form of coercion in which economic measures are employed to achieve political ends by inflicting hardship" (ibid).

Defining sanctions in this way seems straightforward. Economic instruments are used by states to impose economic pain on target states to achieve political objectives. The problem, however, is that sanctions are often imposed without there being any serious expectation on the part of the sender state that the target state will modify its behavior (Jones and Portela 2014). Instead, several other objectives may motivate a sender state when choosing to impose sanctions.

James Barber identified three sets of objectives that motivate sender countries to impose sanctions (Barber 1979). The first set – or the *primary* objectives – broadly approximates the straightforward definition of sanctions outlined above. This means the primary objectives are usually reasonably well defined and include the goal of either inducing a change in the behavior of the target country, either in relation to its domestic or its foreign policy, or of destabilizing or removing a foreign government. There are numerous examples of these types of primary objective being cited by sender countries. For instance, sanctions imposed on South Africa in order to coerce the government into abandoning its policy of apartheid were a clear example of senders seeking to shape the domestic policy of a target state. Sanctions imposed on Iraq immediately after the invasion of Kuwait in 1990 are an example of an effort on the part of sender states to modify the foreign policy of a target state. According to one study, the use of sanctions to promote the destabilization or removal of a foreign government (i.e. regime change) rose from around one-quarter of cases during the Cold War to one-half in the 1990s (Hufbauer, Schott, et al. 2007, p. 131). These primary objectives usually provide the benchmark against which most analysts might assess the effectiveness of sanctions. Primary objectives, according to Barber, also tend to serve as sanctions' "official," publicly stated objectives. However, he argues that *secondary* and *tertiary* objectives are often more important to policymakers in sender countries.

Secondary objectives are often focused not on the target state but instead on domestic constituencies within the sender state(s) (e.g. Barber 1979, p. 379; Drezner 1999; Davidson and Shambaugh 2000; Askari et al. 2003). This may take on a positive form: For instance, states "concerned with the status, reputation and position of the government imposing" sanctions may be prompted to demonstrate "a willingness and capacity to act" (Barber 1979, pp. 379–380). Here, sanctions send a clear signal to the sender's domestic audience that the government is effective and seeking to shape the international environment. However, similar motives may take a more negative form, such as when sanctions are imposed simply to show the domestic audience that the government is not weak, ineffective, or incapable of action. In short, it may wish to be seen to be "at least doing something" (Galtung 1967, p. 411). As Lloyd George, cited by Barber, is said to have remarked of sanctions against Italy in 1936: "They came too late to save Abyssinia, but they are just in the nick of time to save the [British] Government" (Barber 1979, p. 380). Sanctions can also give influence to elements of the government that might not otherwise be able to influence foreign policy in such a meaningful fashion. For instance, the ability of the US Congress to shape sanctions policy today is much greater than its ability to shape other aspects of US foreign policy.

Whether motivated by positive or negative concerns, it is often the case that secondary objectives serve a primarily symbolic or expressive function that is targeted at domestic constituencies. This can be very important. In expressing dissatisfaction with the perceived (by the sender) immorality of the target state's behavior, the sender government may be articulating the views of its population in a forthright fashion that may, while not causing a change in the target's behavior, at least elicit satisfaction in a domestic constituency (e.g. business lobby, activist group, etc.). In politics, this can prove to be a very important achievement.

Tertiary objectives, according to Barber, are "those concerned with the structure and behavior of the international system generally, or those parts of it which affect the imposing states" (ibid, p. 382). Thus, sanctions can be used as a tool to uphold international norms – as defined either by international law or by the sender states – by deterring those who might be tempted to break them in the future. By punishing a state for one such transgression, sender states may wish to deter other states from carrying out similar actions in the future. Of course, as pointed out by Barber, the form of the international structure that is being defended will depend on the way in which international relations are perceived (ibid). As a result, sanctions may be just as likely imposed to uphold international law as they are to maintain, say, a regional balance of power. The use of sanctions to reinforce international norms has been cited as an important tool in both US and EU foreign policy (Biersteker and van Bergeijk 2015).

From a methodological point of view, discerning the relative importance of all three sets of objectives is analytically challenging. After all, how is the analyst to gauge from official statements whether the primary objectives are not taken seriously by the imposing government, or whether the secondary or tertiary objectives are not in fact the most important object-ive? This is not a trivial issue. Accurately assessing the effectiveness of sanctions requires the articulation of clearly defined objectives. Without knowing which objectives were really important in the minds of sender politicians, it is impossible to measure whether sanctions were successful or not. Moral questions might also arise (e.g. Jones and Portela 2014). If, for instance, sanctions were to inflict a significant and negative impact on, say, infant mortality in a target country, and if sender politicians did not seriously expect their primary objectives to be achieved, would it be morally acceptable to persist with a course of action that raised infant mortality in the target country simply to show that "something is being done?"[2]

Assessing the Effectiveness of Sanctions

The multiplicity of objectives outlined above raises problems when assess-ing the effectiveness of sanctions. After all, sender countries may use sanctions "to demonstrate resolve at home and abroad, to express outrage, to punish, to deter future wrongdoers, and to change current policies in the target country" (Hufbauer et al. 2007, p. 157). Very often, sender countries pursue more than one objective simultaneously. Or the relative importance of objectives may change over time. These problems complicate efforts to assess *whether* sanctions are effective and *when* (i.e. under what condi-tions) they are effective. However, these complications have not stopped people from trying.

There are practical as well as academic reasons for taking seriously the measurement of sanctions' effectiveness. Sanctions were increasingly used by the United States, the EU, and Russia after the Cold War to achieve their foreign and domestic policy objectives (e.g. Drezner 1999; Hufbauer et al. 2007; Portela 2010; Biersteker and van Bergeijk 2016; Jones 2016). As a result, policymakers developed an obvious interest in

---

[2] This, of course, is not a purely hypothetical question. In May 1996, Madeleine Albright, the then US ambassador to the UN, was asked during a television interview whether US-led economic sanctions against Iraq, which had been estimated by some – probably unreliable – sources to have caused the deaths of half a million Iraqi children, were worth the price that had been paid. Albright responded by saying: "I think that is a very hard choice, but the price, we think, the price is worth it."

perfecting the sanctions tool by learning about whether and under what conditions sanctions are successful.

In what is perhaps the most well-known large-N quantitative analysis of the effectiveness of sanctions, Gary Hufbauer, Jeffrey Schott, Kimberly Elliott and Barbara Oegg (1985, 2007) periodically documented the effectiveness of sanctions after 1915. In the first edition, the authors argued that sanctions succeeded in what Baldwin would describe as "influence attempts" – i.e. in compelling a foreign state to change their domestic or foreign policies – in around one-third of cases (Hufbauer, Schott, and Elliot 1985). This figure remained stable in both the second and third editions (Hufbauer, Schott, and Elliot 1990; Hufbauer et al. 2007). For these authors, "the bald statement that 'sanctions never work' is demonstrably wrong" (Hufbauer et al. 2007, p. 159). Moreover, they were able to identify factors that helped explain when sanctions were more likely to be effective, stating that "senders should not expect that sanctions will work as well against very large targets that are strong, stable, hostile, and autocratic" (ibid, p. 167).

However, their confidence in their results was not always shared by others. Criticism of the methods used in the construction of their dataset, as well as a more general distrust of the use of quantitative methods to study the nuances of a complex phenomenon, led to their results being challenged (e.g. Drury 1998; Drezner 1999). Perhaps the best-known criticism of their findings came from Robert Pape, who, in a series of articles from 1997 onward, criticized their interpretation of the role sanctions played in contributing toward sender countries achieving their foreign policy objectives (Pape 1997; Baldwin and Pape 1998; Pape 1998). Pape showed that in many cases the outcomes sought by sender countries were determined not by sanctions, but instead by other means, such as the use of military force. Thus, he criticized the use of Germany's defeat in World War I as an example of the successful use of economic sanctions. Likewise, he argued that the role of sanctions in the UK reconquest of the Falkland Islands in 1982 was only of minor significance when compared with the use of military force. Pape suggested that by imposing a more stringent standard on what constituted the effective use of sanctions, the real success rate of sanctions would be closer to 5 percent. For some, expecting sanctions alone to achieve a sender state's foreign policy objectives is an excessively demanding position to take (Weiss and Nephew 2016). After all, if sanctions play even a minor role in achieving the foreign policy objectives of a sender state, then they should be considered to have been effective.

Similar attempts at quantifying the effectiveness of sanctions emerged in the process of scholars assessing *when* sanctions work (e.g. Blanchard and Ripsman 1999; Drezner 1999; van Bergeijk 2009; Biersteker and van Bergeijk 2016). Biersteker and van Bergeijk (2016) were able to summarize the findings from both their own research and the wider extant literature – including the database generated by Hufbauer et al. in the course of their research – to identify factors that help explain when sanctions are more likely to work. In doing so, they formulate "seven conditions for sanctions success" (ibid, pp. 19–27). They suggest that: (1) "pre-sanctions trade volumes need to be important for economic sanctions to bite"; (2) "sanctions tend to succeed most in the initial years of implementation"; (3) "expectations, credibility and strategic interaction play a major role (in explaining when sanctions work)"; (4) "sanctions are more likely to succeed if the target is more democratic (less authoritarian)"; (5) "strong multilateral political commitment makes sanctions more effective"; (6) "narrowly defined goals and multiple policy instruments increase success rate of sanctions"; and finally, (7) "'targeted' sanctions can be as effective as comprehensive sanctions."

Clearly these findings are more nuanced than a simple success/nonsuccess rate indicator. Nevertheless, the formulation of these stylized facts is not sufficient to declare the debate over the effectiveness of sanctions resolved. This is for two primary reasons (Taylor 2010, p. 24). First, the analyst's choice of what objectives need to be met in order for sanctions to be declared a success (e.g. foreign policy objectives, domestic policy objectives, or signaling to the international community), and over whether sanctions' contributions toward achieving these objectives are expected to reach a maximum (i.e. sanctions alone should explain success) or minimum (i.e. sanctions need only make a minor contribution to achieving objectives) threshold, exert a strong influence over what type of conclusions will be generated. Second, most of the focus in the existing literature tends to be on cases in which the United States and European states have used or initiated sanctions. This is understandable, given recent history. However, there are other instances of non-Western states using sanctions in the pursuit of political objectives, including Russia, which employed sanctions on many occasions in the post-Cold War era, especially as a tool to influence its ex-Soviet neighbors (Drezner 1999; Sherr 2013). Widening the sample base beyond those instances of sanctions initiated and used by Western powers, as well as examining these lesser-known cases in greater detail, would surely strengthen the claims made by scholars seeking to measure the efficacy of sanctions.

Assessing the Impact of Sanctions

There are, though, serious problems with studying sanctions purely from the point of view of their effectiveness in achieving the objectives set out by the sender countries. An excessive focus on outcomes neglects the arguably more important question of process – i.e. by examining *whether* or *when* sanctions work, a large body of scholarship either ignores or gives only superficial treatment to *how* sanctions work. As argued by Lee Jones:

> despite extensive sanctions scholarship, the question of how we get from the imposition of economic sanctions to a potential change in policy has been left virtually unexplored. The overwhelming focus on *whether* sanctions work has marginalized the analytically prior question of *how* they are supposed to work, and what they actually do in practice.
>
> (Jones 2016, p. 6)

By seeking to explain how often and under what circumstances sanctions *might work*, while only later thinking about *how sanctions worked*, research on sanctions had evolved in "reverse order" (Portela 2010). This imbalance in scholarly attention is likely to be caused by the fact that "the sanctions subfield has evolved in extraordinarily close connection to policy debates which are typically polarized between advocates and detractors of sanctions as policy tools" (Jones and Portela 2014, p. 3).

This is not to say that scholars have not grappled at all with the question of how sanctions work. Rather, the problem is that what does exist tends to be excessively simplistic and rooted in analytical approaches that tend to neglect "a sense of the domestic dynamics animating state policies, focusing instead on whether or when one can inflict 'costs' sufficient to outweigh the 'benefits' of pursuing an 'objectionable' policy and thereby induce targets to alter their behavior" (Jones 2016, p. 7). Thus, we are usually presented either with large-*N*, statistically driven analyses that reduce the domestic political economy of target states to a few basic quantitative variables (e.g. Hufbauer et al. 2007; Escribà-Folch and Wright 2010; Peksen and Drury 2010; Major 2012), or short case studies, sometimes informed by game theory, that offer only a cursory examination of the political dynamics within target states (e.g. Drezner 1999; Brooks 2002; Taylor 2010). Furthermore, analyses based on in-depth knowledge of target countries are few and far between. Those that do exist tend to be based on English-language secondary sources that belie a superficial understanding of the domestic political economy of the target state under examination. This is unfortunate because while considerable effort is devoted by the scholarly community to generating testable hypotheses concerning sanctions, much less effort is devoted to testing these hypotheses in the sort of rigorous fashion that would lend greater weight to the conclusions formed.[3]

This need not have been the case. One of the earliest studies on sanctions – Johan Galtung's 1967 examination of the impact of sanctions on Rhodesia in the 1960s – placed the domestic political economy at the forefront of his analysis. Galtung, using what he called his "naïve theory of sanctions" as a starting point, suggested that most assessments of the likely efficacy of sanctions were based on an implicit assumption of a direct and linear relationship between economic pain and political compliance. When the economic pain inflicted was low, he suggested, political compliance on the part of the target country would be unlikely. However, Galtung – quite unsurprisingly, given the name he assigned to his baseline theory – suggested that the reality was more complex. In the case of Rhodesia, economic actors adapted to the new environment, while individuals made a psychological adjustment to the new conditions and exploited sanctions to their benefit. Moreover, politicians manipulated sanctions to rally the nation "around the flag," strengthening their political positions and suppressing any possible hope on the part of sender countries that sanctions might favor the domestic political opposition. As a result, he suggested that any effective analysis of the impact of sanctions needed to incorporate an assessment of both the tangible impact of sanctions on economic activity in the target country and the intangible sociopsychological effects of sanctions. Understanding how these two sets of effects interact in each case of sanctions would help further our understanding of *how* sanctions affect the political economy of target countries. Advancing our understanding of this process would be of crucial importance because, he suggested, "the single most important reason (for the failure of sanctions) appears to be the failure of the imposing states to anticipate fully the response to sanctions within the target state" (ibid, p. 376). Thus, understanding how elites in target states might undertake adaptive measures to reduce the tangible economic impact of sanctions, while simultaneously exploiting the intangible sociopsychological impact to their advantage, offered a fruitful avenue for future research.

---

[3] Collaboration between political scientists and Area Studies scholars would seem an obvious solution to this problem. Without the rich contextual knowledge provided by area studies scholars, the scholarship on sanctions will always be limited in its intellectual and practical (i.e. for policymakers) utility.

It is evident, fifty years later, that while some advances were made in understanding how sanctions shape the internal social, political, and economic dynamics within target countries, some important gaps remain. Several broad findings from studies exploring the impact of sanctions on the target country can be discerned.

First, a significant body of research emerged which showed that the impact of sanctions tended to vary according to the type of regime in power in the target country (e.g. Brooks 2002; Allen 2008; Escribà-Folch and Wright 2010; Escribà-Folch 2012; von Soest and Wahman 2015). Differences in the manner in which domestic institutions in the target country mediated the impact of sanctions mean that sanctions can affect elites and social groups in different ways. In their most basic form, Risa Brooks argued that "sanctions that harm the macro economy and thus hurt the 'median voter' [are more likely to] be effective against democratic states," while authoritarian leaders, by contrast, "tend to be insulated from aggregate or macro-economic pressures" and therefore cannot be expected to be as responsive to popular opinion as democracies (Brooks 2002, p. 2). This conclusion was reaffirmed later the same decade when Susan Allen argued that the "domestic political response to sanctions varies greatly by the regime type of the target. As states become more politically open, the domestic public can – and does, to some degree – create political costs for leaders who resist sanctions" (Allen 2008, p. 917).

Second – and building on the observation that the influence of sanctions will vary according to the institutional context of the target state – it has been shown that sanctions can have redistributive consequences in target countries that often serve to strengthen ruling elites rather than weaken them. This is because, as stated by Jonathan Kirshner (1997, p. 42), "states are not unitary economic actors" and, as such, "sanctions affect groups in society differentially." As a result, some groups within the target country may suffer while others thrive (e.g. Rowe 2001; Brooks 2002). According to Brooks, "sanctions act as a protective tariff which bolsters the inefficient domestic competitors of imported goods" and, in some circumstances, "stimulate an Import Substitution Industrialization-style approach in the development of industries to substitute for lost imports" (Brooks 2002, p. 9). Consequently, elites in nondemocracies might be expected to profit from sanctions. Without accountability to the wider public, elites can do this relatively unchecked, as "leaders may actually benefit from sanctions, as domestic publics are unable to impose political costs and the economic constraints of sanctions often allow leaders to extract greater rents while overseeing the trade of scarce goods" (Allen 2008, p. 917). It need not only be elites that benefit, either.

As shown by Galtung (1967), nondemocratic regimes often possess the means to distribute scarce resources not only to allies of the political leadership, in order to strengthen elite cohesion, but also to important socioeconomic constituencies. Initially, this might be done in the hope of "diverting the economic impact away from the politically dominant social groups" (ibid, p. 377). However, over time sanctions can go on to create the conditions for the emergence of powerful socioeconomic constituencies in the target country that have a stake in the perpetuation of sanctions. The role of the state in creating these conditions was discussed by Blanchard and Ripsman (1998, 2008), who focus on how the impact of sanctions is mediated through state–society relations, and particularly on how sanctions affect power relations between the state and important domestic groups. In their view, the autonomy of the target state to "select and implement policies," along with the capacity of the state to "co-opt or coerce key social groups," depends on its ability to mobilize the material, institutional, and ideational resources of state power, something which varies across countries (Blanchard and Ripsman 2008, pp. 378–379).

Third, sanctions can engender a "rally around the flag" effect in target countries, in which sanctions lead to an increase in political cohesion within the target state. The imposition of sanctions enables the leadership in target countries to use the specter of a clear and present external threat as a focal point for a leader to unify the elite and social groups (Coser 1956; Galtung 1967; Downs and Rocke 1994; Smith 1996). As a result, the ruling elite in the target country can shift the blame for any economic hardship endured – whether as a result of sanctions or otherwise – on to the sender state(s) rather than their own political or economic policies. Where successful, target populations might be prompted not to call for a change in policy to satisfy sender countries' demands, but instead to rally against the "enemy" (Galtung 1967; Mueller 1970; Ostrom and Job 1986). However, even this can be an overly simplistic position to take. After all, as pointed out by Lee Jones (2016, p. 9), "entire populations *never* rally 'around the flag'." Therefore, identifying why certain groups act in the way they do in the face of sanctions requires nuanced analysis of the sociopolitical dynamics of the target country.

Fourth, sanctions can affect the relationship between different social forces in target countries in ways that require a more nuanced understanding of the target country than might be yielded by a simple "regime type" or institutionalist approach. In a recent, pathbreaking study, Lee Jones argued that because there is such a diverse range of regime types across the world, many regimes are in fact "hybrids," rendering it almost impossible to detect robust associations between regime types and patterns of sanctions' outcomes (2016, p. 33). Instead, he suggests, it is more fruitful to analyze target countries "in terms of their extant social power relations; that is, in terms of *what they are and how they actually operate,* rather than how well they conform to some idealized benchmark" (ibid, p. 34). In doing this, Jones shifts the analysis away from a focus on formal institutional structures in target countries to the real stuff of politics: the dynamic relationships between social forces. He goes on to argue that "while institutionalism rightly recognizes that domestic institutions mediate the impact of sanctions, it assigns far too much primacy to them in generating political outcomes. The nature and composition of political regimes, their political economy context, and strategies of rule clearly cannot be read off regime type" (ibid).

Instead, Jones formulates an analytical framework that focuses on power relations among key social forces. In doing so, he suggests that an analysis of social forces is important for those concerned with state autonomy and capacity because the ability of states to act in any policy arena is a function of "what local social relations permit" (ibid, p. 36). For Jones, the "real question" confronting analysts interested in how sanctions affect target states "is not how autonomous a state is from society in general ... but which specific forces enjoy access to state power and which do not" (ibid, p. 37). In this, Jones treats the target society as something dynamic, where sanctions can be expected to upset the complex relationships that exist between different social groups, generating "new social conflicts and vulnerabilities" (ibid).

Perhaps most importantly, Jones moves beyond a stale and sometimes facile fixation on whether a target "survives" or modifies the policies that sender states find so objectionable, to instead consider *how* the relationships within the target society might be transformed by sanctions (ibid, p. 9). Rather than characterizing ruling elites as either autonomous or not autonomous, or weak or strong, he suggests that to "capture, retain, and maintain state power, ruling elites must forge coalitions of socio-political forces that extend well beyond their immediate circle." This brings the relationship between elites and social forces into the picture, offering a much more dynamic and useful analysis of the way in which social forces in target countries respond to sanctions. He goes on to elaborate a "social conflict analysis of sanctions" based on the three-step analysis of first identifying the country's leading sociopolitical forces and the strategy they use to maintain state power, then identifying the immediate economic impact of sanctions on the target society, and going on to explore how "the material effects of sanctions condition the socio-political conflicts identified in step one by altering the composition, power, interests, resources, ideologies, and strategies of the coalitions contesting state power, and how this generates political change (or fails to do so)" (ibid, p. 44). Underpinning this approach is a concern for societal actors' *strategic response* to sanctions.

GAPS IN THE EXISTING SCHOLARSHIP

Despite the significant advances made in studying sanctions, several key gaps in the literature remain. These relate to a general failure to: (1) incorporate the institutional environments of target societies beyond simplistic measures of regime type; (2) consider the roles that the economic structure and system of political economy of the target country play in mediating the impact of sanctions; and (3) include an analysis of the nature of the target country's integration with the global economy. All three of these areas, I suggest, are important factors that need to be considered when exploring the impact of sanctions on the political economy of target countries.

First, as in Jones' argument described previously in this chapter, rather than focusing on different formal institutional configurations, especially regime types, it is better to analyze target countries "in terms of their extant social power relations; that is, in terms of *what they are and how they actually operate.*" Jones chose to produce an explanatory framework that focuses on the interaction of social forces within a target society. However, this does not explicitly focus on the nature of the institutional environment, broadly defined by Douglass North as "the rules of the game in a society or, more formally ... the humanly devised constraints that shape human interaction" (North 1990, p. 3). As North earlier argued, "if institutions ... frame human behaviour, it is through organizations that humans undertake myriad forms of social interaction" (North 1981, p. 33).[4] It is through organizations that most choices of a political and economic nature are made. As such, any explanation of political economy

---

[4] There is some ambiguity within institutional literature as to where institutions end and organizations begin. For example, some argue that the state is an institution, while others view it as an organization, albeit the primary organization within a society. Others use the terms interchangeably, seeing the state as both institution and organization.

that focuses on institutional structures must highlight how the institutional structure of a society shapes the kind of organizations that can be created and sustained within it, with certain institutional structures being more or less supportive to the existence of certain organizations (Connolly 2012, p. 43). The nature of these institutional structures will go some way to helping the analyst identify how sanctions might affect the political economy of a target country.

A useful tool for understanding how institutional frameworks shape political economy can be found in the groundbreaking work on social orders by North, Wallis, and Weingast (2009) and North, Wallis, Weingast, and Webb (2012). They articulate the concept of limited-access (LAO) and open-access (OAO) social orders, conceived as representing two broadly defined ends of a social order spectrum. This framework is based on the assumption that a "double-balance" exists between political and economic systems in all societies, and that the intricate relationships between organizations and institutions in both the political and economic spheres of a society are key to understanding social, political, and economic outcomes. They argue that social orders can essentially be distinguished by the nature of competition between organizations and the manner in which rents are created. In open-access systems, open competition ensures that an impersonal, formal rules-based form of contractual organization is prevalent, while in limited-access systems contractual organizations are more informal and arbitrary. Because of the "double-balance" between polity and economy, they see the distribution of rents as intertwined with political power in LAOs, with OAOs tending to be characterized by a clearer separation of economic rents and political power.

What is crucial for understanding how sanctions might affect a target country is that competition is channeled in specific ways in different social orders. Thus, in LAOs, organizations – whether the state or other organizations – limit market entry and competition to ensure that individuals or organizations – whether state-owned or privately owned entities – with market power can accrue rents. More widely, "the purposeful creation of rents by states in LAOs is a consequence of the purposeful creation of differential access for individuals or organizations to the goods and services that the state can provide" (Connolly 2012, p. 44). This might include the enforcement of property rights and contracts, the use of regulations to manage entry and exit in product markets, etc. Conversely, in OAOs, open competition for rents among organizations leads inframarginal rents to accrue to many producers and consumers.

There are good reasons to think that the type of social order prevalent in a target state is of crucial importance to understanding how sanctions might affect a target country. First, target states characterized by LAO institutional frameworks might be well placed to use their position in providing differential access to goods, services, and resources for individuals or organizations, to ensure they are distributed according to the preferences of the ruling elite. In this sense, because economic and political exchange is based on differential access, target states might be able to use their position to divert resources to socially and politically important groups in a way that bolsters the ruling coalition. On the other hand, we might expect to see OAO target states less able to adjust in the same way. Constrained by more intense competition between organizations and by the need to adhere to formal rules, OAO governments may not be able to insulate social groups from the costs of sanctions. This might help explain why, in the sanctions literature, democracies are often considered to be more susceptible to sanctions (e.g. Hufbauer et al. 2007). Therefore, understanding the type of social order existing in the target country forms a vital component in understanding what Galtung described as the "transmission belts" between sanctions and the target society.

Second, very few studies demonstrate a clear understanding of who the ruling coalition is within any target society and what socioeconomic groups that coalition represents. Often this is reduced to either states or ruling regimes. But states rarely exhibit absolute autonomy from other social forces. Instead, states – and the ruling coalitions that hold power – are almost always rooted in a deeper socioeconomic structure. This is particularly important to emphasize in countries such as Russia, where a large number of analysts, especially in liberal accounts, tend to reduce Russian politics to the preferences and choices of either one man – Vladimir Putin – or a relatively small inner circle led by Putin. Other important social groups within society are usually dismissed as passive and inert, with little influence over the political process. Such accounts tend to ignore the strong links that exist between the ruling coalition in Russia and powerful socioeconomic forces located across society.

Consequently, it is important to appreciate how states relate to different socioeconomic groups. A good starting point is to consider the economic structure of the target country: Is it an economy dominated by hightech, knowledge-based industrial sectors? Or is it an economy dominated by agricultural production? Which sector of the economy is the source of the greatest tax revenues? Which sector is most vulnerable to a reduction in access to capital? The answers to these types of questions might help the

analysts identify which social groups are most important to the mainten-
ance of the existing ruling coalition and which might be most vulnerable to
sanctions. Therefore, to identify socially and politically important groups
within any society, it is important to outline the prevailing system of
political economy in that country and to pinpoint the principal sources
of economic power (Karl 1997, pp. 44–45). This should involve identifying
the key economic sectors and sources of tax revenue, as well as the most
important sources of employment, as these inform the strategies used by
elites to extract and distribute resources (Tilly 1992; Herbst 2000). In
addition, it is important to show how targeted sectors of the economy
are organized. So, are they dominated by state-owned firms, or are private
firms dominant? Do private firms enjoy close links with the state? Are the
targeted sectors characterized by relatively open competition, or is competition within and between sectors tightly regulated? Answering these questions helps establish the state's position in the wider system of political
economy, which in turn helps us understand what forms of social conflict, if any, might emerge as a result of sanctions. It also helps understand
the constellation of social forces that might be forced to compete over
scarce resources.

Third, and building on the previous point, many existing accounts fail to
explicitly incorporate any explanation of how a target country's pattern of
integration with the global economy prior to the imposition of sanctions
might shape the manner in which sanctions will affect that country. If,
for example, a target country is closed off from the global economy – i.e.
there is very little in the way of trade or capital flows between it and other
countries – then there is reason to expect that sanctions may not exert
much of an impact. If, on the other hand, the target country is open to
international trade and capital, we might expect, *ceteris paribus*, sanctions
to have a greater impact. However, what is important is not simply
whether a country is open or closed, but more precisely how the target
country's relationship with the global economy affects the distribution of
power and resources among domestic organizations – both political and
economic (Keohane and Milner 1996; Connolly 2012). In this respect, the
pattern of integration with the global economy is usually intimately related
to the target country's domestic system of political economy. The imposition of sanctions may cause a shift in the distribution of resources between
sectors, and in turn cause organizations to adjust the strategies they use to
achieve their objectives. For instance, a firm may rely on foreign capital
and technology, but sanctions may mean that it is forced to seek alternative
sources. Whether this firm is state-owned or privately owned may also be

important. The former may find it easier to access public resources, the latter more difficult. This might be especially important in LAOs, where close relationships between firms and state might be necessary to ensure access to resources. As a result, we might expect some organizations and sectors to be more sensitive to the impact of sanctions than others.

THE ANALYTICAL FRAMEWORK

Taken together, the insights from the literature summarized here provide the foundations of an analytical framework to help understand more clearly how sanctions might shape political economy in a target country. The relationship between the state and socioeconomic forces is placed at the forefront of this approach.

These key insights and assumptions on which the analytical framework is based can be summarized as follows:

- How sanctions affect the domestic political economy of target countries is crucial to understanding whether and under what conditions sanctions might succeed in satisfying the objectives of sender states. As such, assessment of sanctions' impact on the political economy of the target country should be analytically prior to any consideration of their success. This is the most underexplored avenue of research in the sanctions literature.
- The institutional configuration of the target state is an important variable. However, typologies of regime type are too simple. Instead, it is better to focus on how the political systems of target states *actually operate*. This means that identifying the type of social order that exists in the target state at the point at which sanctions are imposed might help us understand better the scope and nature of the target state's response.
- Identifying how sanctions have uneven distributional consequences on target societies is important to understanding how sanctions are mediated by target-state institutional structures. There are with sanctions, as with all political and economic processes, winners and losers. However, the role of states and ruling coalitions in determining who wins and who bears the cost of adjustment with sanctions is often crucial. Depending on the given institutional context, certain groups may be well positioned to use sanctions to their advantage.
- In light of the above, the state's role in crafting a response to sanctions is of paramount importance, as are its relative autonomy from other

social groups and its capacity to act. These indicators of "stateness" vary across countries and sometimes within countries. Consequently, an awareness of the manner in which the state interacts with, and is shaped by, other social forces is required to understand how sanctions might impact a target country. Locating the position of elites and social forces within the target country's system of political economy is important as this helps pinpoint the key nodes of a target country's political and economic resources.

- A vital dimension of a country's system of political economy is the nature of its integration with the global economy. Because sanctions are explicitly designed to alter the terms of the target country's relationship with the wider global economy in the hope that, in doing so, economic damage will be inflicted on it, it is important to understand the precise nature of that country's external economic relations. Again, the prevailing social order is often important, as is the role played by the state in mediating the country's integration with the global economy. States – "Janus-faced" as they are (Skocpol 1979) – are often positioned at the intersection between the domestic and global political economies. As a result, they can, under certain circumstances, be well placed to reshape the nature of a country's integration with the global economy. Determining the state's role in directing the flow of economic resources in a country can offer explanations when formulating its strategic response to sanctions.

- The strategic response of states, elites, and other important social forces is an important factor in understanding how sanctions impact a target country. I propose that the target state's system of political economy – that is, its economic structure, the role played by the state within that economy, and the country's nature of its integration with the global economy – are all crucial to understanding how certain opportunities and constraints are available to ruling elites when confronted by sanctions. Furthermore, this relationship is mutually constitutive in so far as the target country's initial (i.e. at the point of sanctions being imposed) system of political economy can be shaped by the strategic response formulated by the target country.

- Ultimately, whether sufficient pain is inflicted on the target state to cause it to modify its behavior is not simply down to the choice of sanctions by sender states. This assumption is often implicit within the academic literature or policy discourse. Whether sufficient economic pain is inflicted is viewed simply as a function of the sender states' will to "make the right choice from the menu." In practice, the target country's response ⌐ i.e. the adaptive measures taken to reduce the impact of sanctions – is likely to play an important role in mediating the effects of sanctions. It is, therefore, important to identify what options are available to target states.

In order to carry out a rigorous analysis of how sanctions impact a target country based on the assumptions just outlined, it is first necessary to provide an outline of the target country's system of political economy, which encompasses its institutional environment, economic structure, and relationship with the global economy. This helps anchor the subsequent analysis by establishing a starting point against which the impact of sanctions can be traced. Second, only after having established the nature of the target country's system of political economy is it possible to examine how sanctions affect the targeted sectors of the economy. Again, to help provide a firm basis for tracing how sanctions might change the targeted sector, it is necessary to first outline the main contours of that sector's place in the domestic and global economy, highlighting the key actors and organizations, as well as the ownership structure of the sector. Once this has been carried out, it is then necessary to outline the precise nature of the sanctions imposed by sender countries, identifying those areas that sanctions are intended to affect and those that they are not. Third, it is necessary to document the nature of the target state's strategic response. This can be done at both the aggregate, national level and at the sectoral level. This might involve examining both the formal policy response and the instruments used to achieve those policy objectives, including financial, institutional, and administrative resources. Finally, it is then possible to examine the impact of sanctions on the targeted sectors of the economy, examining their effects both on indicators of economic organization and performance and on how the target state's strategic policy response may have altered its domestic system of political economy, as well as that system's relationship with the global economy.

A monograph-length analysis is required to conduct such a detailed analysis of how sanctions affect a target country's political economy. The existing scholarship concerning sanctions is replete with case studies amounting to several pages in length at most. While such analyses are appropriate when generating theories, they do not provide a very sound basis for testing theories. This is perhaps one reason why there is a tendency in the literature "to gloss over the political economy of how targeted states strategically cope and adapt to sanctions" (Andreas 2005, p. 338). In contrast, by contextualizing sanctions within the target state's system of political economy, the analysis used here helps shift the focus toward an examination of the impact of sanctions from the point of view of the target state. For this, a certain degree of empathy is required to carry out a balanced and sober analysis. This should not be conflated with sympathy (Monaghan 2016). It is not the job of a balanced analyst to comment on whether he or she "agrees" with the way in which the subject of analysis behaves. Whether the subject's response is, in the view of the analyst, morally correct or objectionable is of even less importance. But empathy requires viewing the subject of analysis – in this case the target of sanctions – in terms understood by politically important actors and organizations in the target country. To do this requires a detailed understanding of the local context, which in turn should be based on more than a few secondary sources of questionable veracity.

CONCLUSION

This book is about how economic sanctions impact a target country. As I have shown, this crucial question is often not given the detailed attention it deserves. Yet it is of paramount importance because many of the objectives put forward by sending countries require some economic pain to be felt by the target country. How, for example, can we expect the decision-making calculus to change in the target country if sanctions cause, at worst, minor disruption, and even help strengthen elite cohesion in the target country? Or how can we expect sanctions to act as a deterrent to other countries when the target country in any given instance might appear to be coping or even flourishing under sanctions? In short, how can sender states generate political gain without inflicting economic pain?

Having established that the type of social order, system of political economy, and pattern of integration with the global economy are all important to understanding how sanctions might affect a target country, the subject of the next chapter is to identify each of these in Russia, the target country of interest in this book. Understanding these characteristics of Russian political economy can help to: (1) show how Russian policymakers crafted a strategic response to sanctions; (2) show how the country's system of political economy shaped the options available to policymakers; and (3) identify the extent of the economic pain inflicted on those sectors that were targeted by sanctions. In doing so, I hope to show how a target state can adapt to sanctions and what conditions make that adaption possible.

2

Russia's System of Political Economy

INTRODUCTION

Having established that the nature of a target country's system of political economy is an important factor in explaining how target states can formulate adaptive measures in response to sanctions, I use this chapter to provide a stylized outline of the core features of Russia's system of political economy. This system of political economy – described here as a limited-access system of political economy – also exhibits a specific pattern of integration with the wider global economy, which also acts as an important factor in helping explain how sanctions shape the prospects for target states to undertake adaptive measures in response.

Several key characteristics of Russia's system of political economy and pattern of integration with the global economy stand out. First, as a limited-access system of political economy, it is based on the generation of rents from globally competitive sectors of the economy and the subsequent redistribution of those revenues to other less competitive sectors of the economy. This rent distribution system is the core feature of Russia's political economy. Second, the Russian federal state is positioned at the apex of this system of political economy. It is able to use a range of levers – institutional, financial, and diplomatic – to direct resources to areas of the economy that are considered important by the political leadership. The state is also able to use these levers to subordinate economic activity to wider social, political, and geopolitical objectives. Third, while Russia is, in statistical terms, an open economy that is well integrated with the global economy, the Russian state exerts a strong influence over how that interaction with the outside world takes place. This is because state-owned or state-influenced enterprises account for the vast majority of Russia's trade and capital flows. As a result, the state was relatively well positioned to dictate the terms of Russia's interaction with the global economy.

It is these key features of the Russian system of political economy that have proven crucial in explaining how Western sanctions have affected Russia since 2014. Adaptive measures were undertaken by the Russian state in those areas of the economy that were targeted by Western sanctions; that the state was well positioned to formulate and implement these measures was in large part due to the system that had emerged in the aftermath of the failed planned economy. It is the key features of this system that I discuss in this chapter.

RUSSIA'S LIMITED-ACCESS SYSTEM OF POLITICAL ECONOMY

While the dismantling of the Soviet planned economy that took place in the late 1980s and early 1990s created important elements of a market economy – most importantly the liberalization of prices, a decline in the degree of centralized resource allocation, and the formal legalization of private property rights – the process of building a market economy was uneven and subject to reversal from the late 1990s onward (Aslund 1995, 2007; Mau and Starodubrovskaya 2001; Treisman 2010; Sutela 2012). Consequently, what emerged was not a smoothly functioning market economy based on competition and strong property rights (Shlapentokh and Aruntunyan 2013; Frye 2017). Instead, a hybrid system of political economy emerged, in which pockets of relative freedom and competition coexisted alongside large swathes of the economy in which market-oriented economic change proved intractable. This failure to build a fully functioning market economy can be at least partially explained by the heavy influence of Soviet-era legacies – allocational and political – and Russia's natural resource abundance, both of which constrained the development of a competitive market economy (Gaddy and Ickes 2002, 2005, 2014). However, the system of political economy that had crystallized by 2014 was not, by global standards, that unusual. The vast majority of countries across the world are *not* well-functioning market economies, but are instead what have been described as "limited access orders," i.e. economies in which the state interferes in the functioning of the market to maintain ruling coalitions (North, Wallis, and Weingast 2009; North, Wallis, et al. 2012).

As discussed in the previous chapter, social orders can be distinguished according to the degree of competition that exists between organizations and the manner in which the state manipulates access to markets to maintain ruling political coalitions. In limited-access orders, like Russia, the state often engages in the systematic manipulation of markets to ensure that individuals or organizations with market power can accrue rents (North, Wallis, and Weingast 2009; Connolly 2012b). The creation of, and manipulation of access to, rents by states in limited-access orders is a consequence of the purposeful creation of differential access for individuals or organizations to the goods and services that the state can provide, such as the enforcement of property rights. What follows here is a stylized model of the limited-access system of political economy that exists in Russia. This model emphasizes the role of competition in key sectors of the Russian political economy and is a stylized abstraction of a much more complex reality. This abstraction is intended to illustrate the key factors that shape how resources are allocated in Russia, for what purposes, and by whom. Five key elements of the Russian political economy are identified: four broad sectors of the economy, and the state.[1]

Clifford Gaddy and Barry Ickes provide a helpful starting point in their "rent addiction" model elaborated over the course of various iterations (Gaddy and Ickes 2005, 2009). According to their schematic illustration of how the Russian economy functions, the extraction and distribution of resource rents is the most important dimension of political economy in Russia.[2] They present a two-sector schema of the Russian economy. The first sector – the rent-producing sector, or "Sector A," as it will be referred to from now on – primarily comprises enterprises from the natural resources sector of the economy (i.e. oil, gas, and mineral extraction). To this list, we might also add large agricultural conglomerates, firms involved in the construction of nuclear power generation machinery, and perhaps some defense enterprises. Firms in this sector tend to be globally competitive in so far as they sell their goods or services on global markets as well as within Russia. Because these firms have been able to generate substantial profits, they do not, as a rule, require state subsidies to function. As a result of their

---

[1] This stylized model is an augmented version of the model described in Connolly (2015a).

[2] There is some disagreement over the precise nature of economic rents. David Riccardo classically defined rents as a financial return on an asset or action higher than the return derived from the next best opportunity forgone. More recently, there has been a tendency in the literature to refer to directly unproductive rent-seeking activities, wherein economic agents devote resources to gain rents that have no socially useful purpose. The definition employed by Gaddy and Ickes in relation to Russia's oil and gas sector is closer to the classical one, but includes production costs above minimum efficient levels. Thus, rents are not equivalent to profits as they are in the classical definition. Instead they encompass "excessive costs" as well as "more-than-normal" pretax profits.

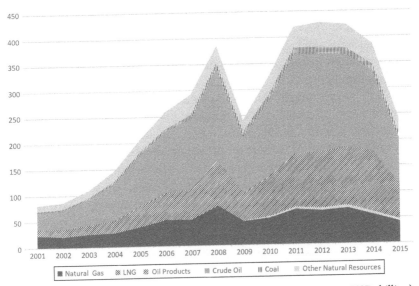

Figure 2.1 Natural resource export revenues, 2001–2015 (constant 2015 USD, billion)
Source: Bank of Russia (2017); author's calculations

high profitability and competitiveness, firms from within this sector accounted for a large share of tax revenues in Russia (Gaddy and Ickes 2005; Kudrin and Gurvich 2014). The volume of resource rents generated from natural resources alone is indicated in Figure 2.1. While this figure does not include costs of production, it does give a clear sense of the scale of natural resource rents generated in Sector A and, as a result, the sector's importance to the wider economy. Indeed, according to Alexei Kudrin and Evsei Gurvich, between 2000 and 2013, cumulative surplus (i.e. compared to the base year of 1999) oil and gas revenues alone totaled $2.1 trillion (in 2013 US dollars). This amounted to 7.5 times the dollar size of Russian GDP in 1999 (Kudrin and Gurvich 2014, p. 6). Export sales of armaments and nuclear power machinery might have added an additional $20 billion annually in recent years, although in these sectors costs tend to be much higher and profits are thus likely to be much lower (Connolly and Senstad 2017).

Although the state is extremely influential in this sector, its role is not uniform. As far as ownership is concerned, the state is dominant in the oil (primarily through Rosneft and Gazprom Neft), gas (Gazprom and, to a lesser extent, Rosneft), nuclear power (Rosatom and its subsidiary entities, including JSC ARMZ Uranium Holding Company [uranium mining],

JSC TENEX [conversion and enrichment], JSC TVEL [nuclear fuel production] and JSC Atomstroiexport [nuclear power plant design and construction]), and defense industries (primarily although not exclusively through Rostec, a large holding company comprising around 700 organizations).

There were, though, notable exceptions to the dominance of state-owned firms in Sector A. For instance, privately owned firms play an important role in the oil industry (e.g. Lukoil), the gas industry (e.g. Novatek), agriculture – where the largest agroholdings were almost always privately owned – and the mining and minerals industries (Fortescue 2006; Wegren, Nikulin, and Trotsuk 2018). Nevertheless, while those privately owned firms present in Sector A might not be directly controlled by the state, strong links exist between the state and owners of these firms which result in the state remaining extremely influential, even where property is nominally privately owned (Hanson 2009). For instance, while Novatek – the second largest firm in the gas industry – is owned by private citizens, these citizens – Leonid Mikhelson and, via Volga Group, Gennady Timchenko – enjoy exceptionally close relations with the ruling elite, including President Putin himself (Henderson 2010). It is these close links that probably explain why Novatek has been so successful in expanding its share on the domestic market and, in the future, in LNG export markets, at the expense of the state-owned behemoth Gazprom (Henderson and Pirani 2014). A similar trend is evident in the agricultural sector, where the largest agroholdings and their subsidiaries tend to be privately owned and the owners or managers tend to enjoy close ties with federal and local government officials.[3] In this respect, the exceptions tend to prove the rule that close links to the state – whether direct or indirect – are crucial to building a viable and sustainable presence in Russia's strategically important Sector A.

A second sector – "Sector B," or the rent-dependent sector – comprises industries that should not be considered as globally competitive in so far as firms from within these industries are not generally successful in selling their goods or services on global markets, and as a result tend to focus their activities on the domestic market. Firms from within this sector tend to rely on subsidies or other forms of support from the state, which may be

---

[3] For instance, the Russian Minister of Agriculture, Alexander Tkachev, has extremely close links with one of Russia's largest agroholdings, Agrocomplex. I am grateful to Stephen Wegren for bringing this fact to my attention. The ownership structure within the agricultural industry is discussed in Wegren, Nikulin, and Trotsuk (2018).

direct (e.g. transfers from the state budget, favorable state procurement rules) or indirect (the use of regulatory mechanisms to suppress competition from other suppliers), and, despite receiving support from the state, tend to struggle to generate consistent profits. In Russia, such industries include automotive machinery, shipbuilding, oil and gas equipment (e.g. drilling rigs, pipelines, etc.), and sections – although by no means all – of the defense industry. In addition to industrial sectors, this category includes social groups dependent on government spending (the so-called *byudzhetniki*, such as pensioners or those employed in the state bureaucracy).

According to the account given by Gaddy and Ickes, the relationship between these two broadly defined sectors lies at the heart of the Russian political economy. In essence, they argue that the rents generated in Sector A are managed by the state to support economic activity in Sector B. This is done for a range of economic, social, and political reasons, and as a result, the primacy of the state in channeling the flow of rents between various constituencies within Russia is of fundamental importance. The state, in this account, uses a variety of instruments to direct rents from the most profitable and competitive firms to the least, with the objective of maintaining output and employment in Sector B. These instruments include direct ownership or control of state-owned enterprises (SOEs). In some instances, the state is able to exert indirect influence over privately owned firms to "encourage" them to perform social or political functions that lie beyond the usual profit-maximizing functions expected of a firm in a market economy.[4] By utilizing a mixture of direct transfers (e.g. by imposing reasonably transparent, formal taxes on the extraction and export of hydrocarbons to fund, for example, state procurement of defense-industrial equipment for Russia's armed forces) and indirect transfers (e.g. Sector A enterprises supplying inputs, such as gas, at below market price to Sector B enterprises, or through the purchase of Sector B products by Sector A enterprises), the state has been able to maintain production and employment in otherwise uncompetitive areas of the Russian economy.

One important aspect of the rent management system that was not explicitly dealt with by Gaddy and Ickes is the suppression of competition that occurs as a result of the operation of this model of political economy. On the one hand, a smaller number of entities are required to facilitate the

---

[4] This is not to suggest that firms in market economies exclusively pursue the maximization of profits. However, this is the general tendency in market economies.

management, monitoring, and taxation of the rent-producing part of the economy. On the other, the use of rents to sustain production and employment in Sector B offers advantages to state-supported firms that prevent the process of "creative destruction" that could ensue if market entry and exit were allowed to occur in a more natural fashion. In its most basic form, this suppression of competition manifests itself in the form of concentrated market configurations, with Sector A characterized by monopolistic or oligopolistic market structures. Although this is to some extent a function of the industries in question – the oil and gas industry elsewhere, for instance, tends to be dominated by a small number of large firms – it is also no doubt true that market concentration facilitates rent extraction by the state. As a result, the degree of competition in Sector A is relatively modest and, to the extent that it does exist, tends to take place between state-owned enterprises (e.g. Gazprom v Rosneft), between SOEs and state-linked firms (e.g. Gazprom v Novatek), or between privately owned firms in relatively concentrated markets, such as the steel industry (Fortescue and Hanson 2015). It is rare indeed that privately owned firms pose a genuinely competitive threat to SOEs, with the likes of Lukoil in the oil industry denied access to licenses for offshore exploration in favor of state-owned Rosneft and Gazprom Neft.

The state asserts the interests of favored firms either through direct management or through regulatory mechanisms, such as awarding licenses for exploration, production, or the right to sell products abroad. This enables the state to utilize SOEs as instruments of public policy, the remit of which is correspondingly broad, with SOEs pursuing objectives beyond that of generating a profit for the main shareholder, i.e. the state, and instead encompassing social and regional development and, in some instances, the pursuit of foreign policy objectives. The suppression of competition results in a system in which the strength of property rights is, in practice if not in law, conditional upon close relations with government, whether that be at the local or the federal level (Hanson and Teague 2005; Sharafutdinova and Kisunko 2014).[5] Property rights have proven especially precarious in the strategically important natural resources sector, perhaps because of the importance the state assigns to maintaining control over the most important sources of rent (Hanson 2005; Tompson 2005; Sakwa 2009). Indeed, one of the key motivations for sharing rents – whether formally or informally – by decision-makers in Sector A is,

---

[5] Although, as pointed out by Timothy Frye (2017, p. 77), "not all forms of political connections are equally effective in reducing perceptions of insecure property rights."

according to Gaddy and Ickes, the belief that their property rights are strengthened by agreeing to share rents with other claimants within the economy (Gaddy and Ickes 2005, p. 564). After all, without the threat to the property rights of owners in Sector A – always implicit, and sometimes explicit – there would be very little incentive to permit the sharing of rents with either the state (in the form of punitive taxation) or other organizations (for instance, through incurring excess costs). In this sense, the conditional nature of property rights is central to the operation of the rent management system and the social order in Russia more widely. What is true for formal owners within, say, the mining and minerals sector is also true for managers of SOEs, who may not enjoy formal property rights but do enjoy access to substantial flows of income.

Within Sector B, enterprises tend to rely on domestic demand because they are not usually competitive in global markets. As in Sector A, competition tends to be suppressed as the state – at both the federal and local level – employs a range of instruments, from regulation to financial support, to maintain high barriers to entry and exit. Direct government spending, subsidies, or the deliberate policy-induced distortion of markets to protect incumbents supports much of the demand in this sector.[6] Economic efficiency – perhaps reduced to the simple measure of profitability – is not required to guarantee firms' survival within this sector. Instead, budget constraints on firms within the sector tend to be "soft" (Kornai 1992; Kudrin and Gurvich 2014). As a result, what tends to be more important to a firm's survival prospects is the degree of what Gaddy and Ickes describe as "relational" capital possessed by a firm's management (Gaddy and Ickes 2002). Firms tend to be endowed with a high degree of relational capital where they act as the provider of local employment and other public services, or where a firm produces goods or services that are considered to be of strategic importance to the state, often because of the role such firms play in enhancing Russia's national security or international prestige.

Perhaps unsurprisingly, the suppression of competition across many markets within the Russian economy exerts a negative influence over productivity growth. According to a significant body of research on the causes of productivity growth and innovation, higher levels of competition tend to result in increased investment in human and physical capital, and in more technological or organizational innovation (Aghion and

---

[6] For instance, official tax exemptions to support business amounted to 2.9 percent of GDP in 2012 (Kudrin and Gurvich 2014).

Bessanova 2006; Aghion and Griffith 2008; Aghion, Blundell, et al. 2009). All things being equal, greater competition should result in faster productivity growth. However, the chronic and systematic intervention by the state in Russia leads to a number of negative outcomes, including high barriers to entry which weaken competitive tendencies within the economy, poor performance in innovative activities, relatively low levels of private investment, and, ultimately, lower rates of growth than would otherwise be possible (Abramov et al. 2017). Because of concerted efforts by state officials in Russia to dampen competition, especially in Sectors A and B, innovation and productivity growth have suffered (Gianella and Tompson 2007; Gokhberg and Kuznetsova 2011; RANEPA 2012; Graham 2013). State intervention in the economy has a number of sources, including the desire to control access to rents for either the state (taxes) or personal interests (corruption), or to support output and employment in socially and politically important parts of the economy that might otherwise fail without state support. This suppression of competition is at least one of the reasons behind the slow nature of structural economic change in Russia, which has resulted in the emergence of very few genuinely new high-technology or knowledge-intensive sectors of the economy (Cooper 2006a; Connolly 2013; Connolly 2015b).

The state-controlled Sectors A and B account for the vast majority of economic activity in Russia. Estimates from a range of different sources, including the IMF and the Russian Federal Antimonopoly Service, suggest that the state-controlled segment of the economy – which includes both the official public sector, SOEs, and enterprises with at least partial state ownership – steadily increased from 2005 onward, to account for as much as 70 percent of Russian GDP by 2015 (Abramov, Radygin, and Chernova 2016). It is therefore clear that despite having undertaken a series of important market-creating reforms in the 1990s, the Russian state remains the single most important actor in the economy today. As a result, it should be no surprise that the deliberate and systematic suppression of competition and other incentives to raise efficiency has caused a widespread slowdown in productivity growth (Kudrin and Gurvich 2014).

By controlling such a large proportion of economic activity in Russia and managing the flows of rents between Sectors A and B, the Russian state has exacerbated the "addiction" to rent sharing that exists in large parts of the economy (Gaddy and Ickes 2009). The relationship between Sectors A and B can be graphically illustrated using several examples. First, the sharp difference in the sources of demand for Sector A and Sector B goods is evident when it is considered that natural resources and unprocessed raw

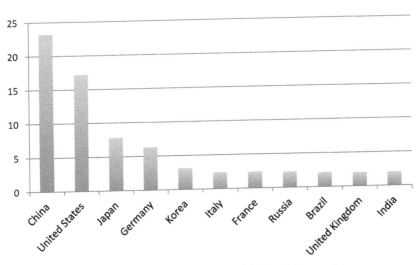

Figure 2.2 Share of global manufacturing value-added, 2013 (percent)
Source: United Nations (2016)

materials account for around 85 percent of Russia's total merchandise exports in any given year. With the exception of armaments and nuclear power generation machinery, there are very few manufactured product categories in which Russian manufacturers are competitive. Nevertheless, Russia remains one of the world's largest manufacturers: In 2013, the year before sanctions were imposed, Russia was the eighth largest manufacturer in the world, accounting for around 3.5 percent of global value-added in manufacturing (Figure 2.2). Clearly Russia is not, as US Senator John McCain once remarked, merely "a gas station masquerading as a country" (Sherfinski 2014). A wide variety of manufactured goods are produced in Russia, and the sector was estimated to employ around ten million people in 2015 (Federal State Statistics Service 2017). However, very little of this large volume of manufacturing output was exported. Instead, domestic consumers bought it. This large gap between the huge volume of Russian manufacturing production and the comparatively paltry volume exported is explained by the fact that it is the rents generated by Sector A that sustain domestic demand for output in Sector B. Without the support and protection granted to Sector B by the Russian state, it is unlikely that domestic consumers would buy as many Russian manufactured goods as they currently do.

A second vivid illustration of the relationship between the two sectors can be found in the strikingly high correlation between output in the

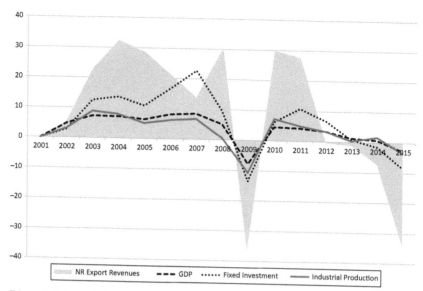

Figure 2.3 Annual changes in natural resource revenues and selected indicators of Russian economic performance, 2001–2015
Source: Bank of Russia (2017); Federal State Statistics Service (2017); author's calculations

rent-generating sector and that in the rent-dependent sector. As shown in Figure 2.3, the historic correlation between annual changes in natural resource rents and annual changes in a number of key economic indicators is extremely high. The statistical correlation between annual fluctuations in natural resource revenues, on the one hand, and GDP (Pearson's $r = 0.88$), fixed investment ($r = 0.84$), and industrial production ($r = 0.83$), on the other, is particularly strong. Although Gaddy and Ickes' model is well over a decade old, the evidence suggests their initial assertion that it is the *rate of change* in natural resource rents that is most important when explaining Russian economic performance, and not the *level* of resource rents, remains accurate. Their model helps to explain precisely how and why the fortunes of the two sectors are so closely intertwined, and why economic activity in Russia remains so dependent on the performance of the natural resources sector.

Nevertheless, while the two-sector model articulated by Gaddy and Ickes provides an extremely useful starting point for understanding the functioning of the Russian system of political economy, it leaves important gaps. For instance, the creation of a market economy in the 1990s led to the emergence of a significant, if somewhat undersized, privately owned

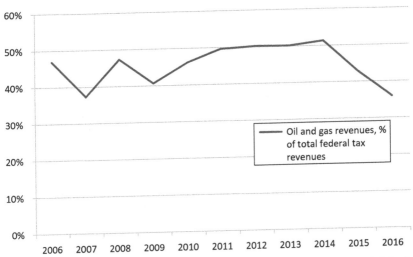

Figure 2.4 Taxation revenues derived from oil and gas as a percentage of total federal tax revenues, 2006–2016 (percent)
Source: Russian Ministry of Finance (2017)

economy that exists largely outside the state-regulated Sectors A and B. Firms operating in this part of the economy are, for the sake of simplicity, part of what is labeled the rent-neutral sector, or "Sector C." This sector includes firms that operate largely outside the rent generation and management system described above. Sector C includes large construction and retail groups, business services, and small and medium-sized enterprises (SMEs) in all industries, but especially in services. These SMEs commonly operate in retail, transportation, business services, and some of the more knowledge-intensive information and communication technologies.

Taken together, firms from within this sector are neither important as sources of taxation – in most years, up to half of federal taxes were derived from the oil and gas sector alone (Figure 2.4) – nor dependent on state support, whether formal (subsidies) or informal (protection from competition or other forms of rent sharing), to survive.[7] Instead, they tend to operate mostly at the periphery of the rent management system that governs economic activity in Sectors A and B. In contrast to firms in Sector B, firms from within this part of the economy are subject to hard budget constraints, which means that their survival depends on their

---

[7] Estimates by the Russian economist Evsei Gurvich suggest that natural resources accounted for as much as 70 percent of federal tax revenues (Gurvich 2010).

profitability rather than their political contacts (Kudrin and Gurvich 2014). However, the state does not systematically interfere with economic activity in this sector; it is, at least compared with Sectors A and B, a relatively free part of the economy, with entry to and exit from product markets less prone to state manipulation. As a result, there is a much greater intensity of competition within Sector C, resulting in correspondingly higher levels of innovation and total factor productivity than elsewhere in the economy (Bessanova 2010; Kuznetsov et al. 2011; RANEPA 2012; Golikova et al. 2017).

There are, however, severe problems that have restricted the growth of this sector. One in particular is the weakness of property rights, which often manifests itself in the form of *reiderstvo*, or criminal corporate raiding (Centre for Political Technologies 2008; Rochlitz 2013; Hanson 2014). This is a social, political, and economic phenomenon, and the term can be used to describe a range of practices that involve the use of a combination of legal and illegal methods to acquire property or other assets from economic agents. More specifically, it can be said to encompass the "illegal . . . seizure of property . . . [and] the winning of control in the widest sense by one company over another by using both illegal and legal methods; the seizure of shares by provoking business conflicts; [it is] . . . a way of redistributing property, which in essence is banditry, but which formally conforms to some sort of judicial procedure" (Centre for Political Technologies 2008).[8] Over time, the nature of *reiderstvo* has changed, moving from being primarily a practice in which private (i.e. nonstate) agents tended to initiate raids and employed corrupt state officials to supply logistical assistance during the 1990s, to a process where state

[8] This type of criminal corporate raiding should not to be confused with the legal type of hostile takeover that occurs in countries such as the United States and United Kingdom. Instead, criminal corporate raids in Russia and the former Soviet Union tend to employ illegal methods, although often alongside other ostensibly legal methods. According to Michael Rochlitz (2013), these include "blackmail, bribery, forged documents, and the use of armed groups to enforce change of ownership." A further distinguishing feature is that raiding frequently involves the connivance of public officials, either as facilitating agents (i.e. state officials whose use of public resources enables other nonstate agents to carry out the raid) or as the initiators, architects, and beneficiaries of a raid themselves. Whereas the type of legal corporate raiding practiced in Western economies is generally considered to be "efficiency enhancing," criminal raiding in the former Soviet Union is considered to be a malign practice that has resulted in a significant weakening of property rights, the business environment, and the wider rule of law in general. This is because, in addition to the direct adverse consequences suffered by the subjects of raiding, other economic agents may be deterred from investing in their businesses due to the fear that their firm will be subjected to criminal raiding in the future.

officials themselves became the initiators or direct beneficiaries of the raids (Volkov 2002; Privlov and Volkov 2007; Gans-Morse 2012). There are, of course, high-profile examples of such raiding, such as the seizure of Mikhail Khodokovsky's oil company, Yukos, in the early 2000s, and the more recent "deprivatization" of another oil company, Vladimir Yevtush-enkov's Bashneft, over the course of 2014–2015 (Hanson 2005; Tompson 2005; Sakwa 2014; Tetryakov 2014). However, perhaps even more perni-ciously, there are reported to be a much larger number of lower-profile instances of *reiderstvo* that affect numerous smaller enterprises across Russia (Gans-Morse 2012; Rochlitz 2013; Hanson 2014).

In essence, this practice is yet another manifestation of the uneven protection of property rights in Russia: Firms with sufficiently strong ties with influential state officials tend to enjoy stronger property rights than those without such ties. As such, property rights in Russia are not homo-genous; rather, their strength in each case depends on a number of variables, not least the strength of an owner's political connections (Frye 2017). This is a problem because the weak protection of property rights results in greater uncertainty for a large proportion of would-be and actual entrepreneurs in Russia. While this sector of the economy might be thought to be the most market-oriented and dynamic sector of the economy – behaving as it does according to the conventional market signals of prices, profits, and hard budget constraints – its size is relatively modest. For example, only around a fifth of the workforce in Russia is estimated to work in SMEs (Federal State Statistics Service 2017). This compares with a European average of 40 percent (European Investment Bank 2013). While many enterprises are likely to exist in the shadow economy in Russia, for a number of reasons – including to avoid taxation – it is still likely to be that case that the size of the SME sector in Russia is comparatively small. The prevalence of *reiderstvo*, alongside other weaknesses in the Russian business environment, is likely to explain why the sector has not grown to the size that reformers in the 1990s had hoped for (Kudrin and Gurvich 2014). While the voice of this sector has grown louder in recent years, it remains a politically and socially weaker constituency than the powerful Sectors A and B described previously in this chapter (Yakovlev 2014; Yakovlev, Sobolev and Kazun 2014).

All three sectors described in this chapter reside in what might be described as the "real" sector of the economy. However, all three sectors require capital to sustain their activities. It is here that a fourth sector – the financial sector – becomes important. The domestic financial sector emerged from virtual nonexistence during most of the Soviet period – with

private banks only appearing in the late 1980s – to become an important
and sometimes vibrant part of the modern Russian economy (Johnson
2000; Kirdina and Vernikov 2013). While much of the progress achieved
over the past three decades has been impressive – with more banks,
providing a wider array of financial services, than ever before in Russian
history – it is nevertheless also true that the financial system has developed
in an uneven fashion. Several key characteristics stand out.

First, the Russian financial sector remains small by international standards, with the total volume of credit extended to the private sector
amounting to just over 50 percent of GDP – compared to a figure of closer
to or in excess of 100 percent in many other middle-income countries
(Connolly 2011; Kirdina and Vernikov 2013). Second, it is a system that
remains overwhelmingly bankcentric, with very few alternative sources of
finance available to would-be borrowers. Equity ownership levels are low,
with a comparatively small stock exchange that is dominated by natural
resource companies. A very thin market for corporate and state bonds
exists, while insurance and pension funds, and other sources of long-term
capital, are relatively limited in number. Third, not only is the financial
system comparatively small, but it is also dominated by state-owned or
state-controlled banks. In 2016, nearly two-thirds of all assets and liabilities in the Russian banking system were held by state-controlled banks
(Vernikov 2017). Privately owned banks, while numerous, tend to be
small in size. Indeed, according to one estimate, they account for 1 percent
of GDP (Movchan 2017). This tendency toward state preeminence within
the financial system became more pronounced after the 2008–2009 global
financial crisis.

These characteristics are important in explaining the role of the financial
system in Russia's system of political economy. First, the relatively small
size of Russia's financial system means that credit is scarce and, as a result,
is subject to a degree of rationing. Second, the key role played by state-
controlled banks has resulted in a corresponding degree of state control
over the allocation of scarce credit. This ensures that politically important
enterprises – usually located in Sectors A and B – are able to access
relatively cheap sources of capital. As a result of these strong links with
the state, enterprises that are not economically efficient on most indicators
are able to enjoy access to capital on a scale not available to enterprises
outside the network of politically well-connected entities. One important
outcome of this network is that competition within Russia's economy is
suppressed as new market entrants are denied access to capital that might
enable them to challenge protected incumbents. As well as channeling

funds to politically favored enterprises, state-controlled banks also act as transmission mechanisms for monetary policy, expanding and tightening credit at the behest of the authorities. In this respect, there are similarities with the structure and behavior of the Chinese banking system (Connolly 2011; Kirdina and Vernikov 2013; Vernikov 2013). Firms situated in Sector C tend to find themselves denied access to credit from state-controlled banks. It is revealing that in any given year, the Russian banking system is the source of less than 1 percent of capital used by SMEs (Gaidar Institute 2017, p. 156).

Russia's state-controlled (through direct or indirect ownership) banks are distinctive in several other respects. They are "too big to fail," enjoy soft budget constraints, and rely on public funds for recapitalization, as illustrated in 2008–2009 and in the anticrisis package developed by the government in response to the 2015 recession. The presence of guaranteed state support ensures that systemically important banks enjoy higher credit ratings than would otherwise be the case. This effective subsidy ensures that the state-controlled banks enjoy a competitive edge over private banks that are unable to raise capital at a comparable rate, which leads them to exhibit relatively favorable results on commonly used indicators of bank performance (Fungácová, Herrala, and Weill 2011). This also leads to state-controlled firms accumulating larger debt burdens than privately owned firms (Abramov et al. 2017). Competition within the banking sector is thus further suppressed as state banks employ administrative leverage to poach the most attractive clients (Vernikov 2013).

These close links with government form a crucial function in the country's system of political economy. Because of the underdeveloped state of Russia's financial system, very few SMEs in Russia are able to access domestic finance, while the larger, more globally oriented firms (such as natural resource companies) are able to access capital from global capital markets (Sutela 2012, pp. 182–186). Indeed, privately owned banks, which tend to offer SMEs easier access to capital than state-owned banks, are estimated to account for less than 1 percent of GDP (Movchan 2017).

In this respect, the financial system in Russia serves to reinforce and perpetuate the three-sector model described previously. The banking system works as a vital lever used by the state to manipulate access to rents in Russia and to protect firms within the state-controlled sectors (i.e. A and B) of the economy by softening their budget constraints, leaving those situated outside to rely on their own means to build successful businesses (Abramov et al. 2017, p. 33). State-controlled banks are also used as instruments of public policy more widely, with the likes of VTB and Vneshekonombank (VEB) used to support economic development projects at home and Russia's foreign policy activities abroad.[9] In short, Russia's financial system plays an important role in the national system of political economy by allowing the state to exert control over the enterprises in Sectors A and B that form the backbone of Russia's system of political economy.

A final sector of the Russian political economy can be said to exist in the form of the state itself. It is the state that shapes incentives in Russia, as it sets the formal rules and regulations that govern economic activity. The decisions made by state actors concerning when to apply those rules and regulations also send important signals to economic agents in Russia. The state either directly owns or indirectly controls large portions of the economy. And it is through the state-owned banks that the majority of decisions concerning the allocation of capital across the economy take place. The decisions made within the state – whether at the federal or local level – affect the distribution of public expenditure. As pointed out by Alexei Kudrin and Evsei Gurvich, Russia has a very "specific structure of public expenditure" when compared with most other countries, largely due to the high proportion of public expenditure that is allocated to spending on social welfare and security (Kudrin and Gurvich 2014, p. 7). These areas of the economy, of course, are both part of what is described here as Sector B – the rent-dependent part of the economy. But what is important to note is that decisions made over the allocation of public expenditure are among the more open and transparent modes of rent-sharing that takes place within the Russian economy.

It is by using these different mechanisms – ownership and management, design and implementation of law and regulation, allocation of public spending, use of state-owned banks, etc. – that the state performs perhaps its most important function of all: that of managing the flow of rents between sectors of the Russian economy to achieve its wider social and political objectives. The influence of the state in all these aspects of public policy in Russia grew after 2000, primarily due to a deliberate policy of centralization under the leadership of Vladimir Putin (Mau and Starodubrovskaya 2001; Monaghan 2011; Taylor 2011; Monaghan 2014). This focus on first centralizing key dimensions of state activity, and then making the state administration work more efficiently, means that the Russian state's role in the economy is now stronger than at any point since, arguably, the late 1980s. Because the state and its leaders had

---

[9] Strictly speaking, VEB is a development bank and therefore is not usually included in calculations of the state's share of the banking sector.

objectives that go beyond economic efficiency, it exploited its augmented position at the apex of Russia's system of political economy to pursue social and political goals. This is not to suggest that the state's autonomy from economic and social forces is anything like absolute; after all, even large state-owned enterprises, such as Rosneft or Gazprom, have exerted a strong influence over government policy, demonstrating that the power to shape policy agendas can work both ways. However, while the relative power of the state varies across policy dimensions, it has since the early 2000s been the most potent actor on the domestic political scene, something that was not necessarily true during the 1990s, when powerful business interests exerted disproportionate power over state policy.

The state's increasingly active role in the economy has, according to a number of researchers, exerted a pernicious impact on efforts at raising economic productivity (Abramov, Radygin, and Chernova 2016; Abramov et al. 2017). Nevertheless, it has enabled the state to achieve a range of significant social and political objectives. For instance, while efforts to strengthen Russia's system of state administration, or *vertikal*, have not always run smoothly, on fundamental measures of state capacity, Russia's performance improved after 1999. One widely used measure of state capacity is the murder rate.[10] Since the late 1990s and early 2000s, the murder rate was reduced from 30.8 per 100,000 people – which at the time put Russia among the worst performing countries outside the low-income group – to 9.2 per 100,000 people in 2012 (United Nations Office on Drugs and Crime 2013). While this figure remained relatively high, certainly when compared with high-income countries, it was not an order of magnitude worse than the average of other middle-income countries. Life expectancy also improved dramatically. In Russia, this fell during much of the 1990s. In 1994, life expectancy was fifty-seven years for men, seventy-one years for women, and just sixty-four years overall. Such figures had not been seen in Russia since the late 1950s. However, as the death rate began to fall in 2003, life expectancy in Russia began to rise again, further increasing since then to exceed 1990 levels in 2011 (Figure 2.5). Over the same period, the officially recorded unemployment rate declined, from 13 percent in 1999 to 6 percent in 2016 (BOFIT 2017). Taken together, these developments show that while the state's role was not always best for economic efficiency, it was able to use the rapid growth of natural resource

---

[10] For a more detailed discussion of the use of murder rate data to measure state capacity in Russia and elsewhere, see Popov (2014). The conceptual utility of identifying the reduction of violence as the first-order duty of the state is discussed in North et al. (2012).

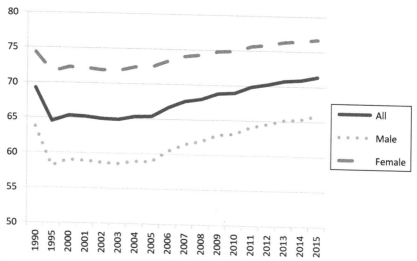

Figure 2.5 Life expectancy at birth, 1990–2015
Source: Federal State Statistics Service (2017), Demograficheskiy prognoz do 2030 goda, Moscow: Federal State Statistics Service

rents in the 2000s to deliver a much more stable system of government that, for many, offered a dramatic improvement on the 1990s.

Thus, the role that the state plays in Russia's system of political economy is crucial to understanding both the sources of Russia's economic inefficiency and the motives that underpin its role in distorting the market. Since 2000, the Russian leadership has centralized formal authority, which has in turn strengthened the state's economic functions. This has led to the state, not the market, being the dominant mechanism for allocating resources in Russia. It does this by utilizing the myriad instruments at its disposal – including its control over much of the financial system – both directly, to coordinate economic activity in Sectors A and B, and indirectly, to suppress the emergence of a dynamic and genuinely competitive Sector C. The state's ability and observed tendency to dampen market signals (prices, hard budget constraints, etc.) and to distort incentive structures (to invest, to innovate, etc.) in order to support favored enterprises has, to date, allowed the state to meet some important social and political objectives, but at the expense of compromising what North et al. (2012) describe as "adaptive efficiency."[11]

---

[11] This refers to the ability of states or societies to adjust in response to changes in the global economy, such as sudden shifts in relative prices (e.g. a collapse in commodity prices) or technological changes that result in a redistribution of economic activity between regions of the global economy.

However, the functioning of this system (smooth or otherwise) is contingent on the generation of rents by Sector A. This in turn means that Russia's economic prospects have been and continue to be shaped by developments outside its borders. It is to Russia's relationship with the global economy that I turn next.

RUSSIA'S RELATIONSHIP WITH THE GLOBAL ECONOMY

Having discussed the contours of what is a very specific form of political economy, I will conclude with a brief summary of the nature of Russia's integration with the global economy. The tools of economic statecraft used by Western countries are designed to impose costs on Russia's domestic economic system by altering the relationship between Russian firms and individuals and those sectors of the global economy targeted by sanctions. As a result, it is vital to appreciate how several key aspects of Russia's place in the global economy might affect the potential effectiveness of sanctions.

The first point to note is that Russia is a large economy. According to World Bank data, at $1.4 trillion, the Russian economy was the thirteenth largest in the world in dollar terms in 2016, accounting for just 1.8 percent of global gross domestic product (GDP). Expressed in current US dollars (USD), Russia's per capita income was around $9,700, which amounts to around 15 percent of per capita income in the United States and around 30 percent of the EU average (World Bank 2017). However, measured at purchasing power parity (PPP) – i.e. adjusted for differences in the cost of living – Russian GDP in 2016 was $3.3 trillion, accounting for around 3.5 percent of global GDP. According to this measure, Russia was the sixth largest economy in the world, and the second largest in Europe. Measured at PPP, per capita income was nearly $25,000, around 45 percent of the US level and 65 percent of the EU average (World Bank 2017).

The second key observation is that Russia is, statistically speaking, an open economy. After decades of quasi-autarky during the Soviet period, Russia has become much more closely integrated with the global economy since 1991 (Connolly 2012b). The role of trade in the Russian economy is comparatively high: The sum of imports and exports as a proportion of GDP (a common measure of trade openness) was 51 percent in 2016. This is comparable to other large, open economies such as China (41 percent), France (61 percent), Turkey (61 percent), and India (42 percent). Russia is, therefore, an open economy for a country of its size. Compared to some advanced economies, Russia is less open than the EU member states taken together (79 percent), but more open than the United States (28 percent) and Japan (36 percent) (World Bank 2017). This means that the Russian economy is sensitive to developments well beyond its own borders and, in most instances, over which it has little control.

However, the structure of imports and exports indicates where these sensitivities are concentrated in a limited number of areas. As far as exports are concerned, natural resources represent the overwhelming majority of Russia's exports (Bradshaw and Connolly 2016). As a result, Russia continues to be as dependent on the sale of natural resources as the Soviet Union once was (Lavigne 1995). Of this, hydrocarbons – oil, oil products, natural gas, and coal – account for between 55 and 75 percent of total Russian exports in any one year (United Nations Comtrade 2017). In addition, other natural resources have served as an important source of export revenue, with nonhydrocarbon natural resources, such as metals, minerals, and forestry products, accounting for nearly 10 percent of total Russian exports in most years (Fortescue 2013). Crucially, however, despite its large share in the global production of a wide range of natural resources, Russia is a price taker, not a price maker, on global natural resource markets (Bradshaw and Connolly 2016; Locatelli and Boussena 2017). Thus, while Russia is remarkably dependent on the extraction and export of natural resources, it wields very little in the way of price-forming influence, which in practical terms, means that Russia's real economic sovereignty is severely constrained (Connolly and Hanson 2016). Moreover, it also means that Russia's sensitivity to events in the global economy is concentrated in a relatively small number of subsectors.

Russia is only globally competitive in a small number of other industries outside natural resources (Cooper 2006; Connolly 2008, 2012a). It has proven especially successful in exporting weaponry, an industry in which it has been the world's second largest exporter (second to the United States) for much of the post-Soviet period (Connolly and Senstad 2017). Russia has also been successful in exporting nuclear power-generation machinery (Oxenstierna 2010; Oxenstierna 2014). In both instances, Russia's comparative advantage was forged during the Soviet era, with both benefiting from favorable legacies bequeathed from the Soviet investment and prioritization of the "privileged heart" of the Soviet economy that was the defense industry (Cooper 1991, p. 1; Josephson 2000). Moreover, the state is dominant in both industries.

Privately owned firms from Sector C account for only a modest share of Russia's exports, with perhaps the only significant example being the software industry (Crane and Usanov 2010; Graham 2013; Russoft 2013). In global terms, Russia is a medium-sized software exporter, albeit among the fastest growing. Barriers to entry and exit in the software industry have been low. Levels of competition are high, there are few state-owned firms, firms are exposed to international competition, and the industry is human capital-intensive as opposed to fixed capital-intensive (Bardhan and Kroll 2006; Russoft 2013; Nazarova 2014). This has allowed software firms to benefit from the positive Soviet legacy of a rich heritage of trained specialists in mathematics (Graham 2013). Nevertheless, the software industry is an exception to the general tendency toward state control, or at least influence, over all the most important export sectors through which Russia is connected to the global economy.

As far as imports are concerned, Russia's import profile is in many ways similar to that of the Soviet Union. Despite its position as one of the world's largest manufacturers, Russia does not tend to produce large volumes of high-quality capital goods (machinery, advanced machine tools, etc.) or consumer products. As a result, according to UN Comtrade data (United Nations Comtrade 2017), capital goods accounted for the highest proportion of imported goods in 2016 (30 percent), followed by industrial supplies (22 percent) and consumer goods (16.7 percent). The concentration of imported goods in these areas has resulted in certain sectors of the Russian economy exhibiting high import-penetration ratios. For example, over the past decade, import penetration ratios in machine-building, manufacturing, retail, and communications have all grown at a fast rate, i.e. by at least 40 percent since 2006 (Berezinskaya and Vedev 2015, p. 104).

On the eve of sanctions, Russia was also a country that was relatively open to flows of both inward and outward foreign direct investment (IFDI and OFDI). Foreign direct investment grew substantially after 1991 (Figure 2.6). The poor performance of the economy in the 1990s resulted in IFDI remaining low until 2003. Thereafter, flows of both IFDI and OFDI grew at a rapid rate, reaching a peak in 2008 before the onset of severe recession caused FDI flows to almost halve. However, direct investment grew again after 2009, reaching near post-Soviet record levels in 2013.[12] The sectoral composition of IFDI varied quite dramatically with each year. However, natural resources, retail, manufacturing, and financial intermediation tended to account for the majority of IFDI in Russia. This was reflected in the fact that Moscow City and the surrounding region, as well as resource-rich regions, accounted for the largest proportion of IFDI.

[12] It should be noted, however, that the high volume of IFDI in 2013 was caused primarily by BP's purchase of an 18.5 percent stake in Rosneft.

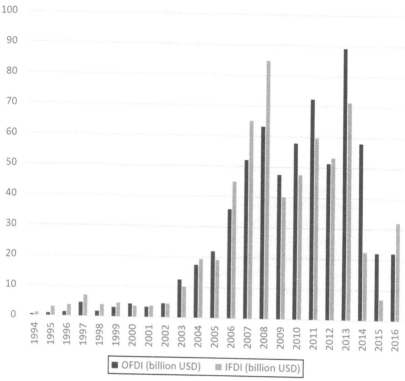

Figure 2.6 Annual flows of IFDI into Russia and OFDI from Russia, 1994–2016 (constant 2015 USD, million)
Source: Bank of Russia (2017)

While Russia did not become as closely integrated with the global value chain (GVCs) as many other postsocialist economies, it was nevertheless true that market-seeking IFDI was evident in certain sectors of the economy, most notably in the automotive sector (Connolly 2012b). Another striking characteristic was that by 2010, Russia's share of global FDI exceeded its share of global GDP, whether measured at market exchange rates or purchasing power parity (Hanson 2010). Indeed, for much of the decade prior to the imposition of sanctions, Russia's stock of IFDI hovered around the level of 30 percent of GDP. This exceeded that of many other large low- and middle-income economies, including Brazil, China, India, Indonesia, Mexico, and Turkey, as well as several high-income economies such as Italy and Korea. In addition, when compared to other middle-income countries, Russia also exhibited a high ratio of OFDI to GDP, as large Russian enterprises were active in the acquisition of foreign companies. Very often this was the result of Russian energy or metals firms acquiring "downstream" assets ("market-seeking" OFDI), or because they wished to acquire foreign technological capabilities and know-how ("technology-seeking" OFDI).[13]

Finally, not only is Russia a large and open economy, but it also engages in foreign economic relations with a diverse range of countries. Indeed, the rapid integration with the global economy that took place in the post-Soviet period has caused a substantial shift in the direction of Russia's trade. While it is true that the majority of Russia's trade continues to take place with the countries of the European Union – with the EU accounting for 46 percent of Russia's exports in 2016, and 38 percent of its imports – it is also true that Russia has developed closer ties with non-Western economies.[14] These include: China – the destination for 10 percent of Russian exports and the source of 22 percent of imports, making it Russia's single largest trade partner; Asia more widely – with south and east Asian economies, including India, South Korea, Japan, and Vietnam accounting for around 10 percent of Russia's exports and 13 percent of imports; and various other rapidly growing economic powers, such as Turkey, which in 2016 was the destination for 5 percent of Russian exports. Perhaps surprisingly, countries from the Middle East and Africa accounted for 3.5 percent of Russia's exports (although only around 1 percent of imports). The United States, the single largest economic power in the group of "sender" countries, accounted for 3.5 percent of Russia's exports and 2.5 percent of imports.

Taken together, these three basic features of the Russian economy make it quite an imposing proposition in the context of applying sanctions. Russia is a larger and more open economy than any other to have been subject to a wide-ranging and multilateral sanctions regime in the post-Cold War period. Moreover, Russia plays a more important role in some strategically important segments of the global economy (e.g. arms and energy) than other significant target countries such as Iran or North Korea. In addition, the fact that the state is dominant in those sectors targeted by sanctions means that it is well placed to divert resources – both institutional and financial – to strategically important yet vulnerable entities

---

[13] Russian companies also tended to invest far more than is normal (by international standards) in tax havens, such as the British Virgin Islands, Bermuda, Cyprus, and Switzerland. In any given year, a substantial proportion of this OFDI is then repatriated in the form of IFDI, thus inflating the "real," non-Russian FDI flows, both inward and outward.

[14] All direction-of-trade data are taken from IMF Direction of Trade Database (2017).

ɔse sectors. Russia's openness to trade and its wide range of
rtners also makes it a difficult target for economic sanctions, as
.. nas, at least in principle, a wide range of potential alternative sources of
technology and capital. The fact that China, Russia's single largest trade
partner, chose not to apply sanctions meant that the world's second largest
economy and largest manufacturing power remained at least potentially a
rich source of technology and capital. To a lesser extent, this is also true of
a wide range of increasingly important economies across the world, from
Latin America to Asia. This meant that – unlike when the Soviet Union
was the target of sanctions during the Cold War – a reasonably wide range
of alternative foreign economic partners were available to Russia when
sanctions were imposed in 2014.

CONCLUSION

Taken together, the key characteristics of the Russian system of political
economy and its integration with the global economy that are described
here were to exert an important influence on how sanctions would affect
Russia. The rent distribution system that lies at the core of Russia's
political economy, its excessive dependence on growth in natural
resource revenues, and the role occupied by the Russian federal state at
the apex of this system, all help explain some of the more negative
features of Russia's economic development over the past decade or so.
These characteristics serve to reduce economic efficiency and productivity growth. They also hamper Russia's longer-term adaptive efficiency
(North et al. 2012).

But those same features that constrain aspects of economic development
in Russia also furnished the state with convenient instruments for
adjusting to sanctions. The state's dominance in economic activity, which
during normal times might have been considered as a weakness, would
prove to be an asset under conditions of sanctions. The state would prove
adept in using a range of instruments at its disposal – institutional,
financial, and diplomatic – to channel resources to areas of the economy
that were considered important by the political leadership. By using these
instruments, the state would be in a position to suppress market signals in
those sectors of the economy in which it was most active, to insulate
targeted entities. The fact that the state exerted a strong influence over
how Russia's interaction with the global economy would take place –
primarily because state-owned or state-influenced firms accounted for
the vast majority of Russia's trade and capital flows – meant that it would

be relatively well positioned to remold crucial aspects of its relationship with the global economy in response to sanctions.

In this respect, the prevailing system of political economy in Russia lent it a certain type of durability that would prove useful when forced to adjust to sanctions from 2014 onward. A series of adaptive measures were quickly undertaken in a reasonably coherent fashion by the Russian state in those areas of the economy that were targeted by Western sanctions. As will be shown throughout the rest of this book, these measures were by no means designed to be, or likely to be, economically efficient. As has been argued throughout this chapter, economic efficiency is rarely the primary objective of economic policy in Russia. But these adaptive measures were intended to reduce Russia's vulnerability to instruments of economic statecraft employed by the West in both the short and long run, and to provide Russia with a more durable pattern of integration with the global economy that would enable it to obtain the benefits of openness (i.e. access to trade and capital, technology and people), but on terms that did not oblige it to relinquish sovereignty and independence in global affairs.

In short, the prevailing system of political economy and the nature of its integration with the global economy gave the Russian state the tools to mediate the impact of sanctions in a way that did not threaten the integrity of the ruling regime. Before I show how this played out in the three strategic sectors targeted by Western sanctions, the next chapter provides a summary of the Western sanctions imposed on Russia over the course of 2014 and beyond, as well as a broad outline of the adaptive measures that were put in place in response to these sanctions.

3

Western Sanctions and the Russian Response

INTRODUCTION

Before examining how the Russian system of political economy described in the previous chapter mediated the impact of Western sanctions, it is first necessary to outline the stated objectives that sender countries set out to achieve by imposing sanctions, to describe the precise nature of those sanctions, and to present the broad contours of the Russian response. The Russian response was multifaceted and included the securitization of strategic areas of economic policy, a concerted effort to support import substitution in strategic sectors of the economy, and vigorous efforts to cultivate economic relations with non-Western countries, especially in Asia. The remaining chapters of this book will be devoted to examining precisely how the Russian response unfolded in three sectors targeted by Western sanctions: the energy industry, the defense industry, and the financial sector.

THE STATED OBJECTIVES OF SENDER COUNTRIES

In line with Baldwin's observation that states may pursue more than one objective when employing techniques of economic statecraft, the statements of Western officials since 2014 suggested that the objectives of the sender countries were multiple (Baldwin 1985). Moreover, it is possible to detect variation in the importance assigned to different objectives by the senders themselves, with the targets of sanctions varying across countries. The variation in importance assigned to each objective is important because the sanctions imposed on Russia in 2014 were – unlike, for instance, the sanctions on Soviet pipeline construction imposed by the United States in the 1980s – multilateral in both design and implementation (Fried 2016).

Sanctions were designed to be multilateral so that they carried what then US President Barack Obama described as a "bigger bite,", although this inevitably meant that the objectives of sender countries were not unified (Baker, Cowell, and Kanter 2014). It is possible to discern at least five broad and interrelated sender-country objectives.

The first objective pursued by Western policymakers was to *express disapproval* of Russia's actions in Crimea and subsequently in Ukraine more widely, and, in doing so, to *provide diplomatic support to the Ukrainian leadership*. In this respect, at least two countries were intended to be directly affected by Western sanctions: Russia (negatively) and Ukraine (positively). Thus, according to Barack Obama, sanctions were designed to "support Ukraine." These sentiments were echoed by the president of the European Council at that time, Herman Van Rompuy, who stated that sanctions were intended to demonstrate to Russia that its actions, including the "illegal annexation of territory" – a reference to Crimea – "and deliberate destabilization of a neighboring sovereign country ... cannot be accepted in 21st-century Europe." Van Rompuy also referred to the "anger and frustration" felt within Europe over the destruction of Malaysia Airlines Flight 17 (MH17) over rebel-held territory in eastern Ukraine on July 17, 2014 (Witte and DeYoung 2014).

The second objective was to affirm the *Western powers' credible commitment to the geopolitical status quo*. As well as signaling disapproval to Russia, both the United States and the European Union were using sanctions as an instrument to promote their wider foreign policy objectives. For the EU, official documents reveal that sanctions are used to "promote the objectives of the Common Foreign and Security Policy (CFSP): peace, democracy and the respect for the rule of law, human rights and international law" and are "not punitive, but designed to bring about a change in policy or activity by the target country, entities or individuals" (EU External Action Service). For the United States, sanctions were intended to act as "a reminder that the United States means what it says, and will rally the international community in standing up for the rights and freedom of people around the world" (Witte and DeYoung 2014). As a result, the sanctions regime was intended to send a signal well beyond Russia and Ukraine, and to emphasize the determination of the United States and Europe to defend the "rules-based order" developed and led by the West in the aftermath of the Cold War. By raising the costs to Russia for transgressing these rules, the Western alliance was demonstrating that it would be prepared to undertake a similar response should any other country pursue policies inimical to the interests of the alliance. The ability to reduce these costs in the future would then serve as leverage – or, as Barack Obama described it, "an incentive to choose the better course" – which could be used by Western powers in negotiations with Russia (The White House Office of the Press Secretary 2014a).

Third, the multilateral nature of the sanctions regime was intended to *demonstrate Western unity* in the face of what the alliance perceived as "Russian aggression." This was intended to be more than simply symbolic. In demonstrating resolve over Ukraine, Western governments were hoping to signal that they were prepared to take serious measures to counteract Russian foreign policy in both Ukraine and beyond. Furthermore, by coordinating their response to Russia's actions in Ukraine, the United States and Europe were also seeking to demonstrate alliance unity, at least in relation to the conflict in Ukraine. For some countries, such as Albania, Iceland, and even Japan, it is likely that participation in the sanctions regime was a signal aimed not so much at Russia as at the United States and the EU. For these countries, demonstrating commitment to their allies may well have superseded any commitment to punishing Russia for its activities. However, for this unity of purpose – impressive and unprecedented as it was – to carry any real weight, sanctions would have to form only part of a wider political strategy, which in this instance might be loosely described as a common "Russia policy." The existence of divergent views within the alliance regarding what form a common policy toward Russia might take would limit the efficacy of any demonstration of alliance unity.

Fourth, the sanctions regime was intended to *inflict economic pain*. By this, we can understand sanctions as an attempt to change the cost–benefit calculations of decision-makers in Russia, in the hope that this might alter the course of Russian foreign policy in relation to Ukraine. Influencing a target country's foreign policy is a longstanding objective in the EU's use of sanctions, which are intended to "bring about a change in policy or activity by the target country, entities or individuals," with sanctions "always targeted at such policies or activities, the means to conduct them and those responsible for them" (European Union 2014).[1] Similar intentions have been expressed by senior US officials. According to Daniel Fried, the senior coordinator of US sanctions policy between 2013 and 2017, one of the key objectives of sanctions is to "influence and not punish" the target state (Fried 2016). This, it is hoped, will occur through the same process

---

[1] For a discussion of the use of sanctions in EU foreign policy, see Portela (2010).

described in EU official documents: by causing discomfort to individuals or entities in the target country so that they are compelled to press for a change in the target country's foreign policy behavior. As Evelyn Farkas, the former Deputy Assistant Secretary of Defense for Russia/Ukraine/ Eurasia, has stated, sanctions against Russia were "tailored ... to affect the people and the companies directly around Putin" in order to "bring about your [i.e. the senders'] objective as soon as possible" (Farkas 2017). Evidently, Galtung's naïve theory was still very much in vogue among policymakers.

The impact of sanctions on shaping decision-making in the target country need not be decisive in order to be considered useful. As argued by Andrew Weiss and Richard Nephew, a former deputy coordinator of US sanctions policy, the goal of sanctions is

to affect the interests of a given state so as to deter or compel it to act in accordance with the interests of the sanctioning state. It does not matter whether sanctions contribute 5 per cent or 75 per cent to this goal. If sanctions, or the threat of sanctions, help tip the scales for the targeted country to make the right choice in its otherwise complex calculation of self-interest, then they represent a particularly useful application of this foreign policy tool (Weiss and Nephew 2016).

In its most extreme form, the desire to inflict economic pain on individuals and entities within Russia meant that, at least for some senior policymakers, sanctions were intended to contribute toward regime change in Russia. While not articulated publicly, this more ambitious objective was stated informally by policymakers from key sender coun- tries.[2] Here, it was hoped that by raising the costs of Russian foreign policy to key members of the Russian elite, they – the perceived "selecto- rate" in Russian politics – would then act to remove Vladimir Putin from power and replace him with a leader who would pursue a foreign policy that was more in line with the preferences of Western policymakers. Regardless of whether this constituted a sensible or, indeed, legal policy objective, it is nevertheless worth stating that this was an objective shared by at least some of the senior policymakers involved in designing and imposing sanctions on Russia.

As the conflict in Ukraine escalated and became further entrenched, the sanctions directed at sectors of the Russian economy became linked to the implementation of the Minsk agreements, which were designed to move

---

[2] Anonymous remarks made to the author by senior US State Department and Treasury officials.

Russia and Ukraine toward a peaceful political solution.[3] Here, sanctions were intended to serve as leverage that could be used to encourage Russia to fulfil its obligations under the Minsk agreements. According to Victoria Nuland, United States Assistant Secretary of State for Europe and Eurasian Affairs between 2013 and 2017, sanctions were intended to "press Moscow to bring an end to the violence in Ukraine and fully implement its commitments under the Minsk agreements" (Tomiuc 2016).

Finally, Western sanctions were intended to *deter* Russia from further expanding its involvement in Ukraine and from behaving in a similar fashion in any other country. In this respect, sanctions were not just seeking to alter immediate Russian calculations concerning the annexation of Crimea and Russia's military involvement in the Donbas region of Ukraine; they were also intended to signal that sanctions could be escalated if, for instance, Russia were to expand the conflict in Ukraine to the port city of Mariupol or to establish a land bridge to Crimea (Weiss and Nephew 2016). Indeed, Victoria Nuland claimed that by 2016, Western "readiness to toughen sanctions even further ... likely played a role in deterring further Russian efforts to grab Ukrainian territory" (Nuland 2016). There are, though, clear methodological difficulties in measuring success in achieving this objective. While it is true that Russia did not (at least up to the point of writing) engage in any concerted effort to expand the conflict beyond the Donbas, it is not clear that this was ever an objective of Russian policymakers. Moreover, Russian military forces were twice deployed to decisive effect in September 2014 and February 2015, even after the "Tier 3" sectoral sanctions were imposed in July 2014 (Charap and Colton 2017, pp. 138–141).

Many, although by no means all, of the objectives outlined here were predicated on the assumption that sanctions at least contribute toward altering the cost–benefit calculations of elite actors within Russia so that those actors might eventually be pushed toward shifting their foreign

---

[3] The Minsk Protocol (and agreement to stop hostilities in the Donbas) was signed by representatives of Ukraine, the Russian Federation, the Donetsk People's Republic (DPR), and the Lugansk People's Republic (LPR) on September 5, 2014. The protocol was signed after protracted negotiations in Minsk, Belarus, under the auspices of the Organization for Security and Co-operation in Europe (OSCE). After numerous violations of the agreement, a new agreement – again overseen by the OSCE – was signed by Ukraine, the Russian Federation, France, and Germany on February 11, 2015, at a summit in Minsk. The new agreement was known as the Minsk II agreement. EU officials stated that sectoral sanctions could only be lifted if and when Russia fulfilled its commitments under the agreement.

policy course. This means, inevitably, that in order to achieve objectives such as affirming commitment to the status quo or deterring Russia or other countries from future aggression, a certain degree of economic pain needs to be inflicted on the target country. How, for instance, can officials from sender countries expect the decision-making calculus to change in the target country if sanctions cause only minor disruption, or, at worst, even help to strengthen elite cohesion in the target country? Or how can policy-makers expect sanctions to act as a credible deterrent to third countries when the target country in any given instance might appear to be coping or even flourishing under sanctions? In short, a significant and negative impact on the target economy is a necessary, although not sufficient, condition for sanctions to be effective.

The rest of this book is primarily devoted to examining whether such economic pain was experienced in Russia after March 2014. An analysis of sanctions' impact on Russia should go some way toward helping those interested in estimating whether sender countries were successful in achieving the political objectives described here. Before that, it is necessary to provide an outline of the scope and extent of the sanctions regime that was developed in the aftermath of Russia's annexation of Crimea.

THE SANCTIONS REGIME

The multiplicity of objectives just stated meant that the multilateral sanctions regime that evolved from March 2014 onward was broad in scope yet also contained important differences, reflecting the variety of policy positions on Russia from within the United States, the EU, and the other countries involved, including Japan, Canada, Norway, Switzerland, Australia, and, of course, Ukraine. While often described as "Russia sanctions," Russia as either a collective entity (i.e. all Russians) or as a state was not sanctioned. Instead, sanctions targeted individuals as well as specific companies and organizations ("entities") within Russia. Analytically, it is possible to separate the sanctions regime into two broad categories: Sanctions imposed in response to Russia's annexation of Crimea – "Crimea sanctions" – which tended to focus on individuals and the economic activity taking place on or in relation to Crimea, or on individuals deemed to have been involved in the political and military operation to annex the peninsula; and sanctions imposed in response to Russia's military intervention in eastern Ukraine – "Donbas sanctions" – which shifted the focus toward companies and sectors of the Russian economy. Although there is some overlap between the two categories, the distinction is useful, because the second set of sanctions was imposed as a means of intensifying economic pressure on Russia as the conflict in Ukraine continued to escalate over the course of 2014.

Crimea Sanctions

On March 5, 2014, more than a week after Russian special forces seized key government buildings in Crimea, the EU adopted a Decision (Council Decision 2014/119/CFSP 2014) that froze the funds and economic resources ("asset freezes") of individuals deemed responsible for the violation of human rights on the peninsula and for the misappropriation of Ukrainian state financial resources. This was followed the next day by an Executive Order (13360), signed by President Barack Obama, that identified events in Ukraine as an "unusual and extraordinary threat to the national security and policy of the United States." This order granted authority for the president to impose sanctions on individuals and entities that were deemed to have "undermine[d] democratic processes and institutions in Ukraine" or misappropriated Ukrainian public assets (The White House Office of the Press Secretary 2014b). At the point that the order was signed, no specific targets were named; the Secretary of the Treasury, in consultation with the Secretary of State, was tasked with determining targets to be included on the US Specially Designated Nationals (SDN) list at a later point.

On March 17, the day after the Crimean referendum, the United States and the EU announced additional sanctions, this time targeting specific Russian individuals and entities. The EU adopted Decision 2014/145, which imposed asset freezes and travel restrictions (visa or travel ban) on, and restrictions on doing business with, individuals and entities that were identified as having compromised Ukraine's sovereignty and territorial integrity (Council Decision 2014/145/CFSP 2014). On the same day, President Obama signed Executive Order 13661, which expanded the legal scope of US sanctions created in Order 13660 – up to this point restricted to asset freezes and travel restrictions – to encompass the "actions and policies" of the Russian government "in respect of Ukraine" (The White House Office of the Press Secretary 2014c). Two days later, President Obama signed an additional Executive Order (13662) which expanded the scope of sanctions even further, this time to include placing restrictions on individuals and entities operating in the financial services, energy, metals and mining, engineering, and defense and related sectors of the

Russian economy (The White House Office of the Press Secretary 2014d). This Order provided the legal foundations for the subsequent imposition of so-called "sectoral" sanctions. Similar asset freezes and travel bans were subsequently imposed by several other countries, including Ukraine, Japan, and Australia. Over time, the list of individuals and entities sanctioned by at least one country/bloc under these terms grew to well over 200 and encompassed Russian and Ukrainian politicians and state officials; business associates of President Putin; combatants in Crimea and eastern Ukraine; and even a Russian journalist, Dmitri Kiselyov, who was working for the Russian government-owned international news agency *Rossiya Segodnya*. Indeed, by April 2014 the list of targeted individuals included senior members of the Russian elite, including Igor Sechin, the executive chairman of Rosneft, and Vyacheslav Volodin, at the time the first deputy chief of staff of the presidential administration of Russia.

Additional sanctions aimed at preventing investment in, or the provision or certain services to, Crimea and Sevastopol were imposed in June 2014 (Council Decision 2014/386 n.d.). These included a ban on imports of goods originating in Crimea or Sevastopol unless they had Ukrainian certificates; a ban on investment in Crimea, including the purchase of real estate, the provision of financial services, or investment in infrastructure projects in six sectors of the local economy; a ban on providing tourism services in Crimea or Sevastopol; prohibition of the sale of goods and technology to Crimean companies, or for use in Crimea, in the transport, telecommunications, and energy sectors, or for use in the exploration of oil, gas, and mineral resources; and the prohibition of technical assistance, brokering, construction, or engineering services related to infrastructure in the same sectors (Council Decision 2014/386 n.d.). Later in the year, President Obama signed Executive Order 13685, which prohibited "certain transactions" – essentially those prohibited by EU Directives 2014/386 and 2014/933 – "with respect to the Crimea Region of Ukraine" (US Treasury 2014a).

Donbas (Sectoral) Sanctions

After March 2014, Russia-backed forces became increasingly involved in fomenting unrest across southern and eastern Ukraine. This process was accelerated as the Russian-supported forces established strongholds in Luhansk and Donetsk, which is broadly described as the Donbas region, and which approximates Slovenia in size.[4] While attempts were made by the insurgents to expand their foothold into other areas, they only proved successful in establishing self-proclaimed people's republics in Donetsk and Luhansk, the two main cities of the region.[5] Even this required the deployment of significant yet undeclared Russian regular military forces to prevent Ukrainian forces from recapturing these areas. As it became apparent that Russian forces were involved in supporting the insurgent forces, Western sanctions were expanded to include Russia's financial, energy, and defense-industrial sectors. While these sanctions were imposed soon after the destruction of Malaysia Airlines Flight 17 (MH17) over insurgent-held territory in eastern Ukraine on July 17, 2014, they were not imposed in response to that atrocity; instead, sectoral sanctions were being prepared even before July 17, and the destruction of the aircraft – carrying 298 passengers and crew – made the political decision to tighten sanctions all the more urgent.[6]

The sanctions imposed in July 2014 targeted specific entities within three strategic sectors of the Russian economy, or denied specific technologies or services used in the three sectors. As such, while the "Tier 3" sanctions have been described as "sectoral," strictly speaking they do not always affect sectors of the Russian economy in a uniform manner. For instance, financial sanctions that prohibited the provision of certain types of financial services to large Russian state-owned banks were not applied to all Russian banks. In the energy sector, technologies used in some parts of the energy extraction process were prohibited while very similar technologies were not. As a result, so-called sectoral sanctions rarely affected all entities in the same sector in the same way. The obvious exception to this lay in the embargo placed on arms trade with Russia, which prohibited all Russian entities from importing weapons from Western countries, although even in this instance the United States and EU differed on the question of whether contracts signed before the imposition of sanctions could still be fulfilled.

The first of the so-called sectoral sanctions was imposed on April 28, 2014, when the US Department of Commerce's Bureau of Industry and Security (BIS) announced that it was expanding its export restrictions on specific items subject to the Export Administration Regulations (EAR) in

---

[4] Military aspects of Russia's involvement in both Crimea and Donbas are documented in Pukhov and Howard (2015).
[5] Neither was formally recognized by any other state, including Russia.
[6] Anonymous conversations between author and senior US and UK officials.

response to Russia's actions in southern and eastern Ukraine (Bureau of Industry and Security 2014). This granted authority to the BIS to deny any pending applications for licenses to export or reexport to Russia or occupied Crimea high-technology items subject to the EAR that were deemed to contribute to Russia's military capabilities. The BIS was also permitted to revoke any existing export licenses which met these conditions. Thus, the United States had, as early as April 2014, imposed a de facto arms embargo on Russia, albeit one that was not especially meaningful given the extremely limited volume of arms sales to Russia by the United States.

The remaining sectoral sanctions were imposed between July and September 2014. On July 17, the United States issued two directives under Executive Order 13662 (signed in April), which brought Russia's financial and energy sectors within the scope of US sanctions. These sanctions prohibited the issuance to specified entities of new equity or debt of longer than ninety days' maturity. Initially, this included the financial entities Vneshekonombank (VEB), Gazprombank, Bank of Moscow, Rosselkhozbank, and VTB, and the energy companies Rosneft and Novatek (Office of Foreign Assets Control 2014). On July 31 the EU adopted Decision 2014/512, which put in place restrictions on the issuance of new equity or debt of longer than ninety days' maturity to specified entities, including VEB, Gazprombank, Sberbank, Rosselkhozbank, and VTB, and which restricted trade in arms or in dual-use goods or technologies intended for military use or military end users (Council Decision 2014/512/CFSP 2014). The EU also restricted the sale of energy equipment and energy-related services to Russia's most technology-intensive energy exploration and extraction projects (e.g. Arctic and deep-water exploration, and onshore shale oil) (Council Decision 2014/512/CFSP 2014). Preferential economic development loans to Russia by the European Bank for Reconstruction and Development (EBRD) were also suspended.

These sectoral sanctions were augmented on September 8, 2014, when the EU modified Decision 2014/512 to reduce the maturity limit on debt issued to specified entities from ninety days to thirty days, and to extend these financial restrictions to entities specified in the defense industry (Oboronprom, Uralvagonzavod, United Aircraft Corporation) and the energy industry (Rosneft, Transneft, and Gazprom Neft). Four days later, four supplementary directives were issued under Executive Order 13662 (Director of the Office of Foreign Assets Control 2014). These directives replicated the EU decision to reduce the maturity limit on debt issued to specified entities from ninety days to thirty days. Sberbank was also added to the initial list of sanctioned entities, and Gazprom Neft and Transneft were prohibited from accessing debt with a maturity of greater than ninety days. The restrictions on the provision of defense or dual-use goods and services were tightened, and financial restrictions that limited the maturity of debt issued by Western entities to thirty days were imposed on defense companies, including the enormous state-owned conglomerate Rostec. The United States also imposed the same energy-sector restrictions that had been put in place by the EU in July.

Once in place, the restrictions imposed by the sanctions regime, with minor adjustments, essentially remained the same until August 2017. Nevertheless, the number of individuals subjected to asset freezes and/or travel restrictions, and entities subjected to financial and/or technological restrictions, rose steadily over time. The United States and EU were joined by other countries, including Ukraine, Japan, Canada, Switzerland, Norway, Australia, New Zealand, Iceland, and Albania, in applying sanctions. In some cases, such as Australia, Canada, Switzerland, and Norway, these sanctions were very similar to those imposed by the United States and EU. In Ukraine, the closeness of precrisis economic relations meant that sanctions were targeted at trade between Ukrainian defense-industrial enterprises and their Russian counterparts, on the one hand, and those individuals deemed to be responsible for activities in Crimea and the Donbas, on the other. Notably, a number of large and advanced economic powers, including the BRICS countries (Brazil, China, India, and South Africa) and South Korea, did not impose sanctions on Russia.

Key Differences in the Western Response

Though the United States and the EU coordinated their sanctions, there were some noteworthy differences, both in terms of the individuals targeted by asset freezes and travel bans and in the manner in which sectoral sanctions were crafted and implemented.

In terms of differences in design, there are notable differences in which individuals and entities were targeted by sanctions, reflecting either differences in sender countries' analyses as to which targets would generate the greatest impact, or more practical concerns relating to the nature of existing economic relations with Russia, which were much closer for most EU member states than for the United States. For instance, some notable Russian officials, including Igor Sechin, Sergei Ivanov, and Vladimir Yakunin, were targeted by the United States, Canada, and Australia, but not by the EU. Gazprom, Europe's single largest supplier of natural gas, was not targeted by EU sanctions, but was targeted by the United States.

There were also notable differences outside the United States and EU. For instance, the composition of Australian sanctions was shaped by government views of who within Russia and the insurgent-held territory was responsible for the MH17 atrocity that resulted in the deaths of thirty-eight Australian citizens. Perhaps most importantly, the world's third largest economy (at market exchange rates), Japan, also chose to impose sanctions that were substantially different to those of the United States and EU. While Japan imposed asset freezes and travel bans on individuals, and participated in the arms embargo and in restricting lending to large Russian state-owned banks, it crucially avoided imposing sanctions on Russia's energy industry. As one of the world's largest net importers of hydrocarbons, it is clear that Japanese officials hoped to facilitate cooperation between Japanese and Russian firms in the energy industry. As a leading technological power, Japan was thus well placed to exploit any reduction in Western involvement in the Russian energy industry. In imposing sanctions that were unlikely to inflict much of an economic cost on Russia (Japan exported only a nominal volume of weapons and dual-use technologies to Russia), Japan was able to make the symbolic gesture of supporting its US ally while also keeping its more commercial options open in the strategically important energy industry. Furthermore, Tokyo also signaled to Moscow that Japan considered good relations to be important, something that was essential if the Japanese government wanted to make progress on reaching an agreement with Russia over the Kurile islands (Streltsov 2015). As the Russian analyst Fyodor Lukyanov noted, "Tokyo has played its cards in the best possible manner. It has restrained the sanctions against Moscow as far as possible so that they are more symbolic than substantial."[7]

As far as differences in implementation are concerned, the most notable disparity between the EU and the United States lies in the EU's "grandfathering" provision, which permits EU firms to perform contracts that were concluded prior to the imposition of the original sanctions. As shown in Chapter 4, this resulted in considerably different outcomes for EU and US firms operating in the areas of Russia's Arctic, offshore deep-water, and shale oil deposits.

It is also important that in the United States, the execution of sanctions is primarily the responsibility of the Department of Treasury's Office of Foreign Asset Control (OFAC), which coordinates the identification of

---

[7] Fyodor Lukyanov quoted in Kitade (2016).

targets alongside the Secretary of State. This means that there is a high degree of cohesion and centralization in the US implementation of sanctions. By contrast, the implementation of EU sanctions is devolved to member states, leaving some leeway in interpreting and executing the sanctions legislation.

Finally, there are considerable differences in how the EU and the United States maintain sanctions. In the EU, unanimity among all twenty-eight member states in regular (annual or biannual) meetings is required to sustain the sanctions regime. This means that, institutionally, sanctions are not difficult to revoke. By contrast, the reduction or removal of US sanctions requires the agreement of both the legislature (Congress) and the executive (the President). Indeed, Congressional influence over the sanctions imposed on Russia was strengthened in August 2017, when additional legislation was passed that both increased the scope of sanctions and reduced the president's ability to remove them.[8]

THE RUSSIAN RESPONSE

As the sanctions regime evolved over the course of 2014, the Russian government did not remain passive. In response, Russian officials employed techniques of economic statecraft of their own, and formulated economic policies designed to reduce the impact of Western sanctions. The Russian response comprised three complementary and overlapping components: (1) the securitization of strategic areas of economic policy; (2) a concerted effort to support import substitution in strategic sectors of the economy; and (3) vigorous efforts to cultivate closer economic relations with non-Western countries, especially in Asia. All three elements were evident in Russia's so-called countersanctions regime, which was introduced in August 2014 and targeted Western agricultural exports to Russia. The Russian response was led by the state and utilized the considerable instruments available to Russia's leaders. As shown in Chapter 2, the influence of the Russian state in key sectors of the economy is significant. This enabled the state to react to Western sanctions in a relatively coordinated fashion, using a range of financial, institutional, and diplomatic measures. Indeed, it is the precise nature of the Russian reaction to sectoral sanctions that is the subject of the remainder of this book. However, before paying detailed attention to how sanctions shaped the development of

---

[8] These additional sanctions – beyond the purview of this book – are contained within the Countering America's Adversaries through Sanctions Act of 2017 (CAATSA).

Russia's energy, defense, and financial sectors, it is first necessary to present a broad outline of the Russian response.

Securitization

Perhaps the broadest way to describe Russia's response to Western sanctions is to suggest that economic policy has, since March 2014, become increasingly securitized. In the academic literature, securitization refers to a two-step process where first a "securitizing move" takes place in which policymakers adopt the rhetoric of national security concerns to justify policies that are no longer "normal" in any given dimension of public policy (Bacon and Renz 2006, p. 10). This is then followed by the second step – the evolution of policy – that occurs after specific key audiences, such as the government, a specific ministry, or other elements of the body politic, have accepted this rhetoric as legitimate. Successful securitization does not always mean that advocates of a discourse of securitization will be successful in advancing their policy agenda. But it does mean that attempts at invoking national security concerns to shape public policy may succeed more frequently than was the case under "normal" politics.

This conceptual framework fits Russian behavior after the annexation of Crimea reasonably well. To be sure, even during "normal" periods, Russian official discourse could appear disproportionately fixated with security concerns. Nevertheless, the balance before 2014 tended to work in favor of "normal" public policy, with the securitized agenda only gaining resonance in either fringe areas of public policy or those areas normally associated with security (e.g. counterterrorism, defense, etc.). There was, for instance, only modest evidence of securitized thinking in the economic sphere prior to March 2014.[9] Afterward, however, a range of economic policy issues that under more normal circumstances might have been considered "technical" were placed in the realm of national security. These included the size of Russia's foreign exchange reserves, the volume of specific food products imported, the geographic direction of Russia's trade relations, and the degree of dependence on imported machinery and services in strategic sectors of the economy. As the geopolitical conflict between Russia and the West intensified over 2014 and beyond, a growing number of Russian policymakers revealed a clear preference for self-reliance and a reorientation of the country's integration with the global economy.

---

[9] An example of a more comprehensive statement of a securitized approach to economic development can be found in Glazyev (2015).

This was justified by reference to security concerns, as policymakers subordinated economic policy to a wider effort to reduce Russia's vulnerability to a growing range of perceived internal and external threats, many of which were seen to emanate from the United States and its allies (Security Council of the Russian Federation 2015).

This shift in thinking became increasingly evident over the course of 2014–2015 and was cemented in the publication of the country's National Security Strategy toward the end of 2015 (ibid). This document clearly stated the view that Russia's economic development was threatened by, inter alia, "economic measures employed by foreign powers" – a clear reference to Western sanctions (ibid., Sections III.51 and IV.57). The threat posed by sanctions deployed by other powers is highlighted several times throughout the document, including a reference to "the restrictive economic measures imposed on Russia" used by the United States and its allies to "contain Russia" (ibid., Sections II.9 and II.12). This led Russian officials present at a meeting of the Interdepartmental Commission of the Security Council to declare the urgent need to protect Russia's "economy from the political and economic decisions of other states that aim to prevent the effective dynamic development of the Russian economy." In order to combat the actions of other states, official thinking emphasized economic policies that would help preserve national sovereignty (*suverennost'*) and independence (*nezavisimost'*). The importance of enhancing Russia's economic sovereignty was reiterated in the Economic Security Strategy to 2030, published in 2017, which stated that economic sovereignty is vital to maintaining and even strengthening Russia's ability to act as an independent foreign policy actor ('O strategii' 2017, p. 2).

This important change in official thinking led to an observable shift in economic policy that contained the core elements of the Russian response to Western sanctions. Efforts to boost Russia's economic sovereignty were focused on two areas. First, it was seen as necessary to replace imported equipment and services with domestic production in a range of strategically important industrial sectors. This became known as "import substitution" (*importozameshcheniye*), although as time progressed it became associated with other state-led efforts to boost domestic economic capabilities, such as "localization." Before March 2014, only a small minority of the economic policy elite supported a concerted import substitution policy. However, it was taken more seriously by a broader audience in the policymaking community after March 2014 as they sought to bolster Russia's domestic productive capabilities, especially in the high-technology goods that were now prohibited by Western governments. Second, import substitution was complemented by efforts to diversify Russia's foreign economic relations. Here, Russian officials stressed the importance of reducing Russia's dependence on importing capital and technology from Western countries and indicated a preference for acquiring larger volumes of capital and technology from non-Western sources.

Import Substitution[10]

A vital component of this overall trend toward the securitization of economic policy in Russia was the import substitution program. Official Russian thinking about the need to formulate a large-scale import substitution program accelerated alongside the intensification of the conflict in Ukraine. Several presidential instructions (*porucheniya*) had been issued by May 14, 2014 (Government of the Russian Federation 2014). At the time – i.e. before Western sectoral sanctions were imposed – these measures were presented primarily as efforts to stimulate economic growth and competitiveness in both industrial and agricultural branches of the economy. This could be seen as a practical step to help combat the effects of the economic slowdown that began over the course of 2012–2013 and which seemed to be pushing Russia toward recession in early 2014 (Zamaraev et al. 2013). However, it was already evident by this point that the Russian leadership was preparing for an expansion of Western sanctions (Kliment'yeva 2014). A new Government Commission for Import Substitution was formed in August 2015 (Ministry of Economic Development 2015). Within less than a year of the program's initiation, Denis Manturov, the Minister for Industry and Trade, presented a detailed plan for import substitution that initially included more than 2,000 projects across nineteen branches of the economy. These projects were to be carried out between 2016 and 2020, and envisaged a total cost of over 1.5 trillion rubles (c.$25 billion at the average 2015 exchange rate), with 235 billion rubles (c.$4.5 billion) allocated to be spent directly from the federal budget (Dzis'-Voynarovskii 2015; Yedovina and Shapovalov 2015). Over the course of 2014–2015, extra resources were also allocated to several strategic sectors of the economy, including those sectors targeted by Western sanctions, such as the defense sector and the oil and gas equipment industry.

Ambitious targets to increase import substitution – i.e. to increase the share of domestic production in goods and services used in the Russian

---

[10] This section draws heavily on Connolly and Hanson (2016).

economy, and its logical corollary, to reduce the share of imported goods and services used in Russia – were set by policymakers. These ambitions were extended to all branches of the economy targeted by Western sanctions but also affected other areas, such as the pharmaceutical and information technology (IT) industries. In order to reach these objectives, the state allocated significant financial resources and institutional support. For example, changes were made to public procurement procedures so the share of imports could be reduced in favor of domestic production. In those areas where existing Russian capabilities were considered to be weak, and where foreign firms were most active, "localization" of production was encouraged. The import substitution program was given extra urgency as the economy entered recession in 2015, with government presenting its efforts to develop new and existing industrial capabilities as a key element of its "anticrisis" strategy (Government of the Russian Federation 2015b).

Overall, the resources allocated to import substitution were substantial. Financial resources, such as the provision of preferential loans to beneficiary companies, the granting of preferential access to state procurement funds, and direct federal budget spending, were all deployed to help stimulate production in targeted sectors of the economy. Financial support for import substitution was given in the form of tax breaks; state-subsidized credit via the state development bank, Vneshekonombank (VEB); and favorable loans provided by the newly established Fund for the Development of Industry (the *fond razvitiya promyshlennosti*, or FRP). Individual credits ranged from 50 million to 700 million rubles, with interest rates of 5 percent, significantly lower than the double-digit rate of inflation in the year they were offered (Kryuchkova 2015).[11] Additional funding was also made available by the Ministry for Economic Development and the Central Bank (Ardaev 2016).

The government also provided considerable institutional support to key sectors of the economy, including the creation of government structures to formulate and implement the import substitution program, as well as creating the legal framework to facilitate the use of public procurement to benefit domestic firms. The import substitution campaign was overseen by the Government Commission on Import Substitution.[12]

---

[11] On January 1, 2016, the Central Bank base rate was 11 per cent. For more on the details of the FRP, see the agency website: http://frprf.ru/.

[12] Details of this body can be found on the government website: http://government.ru/department/314/events/.

This body was chaired by the Prime Minister, Dmitri Medvedev, and was tasked with the identification of strategic objectives and the regulation of state procurement of equipment and the procurement activities of large private companies receiving state support. This was to be carried out with a view to restricting their use of imported machinery to items for which no locally made (i.e. produced in Russia or the Eurasian Economic Union) analogue was available (Medvedev 2016b). Almost immediately, successful lobbying efforts by Russian producers resulted in the extension of the range of products that were subject to restrictions (Malysheva 2015).

While the political, institutional, and financial commitment to import substitution since 2014 has been significant, it is nevertheless important to stress that official statements on the subject continued to emphasize the importance of foreign participation in the Russian economy. As a result, from 2016 onward, "localization" began to replace "import substitution" as a buzzword of state economic policy. Here, the emphasis was not on excluding foreign technology and ownership, but instead on ensuring that Russia was better integrated in global value chains, with a greater proportion of the value-added in the manufacturing process taking place on Russian territory. Nevertheless, while the label may have evolved, the objective remained the same: to use instruments of state regulation and direction to develop domestically-based industrial capabilities.

Overall, the import substitution campaign, in its various guises, represented a core component of what emerged as a wider state-directed effort to boost Russia's domestic industrial capabilities and, in doing so, enhance its sovereignty and economic security. Official statements and documents demonstrated that this shift in thinking was no coincidence, but was instead part of a response crafted to reduce the impact of Western sanctions. The importance of this effort was reiterated when Prime Minister Dmitri Medvedev declared in 2015 that import substitution would be "our strategic priority for the coming years" (Medvedev 2015b). After that, progress in initiating import substitution-related projects across the economy was significant. According to Denis Manturov, by the summer of 2017, twenty-two sectors of the economy were receiving state support to stimulate import substitution, with production initiated in at least 130 projects (Manturov 2017). While Manturov was also quick to highlight areas where progress was still to be made, it was clear that import substitution was considered to be a key component of Russian economic policy.

The Diversification of Russia's Foreign Economic Relations

As well as seeking to bolster Russia's domestic economic capabilities, policymakers also accelerated efforts to impart a more pluridirectional character to Russia's foreign economic relations. As was shown in the previous chapter, the West – and especially the countries that make up the European Union – has historically served as Russia's primary trade partner and source of capital. This was true in the nineteenth century, was true during the Soviet period, and has been true since 1991. However, the past decade has seen a slow yet inexorable shift in Russia's trading relations toward what might be broadly described as Eurasia. This enormous geographic area includes China, now Russia's single largest trading partner, but also India, the countries of the former Soviet Union, and the rapidly growing economies of East Asia and the Middle East. As illustrated in the previous chapter, in recent years Europe continued to account for the bulk of Russia's external trade. It also provided the vast majority of external capital.[13] However, Europe's share of Russia's external trade diminished, especially over the course of the decade before sanctions were imposed. During this period, Russia underwent a gradual shift toward Eurasia. While this process was driven primarily by rapidly growing ties with China, the role of other smaller economies, such as Turkey, Vietnam, India, and South Korea, should not be ignored.

Two observations should be made at this stage. First, the Russian desire to strengthen economic ties with non-Western countries was far from new. For instance, in his 2012 article on Russia's place in the world, Vladimir Putin expressed the hope that Russia would be able to "catch some of China's wind in the sails of our economy" (Putin 2012c). This could, Putin suggested, result in greater mutual investment and a synergy of technological and productive capabilities. If successful, leveraging rapid Chinese growth would also facilitate the development of Russia's domestic economy in Siberia and the Russian Far East. As a result, the institutional framework to develop Russia's Far East and to promote closer ties with the Asian economy was put in place long before Russia's annexation of Crimea (Fortescue 2016; Malle 2017). Thus, it was with a great deal of truth that Putin declared in December 2014 that "our active policy in the Asia-Pacific region began not just yesterday and not in response to sanctions, but is a policy that we have been following for a good many years now" (Putin 2014a).

---

[13] The Russian analyst Vasily Kashin (2016) suggested that official data do not capture the full extent of capital flows between China and Russia.

Second, Russian officials did not present the desire to intensify relations with non-Western countries in binary, zero-sum terms. Instead, policymakers were often keen to stress that Western economies would, where they wished to do so, continue to act as important sources of trade, capital, and ideas. However, by developing a more balanced relationship with non-Western countries, the diversification of Russia's foreign economic relations was intended to help support a wider shift toward a more multipolar order, an order in which Russia's influence would be enhanced precisely because it would not be dependent on economic relations with one political or economic bloc. In this respect, Russian attempts to develop ties with a more diverse array of countries should be seen less as a pivot, and more as a process of rebalancing. It was hoped that this rebalancing of foreign economic relations should in turn grant Russian policymakers greater autonomy in both a geopolitical and a geoeconomic sense ('O strategii' 2017, p. 12; Trenin 2017).

Nevertheless, while the shift toward seeking out partners outside the West, and in Asia in particular, was not new, it was something that became more politically salient after 2014. As Silvana Malle has argued, the "pivot to Asia that predated the Ukrainian crisis has [subsequently] become more pronounced" (Malle 2017, p. 51). In this sense, the conflict in Ukraine and the subsequent imposition of sanctions served to provide the impetus for an acceleration of an existing tendency. This intention was evident even before sectoral sanctions were applied in July 2014, with the Press Secretary to the Russian President, Dmitri Peskov, stating as early as March 2014 that "if one economic partner on the one side of the globe impose sanctions, we will pay attention to new partners from the globe's other side. The world is not monopolar, we will concentrate on other economic partners" (RT 2014). It was perhaps precisely because the shift toward Asia (or, more accurately, toward the "non-West") had taken on such political importance that it led the Russian Foreign Minister, Sergei Lavrov, to triumphantly – and quite uncharacteristically – declare that, by the end of 2014, Russia had succeeded in making "a breakthrough in the development of our strategic partnership with China" (Lavrov 2014).

Further evidence of Russia's commitment to developing economic ties with the non-West can be found in official strategy documents published since 2014. These documents, which seek to define the future direction of Russia's foreign policy and economic development, are consistent in conveying a clear desire on the part of Russian policymakers to diversify the country's foreign economic relations. This was expressed in general terms – for instance, both the National Security Strategy (2015) and the

Economic Security Strategy (2017) cite the increasing use of economic tools of influence by foreign powers as a reason to build closer ties to non-Western centers of economic power. But it was also evident in the narrower, sectoral strategy documents – such as the draft Energy Strategy (2015), the Maritime Doctrine (2015), the Food Security Doctrine (2010) – which all declared the importance of intensifying ties with non-Western economies to boost Russian security and sovereignty.

To sum up: The evidence contained in statements made by senior policymakers and within official strategic planning documents suggests that Russia's aspirations in the realm of its foreign economic relations are both clear and realistic. No ambitions to become dominant in other regions of the global economy are stated. Instead, the declared intention is for Russia to become an active and important actor in all the world's key economic regions. In doing so, Russia would, it was hoped, reduce its own exposure to any deterioration in political (e.g. sanctions) or economic (e.g. poor economic performance) relations with any one part of the global economy, which should then enhance its own economic security and sovereignty.

CONCLUSION

As this chapter has shown, the stated – and sometimes publicly unstated – objectives of the sender countries when imposing sanctions on Russia varied. Moreover, there were subtle but often very important differences in the details of the different sanctions regimes put in place by the United States and its allies. In some instances, these differences were far from trivial and, as will be shown in subsequent chapters, reduced the severity of sanctions in practice. Nevertheless, while the precise nature of sanctions did vary, there was a significant unity of political purpose. Sanctions were intended to demonstrate support for the Ukrainian government, express Western dissatisfaction with Russian foreign policy, and put pressure on the Russian government to change its foreign policy course. Perhaps most importantly, inflicting at least some economic harm on Russia – i.e. having impact – was an important means to achieving the stated objectives. However, the Russian "target" did not prove inert and passive when sanctions were imposed. Instead, the Russian government quickly designed a package of measures that were intended to reduce the impact of sanctions and to insulate the domestic economy from similar measures in the future. Broadly speaking, this response, which was applied in all three of the sectors targeted by the United States and its allies, was focused on enhancing Russia's economic sovereignty through state-directed efforts to boost Russia's domestic economic capabilities (i.e. import substitution and localization) and by diversifying Russia's foreign economic relations. The Russian state found itself in a strong position to shape and implement this response, largely because of the specific characteristics of the Russian system of political economy described in Chapter 2. The remainder of this book will show how these efforts to boost domestic economic capabilities and to forge more pluridirectional foreign economic ties enabled Russia to adjust to Western sanctions in a relatively short period of time. In doing so, the impact of Western sanctions was considerably reduced.

4

Sanctions and the Energy Industry

INTRODUCTION

The energy industry is the most important part of the Russian economy, at least as far as its contribution to aggregate economic activity is concerned, and is the key pillar of the rent-generating sector of the Russian economy described in Chapter 2. After the disintegration of the Soviet Union in 1991, the Russian energy industry became more closely integrated with the global economy. It opened up to partial foreign ownership (inward foreign direct investment, or IFDI) and Russian firms acquired assets abroad (outward foreign direct investment, or OFDI) (Hanson 2010). In Russia, the number of joint ventures (JVs) rose, imports of equipment from a diverse range of countries increased and Russian firms utilized international capital to finance projects.

Due to its strategic importance, and because it is one of the most globally integrated sectors of the Russian economy, the Russian energy industry was also an obvious target for Western economic sanctions. In the summer of 2014, restrictions on access to capital and technology were imposed on Russian oil and gas companies. These tended to affect oil production the most, but the scope of the sanctions meant that some gas projects were also affected. Technological sanctions focused on plans for the development of new "frontier" oil deposits, both offshore in the Arctic and onshore in the shale oil formations (such as the Bazhenov and Domanik formations in Western Siberia and the Urals), although they also affected technology used in enhanced recovery of oil in "brownfield" deposits.[1] Financial restrictions also affected the current operations of

---

[1] The term "frontier" is used here to refer to areas of Russia where production is currently low but scheduled to rise significantly over the coming decades.

Russian energy firms. As a result, it can be seen that sanctions had the potential to reduce Russian oil production in the short term and more significantly in the future. Russia's ability to expand production of off-shore natural gas and to increase its exports of liquefied natural gas (LNG) was also threatened.

Because of the crucial role that hydrocarbons play in the Russian economy, sanctions that threaten Russia's ability to extract hydrocarbons in the future have been described as "highly politicized" and "a threat to national security" (Ministry of Energy of the Russian Federation 2009; Security Council of the Russian Federation 2015; Government of the Russian Federation 2016a). To reduce Russian vulnerability to this threat, policymakers devised a dual policy of Russification and diversification. Russification refers to the support given to the domestic oil and gas equipment industry as one of the priority sectors in the government's wider import substitution strategy. This was accompanied by efforts to increase control over different aspects of the Russian energy industry, including exploration, oil services, and production. Diversification refers to efforts by both the Russian government and by state-owned firms towards greater cooperation with non-Western sources of capital, technology, and demand for Russian energy.

If Russian producers or new foreign suppliers were to emerge as reliable suppliers of viable substitutes for products and services that are sanctioned, as well as new and important sources of demand for Russian energy, the nature of the industry's integration with the global economy could change in several ways.

First, prior to 2014, the Russian oil industry relied on large volumes of imported equipment from a wide range of Western companies. If Russian efforts to substitute Western equipment with domestically produced ana-logues were to prove successful, the role played by Western firms in the Russian oil equipment market would probably diminish. This also has the potential to result in greater competition for Western firms from Russian companies in markets outside Russia and the West.

Second, if Russian producers prove able to produce viable substitutes for Western technology, the need for Western international oil company (IOC) involvement in upstream JVs in Russia might also weaken. After all, Western IOCs were granted access to Russia's energy reserves largely because they currently possess a comparative advantage in technology and knowhow (Overland et al. 2013). If Russia were able to produce viable substitutes for this knowhow and technology, this advantage would obsolesce and the need for Western involvement in Russia's energy industry may diminish, thus reversing many of the steps toward integration with the global oil industry that took place after the disintegration of the Soviet Union.

Third, the Russian energy industry – like the Russian economy writ large – accessed the vast majority of its external capital from Western countries before 2014. This had been the case since the disintegration of the Soviet Union in 1991, and took the form of direct Western equity ownership in Russian energy firms and the provision of loans from Western banks to Russian energy firms. Again, if Russian firms were to prove successful in accessing capital from alternative sources – whether domestic or foreign – it would represent a sea change in the nature of the industry's relationship with the global economy.

Fourth, demand for Russian energy – especially gas – traditionally came from Europe, in a relationship that stretches back to the height of the Cold War (Högselius 2012). However, Russian efforts to diversify the sources of demand for energy exports could, if even only partially successful, enhance both Russia's own energy security – defined in terms of security of demand – and its wider security needs, by reducing its vulnerability to external pressure from Western countries in the future.

Taken together, Russian policies designed to simultaneously Russify and diversify different aspects of the Russian energy industry had the potential to result in a seismic shift in the nature of the industry's integration with the global economy. To effect such changes, the Russian state used its position at the apex of the limited-access system of political economy described in the previous chapter to use the instruments at its disposal – institutional, financial, and diplomatic – to initiate a process of adjustment and adaptation in the Russian energy industry. While this process proceeded unevenly, it managed to minimize the intended impact of Western sanctions, and in doing so reduced Russia's vulnerability to energy-related sanctions in the future.

The remainder of this chapter is organized as follows. First, I give a broad overview of the role that the oil and gas industries play in the Russian economy. The nature of the Russian oil and gas industries' integration with the global energy industry is then discussed, along with an outline of the role played by Russian and foreign technology. After this, the nature of the sanctions imposed on the Russian oil and gas sectors is described. This is followed by an examination of how Russian government policies evolved in response to the imposition of Western sanctions, with a focus on the government's unfolding plans for Russification and diversification. The chapter concludes by considering how, given the adaptive measures initiated by the Russian government, Western sanctions have shaped the development of the Russian oil and gas sectors since 2014.

THE ENERGY INDUSTRY AND THE RUSSIAN ECONOMY

It is difficult to understate the importance of the energy industry – especially oil and gas – to the Russian economy. As illustrated in Figure 4.1, the value of Russia's oil and gas exports are enormous. Crude oil and refined oil products account for the largest share of export revenues. The relative influence of the two has shifted over the past two decades, with higher-value refined oil products accounting for a rising share of oil exports at the expense of exports of crude oil. This occurred as a direct result of government changes to the taxation system to encourage a shift towards the export of higher value-added products (Henderson 2015). As was shown in Chapter 2, the magnitude of export revenues derived from oil and gas sales means that Russia's economic and geopolitical fortunes are shaped primarily by variations in global hydrocarbon prices (Bradshaw and Connolly 2016).

Natural gas also plays an important role in Russia's export profile, although revenues have plateaued since 2009, caused at first by slowing demand from Russia's principal gas customers in the European Union, and then by a concerted effort on the part of Russian producers to reduce gas prices in order to maintain market share in the face of rising competition

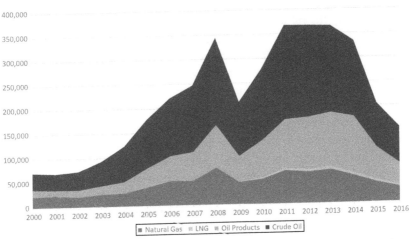

Figure 4.1 Oil and gas export revenues, 2000–2016 (USD bn, constant 2015 prices)
Source: Bank of Russia (2017)

in European markets from liquefied natural gas (LNG) exporters (Boussena and Locatelli 2017). Russia is also emerging as a significant exporter of LNG in its own right, although LNG currently accounts for a relatively small share of Russia's exports (Figure 4.1). Although the Russian government has stated that LNG exports, especially to Asia, will form a key part of its future energy strategy, numerous problems have beset efforts by Gazprom, Russia's largest gas company, to expand LNG exports (Ministry of Energy of the Russian Federation 2009; Henderson and Moe 2016). Other companies, most notably Novatek, have made better progress.

But how do these revenues affect economic performance in Russia? Existing estimates of the relationship between oil and gas production on the one hand, and overall economic performance on the other, have estimated the direct value-added share of the oil and gas sectors in Russian GDP (Ahrend 2005; Kuboniwa, Tabata and Ustinova 2005; Kuboniwa 2016). These estimates suggest that oil and gas revenues have contributed directly to anywhere between 10 and 25 percent of GDP, depending on the value of oil and gas sales at any given point in time.

Focusing on the oil and gas sectors' direct contribution to total value-added in the Russian economy does not give a full picture of the role that it plays. In addition to the direct contribution made by the oil and gas sectors, it is also necessary to consider their indirect contribution. Clifford Gaddy and Barry Ickes describe the various ways in which industry revenues are shared throughout the Russian economy via an informal rent-sharing mechanism. They define this to include price subsidies, informal taxes, and excess costs (Gaddy and Ickes 2005). In addition, revenues generated by the oil and gas sectors are redistributed via a mix of direct transfers (e.g. relatively transparent, formal taxes on hydrocarbon exports to finance the federal budget) and indirect transfers (e.g. through resource sector firms supplying inputs at below market price to other enterprises). As discussed in Chapter 2, this shows how economic activity elsewhere in the economy is driven by the value of export revenues in the hydrocarbons industry. This creates a "demand hunger" in Russia, as state officials seek to ensure that there is a stable, preferably growing, source of income from the sale of hydrocarbons on global markets. However, the oil and gas sector both face significant challenges at home and from abroad that may reduce the flow of income from the sale of hydrocarbons.

In the oil industry, production in many older ("brownfield") oilfields is either diminishing or forecast to decline in the near future (Henderson 2015). This means that production will have to be replaced by Russia's yet untapped "frontier" oil reserves – including those located offshore, mainly in the Arctic – as well as Russia's extensive yet unexploited shale oil formations (Gustafson 2012). Exploitation of these deposits will require the use of expensive extraction technologies. Indeed, as will be discussed later, it was future production at these very deposits that was targeted by Western sanctions. Regardless of how sanctions affect Russian production, it is highly likely that the value of rents that the state will be able to extract from oil firms will decline, either because of lower production (i.e. if Russian firms are unable to exploit new deposits) or because the increased costs involved in carrying out extraction offshore in the Arctic, for instance, necessitate a reduced tax burden on energy firms to incentivize production. Looking abroad, the rapid expansion of oil production in the United States also changed the dynamics of the international oil market, with prices seemingly locked into a lower equilibrium due to the rapid expansion of US tight oil production.

The challenges are different in the gas industry. Domestically, the prospect of lower consumption of gas as Russian industry means greater energy efficiency and, as population growth stagnates and then turns negative, means that exports – which have always been much more profitable than domestic sales – will grow in importance for Russia's gas producers. However, the demand for gas in Russia's traditional customers, Ukraine, and the countries of the European Union is not considered likely to grow substantially in the coming years. In some cases, it may even decline. This is a problem for Russia because its gas producers – including the state-owned Gazprom, which retains its monopoly on the export of pipeline gas, and other large companies such as Novatek and the state-owned Rosneft – have access to vast gas reserves (Boussena and Locatelli 2017). The problem, it appears, is establishing sustainable sources of demand for this gas. But the search for new customers was complicated by increasingly intense competition among gas producers, especially as LNG began to account for a growing share of globally traded gas (British Petroleum 2016, pp. 28–29). This meant that Russia was increasingly faced with competition not just from natural gas producers closer to home, such as Azerbaijan and Turkmenistan, but also from as far as away as Qatar, Australia, and the United States. This competition has the potential to drive down the price and volume of gas that Russia will be able to export in the future, which in turn might reduce the volume of rents available to sustain the existing system of political economy (Boussena and Locatelli 2017).

How Russia confronts these obstacles will be of considerable importance to both the Russian economy – the current system of political economy is founded upon the revenues derived from exports of oil and gas – and the global economy more widely. But to gauge the nature of the relationship between the Russian energy industry and the wider global energy industry, it is necessary to go beyond the simple yet important calculation of Russia's contribution to global supply.

THE RUSSIAN ENERGY INDUSTRY AND THE GLOBAL ECONOMY

The relationship between the Russian energy industry and the wider global energy industry has fluctuated dramatically over the past twenty-five years. During the Soviet period, IOCs were not granted equity shares in upstream hydrocarbons deposits until very late in Gorbachev's leadership (Gustafson 2012, pp. 2–3). Nevertheless, although inward foreign direct investment (IFDI) was limited, the Soviet Union was forced to import considerable quantities of oil and gas extraction equipment, despite possessing one of the largest indigenous oil and gas equipment industries in the world (Campbell 1980).

Yet the sheer volume of hydrocarbons extracted in the Soviet Union, and the input-extensive techniques employed by inefficient Soviet production associations (*ob'edineniya*), meant that imports were, from a Soviet planner's point of view, a necessary evil (Office of Technology Assessment 1986; Gustafson 1990). Where imports were necessary, Soviet planners preferred to source equipment from their socialist allies, which in practice usually meant Romania, the country with the most advanced oil extraction industry within the socialist bloc. However, more advanced equipment, such as offshore drilling platforms, as well as more advanced pumps and drilling equipment, was often obtained from European countries, the United States, and Japan (Campbell 1980, chapter 6).

The 1990s saw Russia create an imperfect but functioning market economy (Sutela 2012). During this first period of post-Soviet oil industry development, the state was fragile, institutions were weak, and the industry suffered from chronic underfunding. A controversial privatization process also resulted in several prize assets being transferred to private owners (Gustafson 2012).

It was in the 1990s that the role of foreign energy companies really changed, as several of them entered production-sharing agreements (PSAs) with Russian producers. At the time, PSAs were considered a mutually beneficial solution to the challenges associated with the uncertain legal and institutional environment of the nascent and chaotic Russian market. A direct contract between an investor and a host government, PSAs offered the advantage of allowing investors to recover costs up front. Once oil started to flow, the initial production revenue went to the investor to cover the costs of investment. After these costs were recovered, the subsequent revenues were split between the investor and the host government. These arrangements were considered to reduce the risks to investors while also facilitating much needed investment into Russia's neglected and badly run oilfields.

As the role of foreign companies in direct ownership of Russia's upstream assets changed, the role played by foreign producers of equipment and oilfield services also began to grow. While many of the more conservative Russian oil companies, such as Surgutneftegaz and Tatneft, continued to source a large share of their oil equipment from local producers, the larger and more ambitious companies, such as Lukoil, Yukos, and Sibneft, increasingly resorted to the use of foreign-supplied equipment and services to boost recovery rates across Soviet-era legacy oilfields (Gustafson 2012, chapter 2). This contributed to a decline in the Russian oil equipment industry. The collapse of the Soviet Union meant that traditional sources of equipment, such as Azerbaijan (extraction tools) and Ukraine (pipe), were no longer as closely integrated with the Russian oil industry. While some defense-industrial plants were converted to produce oil extraction equipment, the share of foreign equipment grew rapidly, especially as an overvalued ruble made foreign-produced equipment more attractive.

The second period of post-Soviet oil industry development coincided with Vladimir Putin's accession to the Russian presidency in 2000. During this period, a more assertive Russian state renegotiated the terms that governed the oil industry in the 1990s. Several of the largest privately owned Russian oil companies were nationalized, including Yukos and Sibneft. Gazprom was also brought back under tight state control. Meanwhile, the Russian government gradually redefined the terms of PSAs – described by Putin as "colonial" (Putin 2007) – to favor Russian state-owned firms (Hanson 2005; Tompson 2005; Fortescue 2006; Sakwa 2014). This reassertion of the state was facilitated by rapidly growing oil revenues. While foreign oil companies were largely left alone – although foreign shareholders in Yukos were not so lucky – Gazprom was able to use support from the state to acquire several foreign assets, including the multinational venture on Sakhalin known as "Sakhalin II" (Hedlund 2014).

As foreign direct ownership was challenged, the role of foreign equipment and oilfield services also changed. The collapse of the ruble that accompanied the August 1998 financial crisis boosted Russia's domestic oil equipment industry. Indigenous producers of low- and medium-technology equipment that were appropriate to Russia's harsh climatic conditions, such as drilling rigs from Uralmash, saw their market share grow. New companies emerged to produce more advanced electrical submersible pumps (ESPs), as well as equipment used for hydraulic fracturing ("fracking"). A plethora of Russian companies also emerged to compete at the lower end of the oilfield services market. However, while the domestic industry showed signs of recovery after the post-Soviet depression, foreign equipment and service providers remained unparalleled in the more technologically and organizationally demanding areas.

The 2010s represents a third period of post-Soviet oil industry development. After the state had reasserted its dominance of the oil industry over the 2000s, and after the resurgence of Russian oil equipment producers and oilfield service providers, distinct roles for Russian and foreign business began to crystallize.

On the one hand, Russian companies, usually state-owned, were the dominant owners of upstream assets and licenses. Russian equipment and oilfield service providers were also dominant in the lower and middle segments of the market, although Chinese producers of, for example, drilling rigs increased their market share. On the other hand, foreign companies – both IOCs and smaller companies – remained important in providing project management experience, capital, and advanced technology for the larger, more technologically demanding projects (Henderson and Ferguson 2014). Foreign oil equipment and oilfield services occupied similar market positions.

This division of labor looked set to continue. As Russia's existing oil deposits – overwhelmingly located in Western Siberia – continue to exhibit rising depletion rates, new sources of oil need to be exploited. Many of these new deposits are located either in remote or geologically challenging regions (e.g. offshore in the Arctic), or onshore in shale oil formations, such as the vast Bazhenov suite. Both areas require advanced technology that is not currently produced by Russian equipment or oilfield service providers. However, the Russian government envisages that these new "frontier" deposits will account for a growing share of Russian oil production over the next two decades. According to the official Energy Strategy, offshore Arctic production should account for at least 20 percent of oil production in Russia by 2030 (Ministry of Energy of the Russian Federation 2009). Without the successful exploitation of offshore oil, Russia's future as an energy superpower may well be in jeopardy.

Table 4.1 *Phases of foreign participation in the Russian energy industry*

Phase	Role of Russian state	Role of foreign ownership	Foreign equipment and services	Role of foreign capital
I 1990s	Weak and permissive	Expanding to include PSAs, JVs, and majority shares	Rapid growth from low base; Russian domestic industry in disarray	Borrower; Western-focused
II 2000s	Rebuilding and intent on nationalization and control over strategic sectors and key dimensions of economic policy	Retrenchment caused by reassertion of state ownership	Consolidation of foreigners in high-end equipment and services; growth of Russian industry at lower end	Outward-focused; listings of majors on foreign exchanges; Western-focused
III 2010s	Resurgent and intent on modernization	JVs between Western IOCs and Russian majors for "frontier" projects	Foreign equipment still dominant for use in "frontier" and shale oil projects; Russian industry competing with China	Western-focused
IV Post-2014	Under sanctions and intent on Russification and diversification	JVs with Russian majors for "frontier" projects where possible	Import substitution campaign to accelerate production of high-end Russian equipment	Diverse sources of capital (Asia, Middle East, Russian public funds)

Aware of the importance of foreign companies in providing technology, capital and knowhow to Russian firms, the giant state-owned oil company Rosneft, as well as the privately owned (but with close links to the state) Novatek, entered into a number of agreements with IOCs, including BP, ExxonMobil, Total, and Statoil. These agreements were intended to cement IOC participation in these high-cost and high-risk projects that are of crucial importance to Russia's future as an oil producer. Deals were later signed with Royal Dutch Shell, BP, and Total to exploit the onshore Bazhenov shale oil formation.

The new deals appeared to offer a better balance between Russian and foreign interests, offering more stability than previous agreements (such as PSAs), while remaining attractive to IOCs. The role of IOC technology and knowhow in attracting overtures from Russian majors cannot be underestimated. As experience in the 2000s illustrated, the Russian state-owned companies tended to eschew foreign involvement where possible. However, due to the technologically demanding nature of exploiting the offshore Arctic deposits and the Bazhenov formation, which could not be addressed with existing Russian capabilities, Russian majors were forced to offer inducements to IOCs to secure their participation (Overland et al. 2013). In early 2014, a close synergy between Russian firms and foreign technology – a "technology partnership," according to Russia's Minister for Natural Resources, Sergei Donskoi – in developing hard-to-reach deposits seemed assured (Interfax 2014).

The Role of Foreign Technology in the Russian Oil Industry before Sanctions

It is useful to gauge the extent to which the Russian oil and gas industry were dependent on foreign – especially Western alliance – technologies before sanctions were imposed. As outlined previously, Russian producers are dominant in lower-end technologies, such as those typically employed to extract oil from Russia's traditional deposits (i.e. Soviet-era legacy fields). According to data from the Russian Ministry of Energy, foreign imports of equipment accounted for just 20 percent of total equipment used in this segment of the oil and gas industry in 2014 (Figure 4.2). Much of this was sourced from China, where, for instance, firms such as the giant Honghua Group increased their share in the Russian drilling rig market.

Western firms however remained dominant in the supply of higher-end equipment used for extraction in offshore and onshore hard-to-recover deposits. According to data from Russia's Ministry of Energy (Figure 4.2),

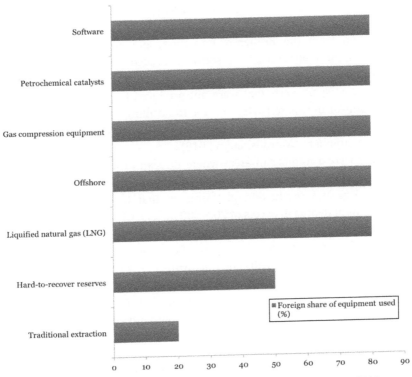

Figure 4.2 Import dependency in selected fields of oil and gas equipment, 2014
Sources: Neftegazavaya Vertikal' (Importozameshchenie, 2015, p. 2)

Russian import dependence was greatest in precisely those areas that were projected to be of strategic importance in the future, with foreigners providing at least 80 percent of the equipment used for the development of offshore oilfields, at least 80 percent of the software used for mapping underground oil reservoirs, at least 80 percent of the equipment used for the processing of LNG, and around 50 percent of the equipment used in, for example, hydraulic fracturing and other types of enhanced oil recovery (RIA Novosti 2015c).

Speaking in 2015, Russian Energy Minister Alexander Novak stated that Western sanctions affected nearly 70 percent of imported equipment.[2] Speaking specifically about the type of technologies used in deposits

---

[2] See Energy Minister Alexander Novak's presentation at the Russian Oil and Gas Forum in Moscow, March 2015, http://oilandgasforum.ru/data/files/Filesper cent200315/Novak .pdf.

affected by sanctions, he suggested that Russian oil companies imported around 50 percent of equipment and 80 percent of software for heavy oil production from the Bazhenov formation, and around 80 percent of equipment and 90 percent of software needed to exploit deep-water deposits from Western suppliers. Controls on the import of technology also affected spare parts that were not produced in Russia. For instance, 90 percent of the spare parts used for the drilling platform of Gazprom Neft in the Prirazlomnoye deposit in the Pechora Sea were sourced from Western suppliers (Mordoshenko 2015).

There were a number of areas where Russian firms were deficient. For instance, while there were numerous companies manufacturing offshore drilling rigs and production platforms, at that time none were fit for operations at depths in excess of 700–800 meters, which would be required to extract oil from the offshore deposits not just in the Arctic, but also in the Black Sea near Tuapse. Elsewhere, there was only modest capacity to produce equipment for hydraulic fracturing and horizontal drilling.[3]

In order to obtain a more precise picture of the role played by Western suppliers of oil extraction equipment in Russia, it is necessary to examine detailed trade statistics that measure cross-border flows of such equipment. In Figure 4.3, data are presented for the Russian imports of equipment under the most important oil and gas extraction equipment-related trade codes (HS, or harmonized system, codes) in which Russia exhibits the greatest import dependency.[4] As is clear, before sanctions were imposed in the summer of 2014, European (and the other Western) firms historically

---

[3] Other areas of high import dependency include: geophysical, drilling, and pipeline equipment for offshore and shelf deposits; subsea production systems; vessels for shelf operations; equipment for the development of shale oil deposits and reserves in the Bazhenov formation; equipment for hydraulic fracturing, including multistage; drilling rigs for offshore platforms; top drives for drilling rigs; advanced automatic drilling tongs, first of all robotic tongs; equipment for MWD/LWD operations; systems of drilling mud treatment (e.g. screen shakers, centrifuges, mud cleaners, sludge pumps). See Ministry for Industry and Trade, Order No. 645, March 31, 2015.

[4] Details are listed in the Appendix to this chapter. Data are derived from the International Trade Centre database, available at www.trademap.org; the UN Comtrade database, available at http://comtrade.un.org/; and the Russian Customs Service, available at http://stat.customs.ru/apex/f?p=201:1:4633879681718756. It should be noted that the trade categories from which the data below are derived may include items that have been destined for other parts of the Russian energy industry (e.g. gas or coal), or for another part of the Russian economy altogether. It is also possible that the data fail to reflect all known transactions. The data also do not capture the equipment used by foreign oilfield services, which were much larger in volume.

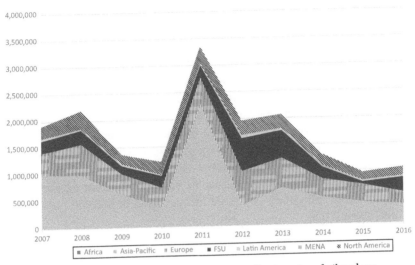

Figure 4.3 Volume and source of Russian imports: all categories of oil and gas extraction equipment, 2007–2016 (current USD, thousand)
Sources: International Trade Centre (ITC); United Nations Comtrade database; author's calculations

played an important role in supplying oil and gas extraction equipment, particularly in the high-end segment of the market.[5]

Within the overall figures presented here, the data for drilling equipment show that European firms, and Western firms more widely, occupied an important position. Average annual Russian imports of drilling tools amounted to around $270 million, with European firms occupying around 30 percent of the Russian market. Firms from the United States supplied around 25 percent of Russia's imported drilling tools, with China supplying around a third. As in most other product categories, Western firms tended to supply the higher-tech products.

The Russian market for drilling rigs and associated equipment was considerably larger. From 2005 onward, Russia imported an average of around $750 million worth of drilling rigs and associated equipment (such as parts) annually, although imports declined significantly since 2008. This is for two reasons. First, Russian domestic production of drilling rigs increased. However, domestically produced rigs, with one or two rare exceptions (such as some higher-end models produced by Uralmash and

---

[5] Moreover, this equipment does not include that brought in by oilfield services companies, or the equipment that foreign investors might bring (e.g. Shell, BP, Total, Exxon, Statoil).

Izhneftemash), were not capable of carrying out the deep and horizontal drilling operations performed by Western analogues. Second, fewer new rigs were imported because Russian companies used existing stock for longer. This caused a steep rise in the average age of Russia's drilling rig fleet. In 2013, it was estimated that 57 percent of Russia's 1,835-strong rig fleet was more than twenty years old (VTB Capital Research 2013). This shortage of modern rigs may present a problem in the future because large numbers of modern rigs are required for the exploitation of, for instance, the shale oil deposits in the Bazhenov formation (Henderson 2015). By way of comparison, US firms are believed to have built up about 25 million horsepower for hydraulic fracturing, mostly over the past decade, while Russian firms collectively possessed in the region of 850,000 horsepower (Bloomberg 2013).

Russia also tended to exhibit high levels of import dependency in offshore drilling platforms, floating and submersible vessels, and auxiliary vessels and equipment. Russia imported an average of $2.7 billion annually over the past decade. A large portion of these imports came from Korea, where the country's shipping industry has supplied a high number of either complete vessels or sections of vessels. Perhaps the most high-profile sale from Korea was the topside of the giant Berkut ("golden eagle") drilling platform – the largest of its kind in the world – that was constructed at Daewoo Shipbuilding and Marine Engineering's (DSME) yard. Samsung Heavy Industries also fabricated the drilling rig. This sale alone explains the spike in imports of oil and gas equipment observed in 2011.

SANCTIONS AND THE RUSSIAN ENERGY INDUSTRY

As illustrated in the preceding section, international – and especially Western – participation in the Russian energy industry has played an important role over the past two decades or so. Immediately prior to the outbreak of conflict in Ukraine, the partnership between Western IOCs and foreign providers of advanced equipment and services, on the one hand, and Russian firms, on the other, was of strategic importance to the Russian government, and looked set to continue into the future, especially as Russian firms moved towards exploiting "frontier" oil and gas deposits. Russian oil and gas companies also made considerable use of Western capital markets. However, the Russian annexation of Crimea, and the subsequent outbreak of war in Ukraine, resulted in the imposition of a wide range of economic sanctions on the Russian energy industry by the United States, the EU, and their allies.

Western sanctions against the Russian energy industry were introduced in several phases. The first phase applied to deliveries of equipment and was introduced over the course of July–August 2014. The
second phase of sanctions was applied in September 2014. This expanded
the scope of sanctions to include not only deliveries of equipment, but
also the provision of services, the exchange of technical information with
Russian firms, and, perhaps most importantly, the engagement of Western companies in JVs that were focused on the most technologically
challenging projects. Sanctions were targeted at adversely affecting
Russia's future production of oil; the short-term impact on production
was not expected to be significant. Gas projects were also affected, if
either deep-sea drilling equipment was used in extraction or the gas field
also produced oil. Production at the Yuzhno-Kirinskoye gas and conden-
sate field, located around 35 km northeast of Sakhalin Island – which was
intended to supply gas to both the Sakhalin II and Sakhalin III JVs – was
perhaps the most notable of the affected gas projects (Fadeyeva and
Derbilova 2016).

For deep-water, Arctic and shale oil projects, the following equipment
was prohibited by the sender countries for export to Russia: drilling rigs;
parts for horizontal drilling; drilling equipment and well-completion
equipment; offshore equipment for Arctic operations; well-logging equipment; well pumps; drill pipes and casing pipes; software for hydraulic
fracturing; high-pressure pumps; seismic exploration equipment; remotely
controlled underwater vehicles; compressors; tube expanders; and distribution cocks. In addition to prohibitions on the acquisition and use of
technology, Western financial sanctions were also targeted at the key
Russian energy companies. As a result, a ban on trading bonds and equity
and related brokering services for products whose maturity period exceeds
thirty days (initially ninety days, but reduced in September 2014) was
imposed on the likes of Rosneft, Transneft, Lukoil, Gazprom Neft, and,
in the case of US sanctions, Gazprom and Novatek.[6]

As a result of the sanctions regime, a number of the "Phase III" projects
described previously in this chapter, in which foreign IOCs were involved
with Russian partners to provide technology and know-how, were suspended. For instance, ExxonMobil was forced to suspend cooperation with
Rosneft in the Sakhalin I deep-water project and the production of heavy
oil from the Bazhenov formation (Topalov 2014). Perhaps the most

---

[6] Although Gazprom was excluded from EU sanctions, it was subject to US sanctions.

high-profile example was the JV between Rosneft and Exxon to develop deposits in the Kara Sea, which was suspended immediately after the announcement that the project had discovered commercial quantities of recoverable oil (Oilcapital.ru 2014). However, without Exxon's participation, Rosneft was unable to exploit this or other similar deposits.

Nevertheless, while the sanctions regime was broad in scope and precise in the financial and technological instruments that were targeted, there were several important loopholes that would dilute their full impact.

First, the sanctions did not affect the subsidiaries of Western oilfield service companies operating in Russia (RBK.ru 2014). As a result, the likes of Schlumberger and Baker Hughes were still able to operate in Russia, helping, for instance, Gazprom Neft in the development of the offshore Prirazlomnoye deposit in the Pechora Sea.

Second, the sanctions imposed by EU countries differed from those imposed by the United States in so far as they deliberately avoided targeting gas production. As a result, the United States and not the EU imposed financial sanctions on the major gas producers Gazprom and Novatek. Although this still caused considerable complications for EU companies who did not want to fall foul of US law, it did leave enough leeway for EU companies to maintain their exposure to the Russian market. There were also small but important differences between the US and EU legislation in the definitions of prohibited oil and gas extraction equipment.[7]

Third, the EU also introduced a preapproval procedure for deals involving the supply of equipment to Russia. The authorized government bodies of the countries in which the exporting companies are registered must grant approval for the sale of such equipment. Moreover, the European authorities may issue a permit for delivery if the export is related to a commitment arising from a contract or agreement executed before August 1, 2014, i.e. before the EU sanctions were imposed.[8] Known as the "grandfathering" provision, this has enabled some JVs to continue. By contrast, the US restrictions – enforced more consistently and vigorously by the Office of Foreign Assets Control – do not provide any exemptions for

---

[7] US sanctions apply to the licensing of Russia-bound supplies of equipment used in deep-water (i.e. more than 500 feet, or 152.4 m) in hydrocarbon production, in the development of the Arctic shelf, and for extraction in shale oil deposits. The EU sanctions, by contrast, apply to deep-water hydrocarbon production, but do not specify the minimum depth of production.

[8] EU sanctions are described in detail at http://eur-lex.europa.eu/legal-content/EN/TXT/?uri=celex:32014R0833.

contracts executed before August 6, 2014.[9] This has caused some US firms, such as ExxonMobil, to suffer from a competitive disadvantage vis-à-vis EU firms operating in Russia (Crooks and Foy 2017).

THE RUSSIAN RESPONSE TO WESTERN SANCTIONS ON THE OIL INDUSTRY

Faced with a clear threat to Russia's energy, economic, and national security, the sanctions imposed by the West were met with a wide-ranging response that included efforts to: (1) substitute strategically important Western technologies with Russian-produced equipment, or if not, acquire analogues from non-Western alliance countries with whom Russia continued to enjoy normal trade relations; (2) acquire alternative sources of finance – both domestic and foreign – to complement, if not replace, traditional capital markets in the West, so that state-owned (Rosneft and Gazprom) and state-favored (Novatek) companies were insulated from the worst effects of the Ukraine-related sanctions; and (3) undertake diplomatic and commercial initiatives to open up new sources of demand for Russian energy.

Realizing these ambitions will be no mean feat. To work toward achieving them, the Russian state used its position at the apex of the country's system of political economy to channel resources to favored organizations that were considered to be strategically important, cushion key organizations from the worst effects of sanctions, seek out alternative sources of demand for Russian energy, and build constituencies within Russia that would benefit from sanctions.

Policies to Support Import Substitution in the Oil and Gas Equipment Industry

One of the key sectors identified as in need of state support in the import substitution strategy was the oil and gas extraction equipment industry (Medvedev 2015d; Zhernov 2015). Because of the vital role that high-technology oil and gas extraction equipment is projected to play in the development of Russia's "frontier" oil deposits, import substitution in this sector was considered to be perhaps the most important area, at least in the civilian branches of the economy (RIA Novosti 2015d). According to

---

[9] US sanctions are described in detail at www.treasury.gov/resource-center/sanctions/Programs/Pages/ukraine.aspx.

Table 4.2 *Import substitution targets for Russian oil extraction equipment industry*

Type of technology	Imports, 2014 (percent total equipment)	Target imports, 2020 (percent total equipment)
Technology, equipment, and services for enhanced oil recovery	67–95	50–80
High-pressure pumps (1,200–1,500 ATM)	80	65
Technology and equipment for slant hole directional drilling, horizontal drilling, and drilling in multilateral wells	60–83	45–60
Drilling equipment, rotor-managed systems, navigation equipment for drilling equipment, equipment for onboard drilling device	83	60
Technology and equipment used in offshore projects	80–90	60–70
Equipment for floating drilling platforms	80	60
Submersible extraction systems	90	70
Technology and equipment for geological exploration	40–85	30–70
Geological, geophysical, and seismic equipment	85	70

Source: Ministry for Industry and Trade of the Russian Federation (2015)

the Minister for Energy, Alexander Novak, the priority areas for work in the area of import substitution in the oil and gas industry are technologies for hydraulic fracturing and directional drilling, both of which are projected to become increasingly important for Russia as production moves away from legacy oil fields to "frontier" deposits (ibid).

The sectoral import substitution plan agreed by the Ministry for Industry and Trade in March 2015 defined a number of ambitious objectives for reducing imported equipment's share in the total equipment used in different areas of the energy industry (Table 4.2). At a meeting of the Presidential Council for Economic Modernization and Innovation-Based Development of Russia, Prime Minister Dmitri Medvedev declared that these areas of industry were "high-end" but were "highly politicized," as shown by the Western imposition of sanctions in precisely these areas (Medvedev 2015a). Medvedev also outlined a comprehensive action plan for the development of the industry that coordinates the activities of not only the Ministry of Industry and Trade but also the Ministry of Education, the Ministry of Environmental Protection, and the Ministry of

Energy, as well as the Russian manufacturers, research and engineering organizations, and oil production companies that determine demand in this area.

As indicated, the stated objective was not to move Russia towards full self-sufficiency (autarky) in these areas of strategic importance; instead, the objective was to build, in a relatively short period of time, domestic capabilities that would reduce Russia's vulnerability to the use of economic sanctions by countries with the ability to prevent supplies of technologically advanced equipment and services to Russia in the future. As acknowledged by the Russian Minister for Natural Resources, Sergei Donskoi, a shift towards the more widespread use of domestically produced, high-end equipment would not be successful in isolation. It would, he stated, need to be supplemented by an increase in imports from non-Western countries, such as China and South Korea (Starinskaya 2015b).

In addition to the institutional architecture that was put in place to help support import substitution in Russia, the government allocated considerable financial resources to support the development of the energy extraction equipment in Russia. Within the first eighteen months, funds were allocated to support the development of twelve priority technologies in the oil and gas equipment industry.[10] Direct funding of projects was supplemented by access to subsidized loans from the Fund for Industrial Development (FRP) (Putin 2015). Coordination of industry requirements for oil extraction equipment is now managed by an automated system that monitors supply of and demand for such technologies (Ministry of Energy of the Russian Federation 2015b).

The allocation of significant institutional and financial resources to the development of a more competitive oil equipment industry represents a deviation from the previous trajectory of economic policy, which had largely left the industry to the vagaries of the market. A good illustration of this change in policy course is the fact that very little mention was made of the need for high-end domestic equipment industry in the Russian Energy Strategy to 2030, published in 2009. However, the current draft Energy Strategy to 2035 contains a section that articulated the urgent need to develop greater domestic capabilities (Ministry of Energy of the Russian Federation 2015a). To build these capabilities, the Russian state was able to use the instruments available to it as a limited access system of political

---

[10] A total of nineteen projects in the civilian branch of the economy received state support (Teksler 2015).

economy, including financial and regulatory means and the robust deployment of state-owned entities in key sectors.

The Offshore Oil Extraction Equipment Industry

One of the most important gaps in Russian domestic equipment manufacturing existed in the area of offshore platforms and extraction equipment. This branch of Russian industry was considered strategically important precisely because offshore Arctic deposits were projected to become an important source of oil production up to 2030–2040 (ibid). Consequently, offshore exploratory and production platforms, floating drilling rigs, and associated equipment, such as submersible vessels and other auxiliary and service vessels, were identified as important technologies that should be produced domestically. According to the Krylov Shipbuilding Research Institute, the expansion of Arctic extraction would, by 2030, require the use of at least fifty-five exploratory and production platforms, thirty-five offshore drilling platforms, and nearly one hundred support, service, and auxiliary vessels.

However, this was an area where, due to Russia's historic preponderance of onshore deposits, there was a significant dearth of domestic capabilities. Even during the Cold War, offshore equipment was often sourced from Scandinavia and other European countries. More recently, South Korea has emerged as the most important supplier of offshore vessels. To address this gap in Russian capabilities, considerable resources were allocated to the development of the Zvezda shipbuilding complex in Bolshoi Kamen in Russia's Far East, with Dmitri Medvedev stating that the ultimate objective for Zvezda was to reduce Russian dependence on foreign-supplied equipment (Medvedev 2015c).

Zvezda was intended to become Russia's first large-tonnage dockyard. Rosneft CEO and long-time Putin ally Igor Sechin was charged with supervising its development. In addition to contributing to military production, it was envisaged that the Zvezda complex would be able to build tankers with a displacement of up to 350,000 tons, as well as LNG carriers, ice-breaking vessels, and other specialized vessels and structures for operation on the Arctic shelf.[11] Zvezda was also seen as a means of revitalizing industry in

---

[11] The Zvezda complex forms part of a larger Far Eastern Shipbuilding and Ship Repair Centre (FESRC), which also comprises the major ship repair and shipbuilding industrial capacities of the Far Eastern Federal District, such as Dalzavod Ship Repair Plant (Vladivostok) and the North Eastern Repair Centre (Vilyuchinsk). As well as enhancing

Russia's Far East, which has also been labeled as one of the Russian government's strategic objectives, forming an important component of the much heralded "Asian pivot." The project was initiated by Russia's state-owned United Shipbuilding Corporation (USC) and Daewoo Shipbuilding and Marine Engineering (DSME). However, DSME withdrew in 2012, and USC's majority stake was taken over by the Modern Shipbuilding Technologies consortium established by Gazprombank and Rosneft.

Because the project serves the objectives of both regional development in Russia's Far East and supplying domestically produced technologies for the development of energy deposits in the Arctic, Zvezda was considered to be a project of immense political importance (RIA Novosti 2015b). Indeed, the Secretary of the Security Council of the Russian Federation, Nikolai Patrushev, declared that the success of the project would be a matter of national security. As a result, he stated, the project is supervised directly by the president; this was further emphasized when Bolshoi Kamen was labeled a Priority Development Area in December 2015 (Pettersen 2015).

The scale of financial resources allocated to the project's implementation illustrates the extent of its importance. Total estimated costs were around 145–150 billion rubles (c. $2 billion), a substantial increase from Rosneft's initial 2013 estimate of 89 billion rubles, to be raised by the operating consortium (Popov 2015). Due to a combination of rising costs and financial difficulties associated with an onerous volume of external debt, Rosneft requested 89 billion rubles from the National Welfare Fund (NWF) to help with the project (RIA Novosti 2015a). In response, the Finance Ministry suggested NWF funds should not be used, instead preferring that Rosneftegaz holding would be the main investor (providing at least 50 billion rubles), alongside CJSC Modern Shipbuilding Technologies, banks, and non-state pension funds (Farchy 2015). One of the reasons for the Finance Ministry's reluctance to allocate funds to the project was that the significant expected return on investment was expected to facilitate access to private sector sources of funding.

Overall, the effort to develop substantial capabilities in the area of offshore hydrocarbon extraction at Zvezda proceeded with significant financial support from state-owned companies and with high-level political support. It was reported that the first large vessels would be launched by the end of

---

the production capacity of the military industrial complex for the production of naval vessels, this cluster of facilities was intended to help modernize Russia's shipbuilding and marine facilities to boost Russian offshore and civil shipbuilding. Details of the project's history can be found at www.fes-zvezda.ru/about/.

2018 (RIA Novosti 2016d). The fact that demand for Russian ships should be high due to the ambitions attached to the development of the Arctic, and the fact that Arctic exploration itself was considered to be strategically important by the state, suggest that the Zvezda project would be of central importance to the wider import substitution strategy (Rotnem 2017).

Diversification of Supply of Equipment

While much attention was paid to state-directed plans for developing Russian industry, it was also noteworthy that Russian officials saw a switch away from importing equipment and services from Western firms and toward non-Western firms as forming an important component of the plan to enhance Russia's economic security, especially if domestic measures should prove insufficient (Agenstvo Neftegazovoi Informatsii 2016). In this respect, the Russian strategy was not so much focused on "deglobalization" (i.e. achieving full self-sufficiency), but rather on "reglobalization," or diversifying the range of sources from which Russian firms source strategically important supplies.

As revealed in Figure 4.3, overall imports of oil and gas extraction equipment declined considerably after 2013. This was largely because the decline in oil prices that started in the autumn of 2014 reduced sales of such equipment across the world. Nevertheless, several broad trends can be observed. First, while the share of North America in Russian imports of oil and gas extraction equipment remained stable between 2013 and 2016, the European share (including non-EU members such as Norway) declined at the expense of a rise in the shares of former Soviet (FSU) states and countries from the Asia-Pacific region (primarily China). The fact that the rise in imports from FSU states was concentrated in Belarus and Kazakhstan – both members of the Eurasian Economic Union (EAEU) – suggests that prohibited European equipment may have been exported to Russia through more circuitous routes than would have been the case before sanctions were imposed. Such diversionary activities would, of course, have raised the final cost to Russian buyers.

However, it is clear that Western sanctions gave non-Western countries, especially China, the opportunity to increase their market share. This is evident when looking at data at the subsector level. For instance, the Chinese share of the drilling rig market grew from 19 percent in 2013 to more than 35 percent in 2016. In offshore drilling platforms, competition from Chinese-produced vessels grew after 2013, rising from next to nothing to account for around a fifth of Russian imports in 2016.

The Russification of the Oilfield Services Sector

After 2014, the Russian government promoted the Russification of the oilfield services industry. In January 2016, the Prime Minister bemoaned the fact that Russian firms were so dependent on foreign sources of oilfield services, arguing that "we need our own technology, our own production and our own services market" (Medvedev 2016a). These sentiments were later echoed by Alexander Novak, the Minister for Energy, when he stressed the need to "significantly reduce" Russia's dependence on foreign sources of oilfield services (Ministry for Energy of the Russian Federation 2016). High-end technologies used in oilfield services are contained within the Government Commission on Import Substitution's list of strategic technologies that require state support.

The oilfield services market in Russia is one of the largest in the world, and is one of the key channels for technology transfer to Russia. An analysis of the sector carried out by Deloitte estimated that the market was worth around $23 billion in 2015 (Deloitte 2015). This included production and exploration drilling, well maintenance, enhanced oil recovery, and geophysical services.

The role of foreign firms varied across the sector. In some subsectors, it appeared as though Russian firms were already dominant. For instance, seismic research was dominated by IGSS (IG Seismic Services), which accounted for nearly half of all seismic services in 2013, with the rest of the services provided by other domestic firms. However, this picture of Russian supremacy was misleading: IGSS is a joint venture between Schlumberger and Integra in which Schlumberger provided the advanced technologies. The drilling market – the largest by value of the oilfield services – was more evenly distributed, with Eurasia Drilling (EDC) and Surgutneftegaz, both Russian firms, accounting for over half of the domestic market, while foreign firms such as Weatherford and ERIELL until recently accounted for more than a third of the market. However, because the oilfield services sector was considered an area of strategic importance by the Russian government, several important developments reshaped the industry after sanctions were imposed in 2014.

First, a number of mergers and acquisitions took place that expanded and consolidated Russian firms' hold over segments of the oilfield services markets. In July 2014, Rosneft struck a deal to buy the drilling and well-servicing assets of oil and gas service company Weatherford

International in Russia and Venezuela. Weatherford accounted for around 3 percent of the Russian oilfield services market by revenue in 2012.[12]

Second, Rosneft then reached an agreement with Seadrill in July 2014 to acquire a 30 percent stake in Atlantic Drilling Limited. However, Western sanctions resulted in the deal being suspended, with the two parties subsequently agreeing to extend the termination date of the Framework Agreement signed on August 20, 2014, until May 31, 2017. This was again extended until May 31, 2019 (Offshore Energy Today 2015). If the deal is eventually concluded, it will significantly enhance Rosneft's offshore capabilities, as the deal involved the transfer of up to eight drilling units, including four semi-submersibles, a drillship, and three jack-up rigs (Rosneft 2014). Rosneft also acquired a subsidiary of the Canadian firm Trican Well Service Ltd, which provides high-quality pressure pumping services focused on the enhancement of production within the conventional oil industry in Russia (Rosneft 2015). Rosneft also intensified its efforts to enhance its own in-house technical expertise in horizontal drilling and fracking (Starinskaya 2015a).

Third, a clear signal of the Russian government's intention to curtail the influence of foreign firms was given when the Federal Anti-Monopoly Service refused to sanction Schlumberger's proposed $1.7 billion acquisition of a minority stake (46 percent) in Eurasia Drilling in 2015. This deal would have expanded Schlumberger's share in the lucrative Russian drilling market, and would likely have been a significant supplier of technology and knowhow to Russia. However, it was rumored that the failure to secure regulatory approval was caused by resistance from security officials concerned that Schlumberger's enhanced role would have presented a potential threat to national security (RBK.ru 2015). In June 2017, the sale of a minority stake in the firm to a consortium from China, UAE and Saudi Arabia was agreed at the St Petersburg International Economic Forum (Peremitin and Fadeyeva 2017).

Finally, another significant indication of state policy was the continued expansion of the 100 percent state-owned exploration firm Rosgeologiya, which has been charged with enhancing domestic provision of exploratory drilling and turning the company into the dominant player in geophysical

---

[12] The Russian rig operations acquired by Rosneft included sixty-one land drilling crews and a fleet of workover rigs, while the Venezuela operations included six land drilling rigs. The rig staffing was approximately 7,800 in Russia and 375 in Venezuela. See Golubkova (2013).

exploration. To this end, twenty-five smaller geophysical and scientific research companies were transferred to Rosgeologiya by presidential order in February 2015 (Rosgeo 2015).

Thus, it is clear that a determined and sustained effort to expand the control of Russian (state-owned) firms over a variety of oilfield services was underway soon after the imposition of sanctions. This is consistent with the stated aims of the Government Commission for Import Substitution, the Ministry of Energy, and state-owned firms such as Rosneft and Gazprom Neft (Ministry of Energy of the Russian Federation 2016).

Diversification of Finance

The imposition of financial sanctions meant that Russian energy firms suffered from an immediate "sudden stop" in access to external finance, at least on the terms enjoyed before the Ukraine conflict. This was a serious problem due to the large volume of external debt accumulated by Russia's energy sector prior to 2014. Moreover, the reduction in access to capital affected firms well beyond those officially sanctioned – Rosneft, Gazprom Neft, Novatek, and Transneft – because of the fear outside Russia that sanctions could be expanded at a later point to encompass a wider range of companies. These restrictions meant that some Russian firms – especially the most highly leveraged, such as Rosneft – faced immediate liquidity crises and struggled to refinance their existing stocks of external debt.

To deal with the threat posed by financial sanctions, the Russian state used public funds to support those energy firms deemed to be most in need. A few months after the imposition of sanctions, the sudden stop of external capital flows particularly affected Rosneft, due to its large stock of external debt (Mordyushenko and Melnikov 2015). In order to repay a $6.9 billion tranche of debt due at the end of 2014, Rosneft sold bonds to commercial banks in domestic currency and then immediately exchanged the ruble-denominated bonds for dollars in a closed auction in the Bank of Russia – an operation that caused a precipitous depreciation of the ruble (Barsukov 2014). A similar exercise was performed a month later as Rosneft raised foreign currency at another closed auction to service another debt repayment due in January 2015 (Forbes.ru 2015b).

While the assistance granted to Rosneft was the most high-profile case, and certainly took place under opaque circumstances, it was not the only one. Dozens of applications were made to access funds held in Russia's National Welfare Fund (NWF), which was designed to fund long-term investments that would help finance state pension obligations in the future.

Most were unsuccessful. However, while Rosneft's privileged position with the Russian political economy enabled it to access much needed financial resources, public funds were far from inexhaustible. As a result, energy firms also sought out new sources of external finance. In the short term, this proved frustrating. While Novatek and Sibur, for example, were able to attract Chinese finance, these proved to be the exception rather than the norm, at least in the first year or so after sanctions were imposed (Interfax 2015, Forbes.ru 2015a). As will be discussed in the next section, the diversification of sources of external funding took longer than policy-makers may have initially anticipated.

Diversification of Demand: Toward an Asian Pivot?

The imposition of sanctions also accelerated the desire in Moscow to seek out alternative sources of demand for Russia's primary source of export revenues. Traditionally the main source of demand for Russian hydrocarbons, especially gas, has been Europe. However, the geopolitical conflict between Russia and the West prompted Russian officials to hasten their efforts to expand Russian energy exports to Asia. To be sure, this was not an entirely new development. Policymakers in Russia had been seeking out new markets in Asia for many years.[13] Initially this effort was motivated by commercial considerations: The forecast for growth in oil and gas consumption was much higher in Asia than it was for Europe (Thomson and Horii 2009; Henderson and Mitrova 2016). But the conflict in Ukraine prompted Russian policymakers to view Russia's search for stable sources of energy demand as a matter of national security. As a result, official thinking quickly settled on the need to cement closer energy ties with Asian countries, especially China, as part of a broader rebalancing of Russia's foreign policy away from excessive dependence on ties to the West.[14]

---

[13] Putin specifically identified the importance of China in this respect. As previously noted, in 2012, he expressed the hope that Russia might "catch the Chinese wind in the sails of our economy." See Putin (2012c) and Bradshaw and Shadrina (2013).

[14] East Asia, and especially China, was described as the new source of power and vitality in the emerging global "polycentric" order. As such, many in the elite feel that Russia should be an integral part of East Asian political and economic structures so that Russia might maintain its status as a great power through a growing presence in the fastest growing geographic region of the global economy.

The energy component of this *povorot na vostok* ("turn to the east") formed a crucial part of Russia's response to Western sanctions.[15]

Expanding energy ties with Asia was a stated aim of government policy before 2014, and was clearly expressed in the Energy Strategy to 2030, published in 2009 (Ministry of Energy of the Russian Federation 2009). However, evidence of a significant shift in thinking can be found in the draft Energy Strategy to 2035 (Government of the Russian Federation 2014a; hereafter referred to as ES-2035). Produced in late 2014, the draft ES-2035 was clearly shaped by the imposition of sanctions, with several references made to the "geopolitical crisis which started in 2014 and which has resulted in the imposition of financial, technological and other sanctions by several leading powers" (ibid, p. 4). Threats to Russia's energy security – and by extension its national security – were identified as structural rather than cyclical, i.e. related to the intensification of competition from other hydrocarbon producers, especially the United States; the weak growth in demand from Europe; and the use of sanctions as a weapon to undermine Russia's position as one of the world's three most important energy producers, alongside the United States and Saudi Arabia (Mehdiyeva 2017).

In order for Russia to maintain its position as a leading energy supplier against the backdrop of sanctions and the broader geopolitical conflict between Russia and the West, the ES-2035 stated that it was imperative that Russia should diversify the sources of energy demand, energy transit, and the technology used to extract energy, and also ensure that exports grow faster than production. Indeed, by stating that the export of energy will remain "the key factor in national economic development and the economic and political position that Russia holds in the international community," the document amounts to an explicit statement of the "demand hunger" that drives Russian energy policy and, by extension, much of its foreign economic policy.[16] To achieve the desired diversification, the ES-2035 highlights the crucial importance of increasing sales to Asia, and especially China.

The statement of objectives contained in the ES-2035 was accompanied by tangible progress in intensifying energy ties with China. In addition to the rising share of Chinese equipment used in the energy industry, discussed earlier in this chapter, a thirty-year deal – estimated to be worth US

---

[15] On Russia's Asian pivot, see Lo (2009); Lo and Hill (2013); Malle and Cooper (2014); and Fortescue (2016).
[16] ES-2035 quoted in Mehdiyeva (2017, p. 7).

$400 billion – for Russia to build the *Sila Sibiri* (*Power of Siberia*) gas pipeline to deliver up to 38 bcm per year of gas to China was signed in May 2014 (Topalov and Falchev 2014). Although the precise terms of the deal led some to suggest that the deal may not prove to be commercially advantageous to Russia, the political gains cannot be exaggerated. In simple terms, *Sila Sibiri*, alongside the sale of LNG from Yamal, should result in considerable growth in Russia's energy footprint in Asia, thus going some way to achieving the objectives stated in the ES-2035. Moreover, the nature of Russia's system of political economy means that commercial profitability is less important than geopolitical gains: excess costs in the production of infrastructure will be shared among contractors in Russia's Far East, while the prospect of a large and stable source of demand in future decades will help shift Russia's gas sales toward a faster growing pole of the global economy. Moreover, the fact that state-owned firms or firms with close links to the senior leadership – all of whom perform social and political functions, as well as economic – have benefited most from cooperation with Asian economies helps explain how commercial imperatives can be subordinated to political objectives (Gabuev 2017).

Japanese and Indian firms also sought to strengthen their relationship with Russian energy firms, which opened up new possibilities for Russian firms to avoid the full impact of sanctions. For instance, a Japanese consortium comprising Japan Oil, Gas & Metals National Corp. (known as Jogmec), Inpex Corp, and Marubeni Corp, signed a preliminary deal with Rosneft in December 2016 to carry out exploration of an offshore area to the south west of Sakhalin Island (Central Tatarsky). Officials from the United States claimed that exploration in at least some of this area would take place at depths of greater than 500 feet, placing it within the reach of sanctions. Elsewhere, Rosneft's acquisition of a 49 percent share of the Indian firm Essar, for around $13 billion, strengthened its presence on one of the world's fastest growing oil markets (Foy 2017a). This deal also raised the possibility of Rosneft's "daughter" – not being subject to restrictions – purchasing sanctioned Western equipment at a future point for subsequent transfer to Rosneft.

THE IMPACT OF SANCTIONS ON THE RUSSIAN ENERGY INDUSTRY

The Russian state's response to Western sanctions on the energy industry was clearly sophisticated, substantial, and displayed evidence of clear coordination. This is not to say that sanctions did not cause considerable disruption. However, after the first year, most of the necessary adjustment had taken place and Russian energy firms were able to invest in future production and produce oil and gas at levels close to post-Soviet peaks. A concerted effort to reduce dependency on certain types of imported oil and gas extraction equipment was also progressing.

Finance and Investment

In the first year, sanctions certainly disrupted activity in the Russian energy industry, with the situation exacerbated by the steep decline in oil prices that began in September 2014 and which took oil prices from more than $100 per barrel to closer to $30 in early 2015. Rosneft and Novatek, in particular, were forced into restructuring their external debt and financing arrangements so that they could continue to undertake investment in future production and finance existing operations.

However, several factors cushioned the industry from sanctions.

First, state help was given to the strategically important companies that faced the most distress. Rosneft, as already discussed, was given access to resources denied to all other Russian firms, while Novatek was able to secure 150 billion rubles (c.$2.2 billion in 2015) of finance from the National Welfare Fund (TASS 2015a). Less well-publicized but often more frequent loans from state-owned or state-influenced banks, such as Sberbank and Gazprombank, also helped targeted firms.[17]

Second, Russian firms were able to create new instruments to finance their activities. Rosneft, for instance, made extensive use of prepayment arrangements with oil traders and Chinese firms to ensure that it had access to sufficient volumes of foreign currency.

Third, Russian energy firms gradually made greater use of alternative, non-Western sources of finance. Rosneft, for instance, sold a stake in its subsidiary Vankorneft to the Indian ONGC Videsh Limited, and sold 20 percent of its subsidiary Verkhnechyonskneftegaz (VChNG) to Beijing Gas for around $1.1 billion (TASS 2016a; Golubkova 2017). Rosneft also accessed Middle Eastern and Asian capital when it sold a 19.5 percent stake (worth around $11 billion at the time) in itself in December 2016. An agreement was later reached to sell this share to a Chinese energy company with close links to the state, cementing even closer ties between the leaderships of Russia and China (Petlevoy 2017). Yamal LNG (loans from

---

[17] In July 2017, for instance, Rosneft borrowed 125 billion rubles from Sberbank. See Neftegazovoe Novosti (2017).

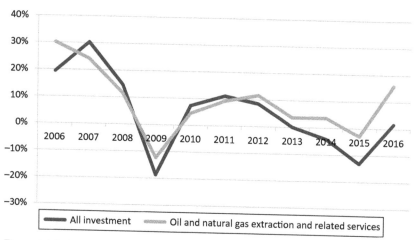

Figure 4.4 Investment in the Russian oil and gas industries, 2010–2016 (per cent annual change in value of investment, constant 2015 rubles)
Source: Federal State Statistics Service (2017); author's calculations.

the Export-Import Bank of China and the China Development Bank; equity shares held by China National Petroleum Corp and China's Silk Road Fund), Sibur (equity stake sold to Sinopec) and Gazprom (loans from Bank of China) were also able to tap Chinese sources of capital (Soldatkin and Astakhova 2016). Elsewhere, in June 2017, the sale of a minority stake in Eurasia Drilling to a consortium from China, UAE, and Saudi Arabia, alongside the Russian Direct Investment Fund, was agreed at the St Petersburg International Economic Forum, shortly before it emerged that Schlumberger was attempting to resurrect the deal to acquire a controlling share of the company (TASS 2017b).

Finally, the sharp depreciation of the ruble that accompanied the decline in oil prices helped boost the competitiveness of energy firms by reducing costs (largely denominated in rubles) relative to income (largely denominated in dollars). The existence of a tax regime that imposes a higher marginal rate of tax on the extraction and export of oil when prices are higher meant that that it was the Russian state that absorbed much of the reduction in income rather than the firms themselves (Henderson 2017).

Taken together, the factors just listed resulted in the rate of investment in the oil and gas sector growing significantly faster than overall national fixed investment (Figure 4.4). Given the support provided to the industry – in terms of both direct support to cushion it from sanctions, and the

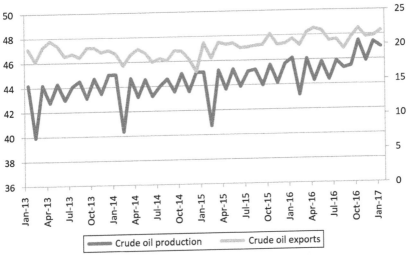

Figure 4.5 Crude oil production and exports, 2013–2017 (million tons per month; production, left axis; exports, right axis)
Source: Minenergo (2017); author's calculations

indirect support provided by the exchange rate depreciation and tax regime – it is perhaps not surprising that investment has remained strong. As James Henderson has noted in his analysis of the Russian oil industry, "operating cash flow … exceeded total capital expenditure for the past three years [i.e. 2014–2016]" and, as a result, the Russian oil industry "has been able to self-fund itself during periods of high and low oil prices, despite the imposition of sanctions since 2014" (Henderson 2017, p. 7). Indeed, even when overall investment slowed in 2015, the ruble value of capital expenditure in upstream investment grew in each year between 2014 and 2016 (ibid). The relatively healthy financial position of Russian oil firms enabled them to expand production drilling activity, which has in turn stimulated a faster rate of extraction (ibid., p. 4).

Production

While it has been stated by Western policymakers that the sanctions that prohibit the transfer of technology and knowhow are intended only to affect future production in Russia's "frontier" deposits, it was clear that financial sanctions on Russian energy firms were intended to disrupt current operations. However, sanctions did not adversely affect oil and gas production in Russia. As illustrated in Figure 4.5, crude oil extraction grew by 6.3 per cent between January 2013 and January 2017, while exports grew even faster, rising by 10.5 per cent over the same period. Indeed, before the end of 2016, when Russia entered into an agreement with OPEC countries to limit oil production, Russian output was at post-Soviet record-high levels of 11.7 million barrels per day.

The rate of oil extraction was driven primarily by rapid growth in production in Russia's small- and medium-sized producers. Thus, while the three largest producers – Rosneft, LUKOIL, and Surgutneftegaz – experienced stagnation in production, Gazprom Neft, Novatek, and Bash-neft all grew briskly between 2014 and 2016 (ibid). Novatek's production increase was largely due to the start of operations in the new Yarudeyskoye field, while Gazprom Neft expanded growth in its Prirazlomnoye and Novy Port fields in the Arctic and the Messoyakha field (with Rosneft). Indeed, Gazprom Neft's strong performance illustrates the resilience of at least some of the Russian oil industry in the face of sanctions: much of its growth is explained by the successful exploitation of hard-to-recover oil using horizontal wells with multiple fracking technologies (Golubkova and Astakhova 2016). Indeed, senior officials from Gazprom Neft are also confident that they will soon be able to exploit hard-to-recover deposits located in Russia's vast Bazhenov formation and offshore in the Arctic (Farchy 2017; Foy 2017b).

Joint Ventures with Western IOCs

The JVs between Western IOCs and Russian oil and gas companies that were formed in the early 2010s to help develop Arctic (onshore and offshore), deep-water, and hard-to-recover oil and gas deposits were among the primary targets of the sanctions imposed in the summer of 2014. However, these sanctions were enforced unevenly (Rozhdestvens-kaya 2017). As illustrated in Table 4.3, US firms – most notably Exxon-Mobil – were forced to freeze JVs on Russian soil in those areas affected by the sanctions regime as sanctions were enforced strictly by the Office of Foreign Assets Control (OFAC), the body tasked with monitoring the implementation of sanctions. By contrast, EU firms enjoyed more lati-tude. This is because of both the "grandfathering" provision that enabled the continuation of projects that were initiated before sanctions were imposed, and the fact that home countries rather than the supranational EU bodies were tasked with implementation. Other means were used to ensure that projects were not frozen. Statoil, for instance, was able to continue work in the Domanik formation by successfully classifying its

Table 4.3 *Status of selected joint ventures between Western IOCs and Russian oil companies, 2017*

Deposits to be developed by JVs	Stakeholders	Status
Arctic offshore deposits in Kara Sea and offshore deposits near Tuapse in the Black Sea	Rosneft (51 percent) and Exxon (49 percent)	Stalled
Shale oil extraction in Bazhenov and Achimov formations in Western Siberia	Rosneft (51 percent) and Exxon (49 percent)	Stalled
Arctic offshore in Barents Sea and offshore in the Val Shatsky field in Black Sea	Rosneft (67 percent) and ENI (33 percent)	Active
Shale oil extraction in Domanik formation near Samara	Rosneft (51 percent) and Statoil (49 percent)	Active
Yamal LNG plant	Novatek (50.1 percent); Total (20 percent); CNPC (20 percent); Silk Road Fund (9.9 percent)	Active
Shale oil extraction in Domanik formation in Volga-Urals	Rosneft (51 per cent) and BP (49 per cent)	Active
Sakhalin II LNG plant	Gazprom (50 percent + 1 share); Shell (25 percent – 1 share); Mitsui (12.5 percent); Mitsubishi (10 percent)	Active
Shale oil extraction in Bazhenov and Achimov (Salym project) formations in Western Siberia	Gazprom Neft (50 percent) and Shell (50 percent)	Active (Achimov formation)

Source: author's assessment

project as a "limestone" deposit, which placed it outside the existing sanctions legislation (Farchy 2017). As a result, most of the major joint ventures between European and Russian firms were able to continue. In some instances, the low value of oil sales caused progress to be slowed, but in most instances sanctions were not the cause of slow progress.

Import Substitution in the Oil and Gas Extraction Equipment Industry

Over the course of 2015 and 2016, significant progress appeared to have been made in stimulating production of equipment used in the extraction of oil and gas. This was, of course, one of the primary objectives stated in the original import substitution plan drafted in 2015. In May 2017, Prime Minister Dmitri Medvedev chaired a meeting in St Petersburg where he and other key officials summarized progress with import substitution (Government of the Russian Federation 2017). The results were encouraging. According to Medvedev, the original schedule envisaged a reduction in import dependency in the oil and gas equipment industry to 56 percent by the end of 2016, yet the actual share was 45 percent. At the same meeting, Gleb Nikitin, Deputy Minister of Industry and Trade, stated that annual output in the oil and gas equipment grew by 4 percent in 2015 and 14 percent in 2016. This was, he suggested, all the more impressive given that the wider fuel and energy industry had been suffering under the weight of low oil prices and an economy in recession, which had depressed activity in subsectors like power generation equipment.

Considerable government resources were allocated to meeting these objectives. According to Medvedev, nearly 375 billion rubles (c. $6 billion at average 2016 exchange rates) was assigned to support import substitution activities in 2016, which, as he stated, was "a lot considering our economic position." A large proportion of this sum was allocated to the oil and gas equipment industry, and it included direct state funding as well as capital released from Russian state investment funds. These funds were used in the successful development of intelligent geonavigation equipment used in drilling by Surgutneftegaz, as well as advanced drills used in horizontal drilling by Gazprom Neft (ibid).

The fact that the share of imported equipment used to extract oil and gas declined since 2013 is also likely to be explained by the historically weak value of the ruble during the period in which the import substitution plan was in effect. Nevertheless, it is revealing that investment in the machinery and equipment industry (i.e. all machinery and equipment, not just oil and gas equipment) grew significantly faster than overall investment between 2014 and 2016. Whereas the overall rate of investment in Russia was negative during 2014–2015, and grew only modestly in 2016, investment in machinery and equipment grew at an average annual rate of 14 percent over the same period.[18] The fact that investment and output was rising in precisely those sectors targeted by state industrial policy suggests that firms were probably responding to both the incentives offered by the state and the price signals displayed by the depreciation of the ruble.

The fact that import substitution seemed to be yielding some positive results, alongside the gradual diversification of sources of imported oil and gas equipment, suggests that the Russian government was moving some way toward its stated objectives. Progress was uneven, and slow in some subsectors, and the officially reported data may be exaggerated.[19] Nevertheless, the trajectory appeared to be well in line with policymakers' hopes expressed after sanctions were imposed in the summer of 2014. Moreover, as Alexander Novak, the Minister for Energy, pointed out at the St Petersburg meeting in May 2017, import substitution was progressing in other areas of the oil and gas equipment industry that did not fall within the purview of the sanctions regime. These areas included gas turbine production, LNG technology, and catalysts used in oil refinery (Government of the Russian Federation 2017; Ministry of Energy 2017).

Conclusion

The Russian energy industry experienced disruption and increased costs as a result of Western sanctions. This was especially apparent in the first few months after financial sanctions were imposed, when several targeted Russian firms experienced difficulties dealing with the sudden halt of Western capital to large energy firms such as Rosneft and Novatek. Several of the high-profile joint ventures with Western IOCs were also frozen, with US firms especially hard hit. (Although the fact that oil prices dropped precipitously just as sanctions were put in place suggests that expensive projects, such as those planned for the Kara Sea, would probably have been shelved until prices returned to those prevailing in the summer of 2014.) Some Russian firms operating in areas of hard-to-recover deposits also noted some difficulties in accessing the necessary technology.

---

[18] Rosstat, "Promyshlennoye proizvodstvo v Rossii – 2016 g," Moscow, 2017, www.gks.ru/bgd/regl/b16_48/Main.htm.

[19] It is possible that what was reported as Russian production was local production by foreign multinational firms operating in Russia. While, strictly speaking, this type of production is indeed Russian, the role of Russian companies may be exaggerated. The conflicting views from Russian government ministries and enterprises on what exactly constituted "Russian" production are discussed in Kozlov (2017).

Nevertheless, it is important not to exaggerate the impact of sanctions on the Russian energy industry, nor to expect that they will exert any significant impact in the future. The state's response to sanctions was comprehensive and sophisticated. A range of instruments – financial, institutional, and diplomatic – was used to cushion domestic energy firms from the immediate impact of sanctions and to change the trajectory of the industry's integration with the wider global economy. Recognizing the crucial role that energy sales make to Russia's economy and national security, the Russian government securitized energy policy by using the instruments at its disposal to ensure that the impact on Russia's most important economic sector was dampened.

From the Russian perspective, much was achieved in just three years. A determined effort to expand investment in the oil and gas equipment industry was gathering momentum. Alongside attempts to reinvigorate the domestic oil and gas equipment industry, rising imports of equipment from non-Western countries have meant that the trend toward increasing reliance on Asian sources of equipment, already evident pre-2014, is resulting in a slow but steady reduction in Russian dependence on the West for technology. If this process is only even partially successful, it will reduce, if not obviate, the need for Western IOC involvement in Russia's energy industry in the future. The substitution of technology has been accompanied by a steady increase in the use of non-Western sources of capital, with China leading the way in supplying capital to Russian energy projects on an increasingly large scale. Finally, diplomatic resources have been used to open up a closer gas-trade relationship with China. Alongside Russia's emergence as China's single largest supplier of crude oil, the intensification of energy trade between the two countries means that Russia is moving closer to achieving the objectives stated in the draft ES-2035.

It is also true that progress in achieving the wide range of objectives discussed in this chapter has been uneven, and in some instances was costly. Developing the domestic oil and gas equipment industry, for instance, will require many years of sustained and successful investment before Russia is in a position to supply the high-technology equipment required for deep-water extraction in the Arctic. A long-term commitment to import substitution will also be required, and even more so should the ruble strengthen in the future and thus lower the relative cost of imported machinery (Connolly and Hanson 2016).

The energy industry may also encounter obstacles in the future. For example, much of the economic shift toward Asia is predicated on rising

Chinese demand for hydrocarbons, which may not ensue. Nevertheless, the direction of travel for the Russian energy industry is clear: it is moving away from what Russian policymakers consider to be an excessive dependence on technology, capital, and demand from Western countries. This should reduce Russia's future vulnerability to Western sanctions, although the logical corollary is that potential exposure to similar instruments of economic statecraft being used by Asian countries – especially China – will rise.

The Russian response to sanctions in the energy industry also helps further our understanding of how target countries can, under certain circumstances, adapt to sanctions, and in doing so dilute the impact intended by sender countries. In this instance, a country that possessed one of the largest energy industries in the world, and which was connected to both a relatively sophisticated domestic industrial base and a wide range of foreign suppliers and consumers, was able to weather the initial storm created by sanctions. That it was able to do this was almost certainly a function of its system of political economy. Enterprises either owned by or close to the state were at the forefront of nearly all the instances in which adaptation took place.

While Russia's highly centralized system of resource allocation can often prove unwieldy and inefficient under normal circumstances, the fact that the state was able to employ a wide range of instruments – including the central bank, state-owned companies, state-owned banks, etc. – to coordinate a relatively swift and coherent response to sanctions demonstrates the difficulties faced by sender countries when trying to inflict economic pain for political gain. Instead, sender countries were confronted by a moving target that was able to reallocate resources to its weakest points to cushion the blow of sanctions. Regardless of whether Russia is fully successful in achieving the objectives its policymakers have set out since 2014, the fact that its actions in the first three years reduced, if not quite eliminated, the economic disruption caused in the energy industry almost certainly helps explain why the political gain sought by Western policymakers proved so elusive.

Appendix

International trade categories for oil and gas extraction equipment. Trade categories include:

(HS-72) Tubes, pipes, casings and fittings of metal products that are used in oil extraction

HS-730100 – Sheet piling, etc of iron/steel;

HS-730422 – Drill pipe, seamless, of stainless steel, of a kind used in drilling for oil and gas;

HS-730423 – Drill pipe, seamless, of a kind used in drilling for oil or gas;

HS-730424 – Casing and tubing, seamless, of a kind used for drilling for oil or gas;

HS-730429 – Casings, tubing, drill pipe, for oil drilling use;

HS-730520 – Casings, i/s, int/ext circ c sect, wld ext dia >406.4 mm, oil/gas drill, nes;

HS-730621 – Casing and tubing of a kind used in drilling for oil or gas, >=406.5 mm;

HS-730629 – Casing and tubing of a kind used in drilling for oil or gas, <=406.4 mm.

(HS-82) Drilling tools and parts

HS-820510 – Drilling, threading or tapping tools;

HS-820713 – Rock drilling/earth boring tools, working part cermets;

HS-820719 – Rock drilling/earth boring tools, nes, parts;

HS-820750 – Tools for drilling, other than for rock drilling.

(HS-84[+7]) drillings rigs and associated equipment

HS-843041 – Boring or sinking machinery nes, selfpropelled;

HS-843049 – Boring or sinking machinery nes, not self-propelled;

HS-845921 – Drilling mches nes; numerically controlled for removing metal;

HS-845929 – Drilling mches nes, for removing metal;

HS-870520 – Mobile drilling derricks

(HS-8905) Floating and submersible vessels and drilling platforms

HS-8905 – Light vessel, dredger; floating dock; floating/submersible drill platform.

5

Sanctions and the Defense Industry

INTRODUCTION

Historically, the defense industry, or OPK (*oboronno-promyshlennyi kompleks*), has occupied an extremely important position within Russia's political economy. It is strategically important, in so far as it provides Russia with a large and relatively independent defense-industrial capability that enables it to supply its armed forces with a wide range of weaponry. It is also an important source of industrial employment and represents one of the few areas of technology-intensive manufacturing in which Russian firms are successful as exporters. Nevertheless, because of the fact that its success is, to a large degree, dependent on demand from the state, I characterize it as a large and politically important component of the rent-dependent Sector B described in Chapter 2. In contrast to the energy industry, the defense industry relies on state expenditure and support to maintain output and employment. Direct state ownership and control is also even greater than in the energy industry. Moreover, unlike the energy industry, the defense industry did not embark on a path of widespread integration with the global economy after the disintegration of the Soviet Union in 1991. Although Russia was and remains the world's second largest exporter of weaponry, and while many Russian firms began to source components used in the production of weaponry from outside the traditional suppliers in the former Soviet Union, the role of foreign capital and ownership within the industry remained low, as did the number of joint ventures undertaken. To the extent that cooperation with non-Russian firms did take place, it was mainly as a result of the legacy of Soviet-era production networks which persisted with firms located within former Soviet states, such as Belarus and Ukraine.

It is perhaps no exaggeration to state that Russia's defense industry is one of the most important components of its position as a power of global significance, and one with the capacity to pursue interests that are times inimical to those of Western powers. It is, after all, the defense industry's ability to produce a wide range of sophisticated and effective weaponry – both conventional and nuclear – that furnishes Russia with the military capabilities that underpin its independent role in international politics (Kotkin 2016). Without these capabilities, it would be difficult to maintain Russia's high-profile position in global affairs. This sentiment was expressed clearly by the Prime Minister, Dmitri Medvedev, who declared: "if we do not have effective armed forces we will simply have no country" (Medevdev 2015d). In addition to its strategic value, the defense industry is also one of the few technology-intensive economic sectors in which Russia can be considered a world leader. As a result, it has an elevated status among the policy elite in Russia. Such is the importance attached to the defense industry that in 2012, President Vladimir Putin affirmed the potential of defense-industrial activity to "serve as fuel to feed the engines of modernization in [Russia's] economy" (Putin 2012b).

Given its clear economic and strategic value, the Russian defense industry was also an obvious target for Western economic sanctions. In the summer of 2014, Russian defense enterprises were restricted from accessing capital and technology from sender countries. Western sanctions were buttressed by a moratorium on the supply of defense-industrial equipment by Ukraine. Unlike in the energy industry, where access to only specific items of technology was prohibited, here a blanket ban on the export of items that might be used in military production was imposed. This included final weapons systems, but also components and dual-use items that could be used to support defense-industrial activities. Consequently, sanctions by both the West and Ukraine carried the potential to disrupt defense-industrial production in Russia and, in turn, to disrupt Russia's domestic military modernization program as well as its ability to export a high volume of weaponry.

As in the energy industry, the Russian response to the sanctions imposed on the defense industry has consisted of a combination of Russification and diversification. In the defense industry, Russification encompassed an ambitious import substitution program that sought to replace prohibited components and weapons systems with domestically produced analogues. This was accompanied by efforts to intensify defense-industrial cooperation with several non-Western states, such as China and India. Taken together, the Russian response to sanctions has the potential to practically eliminate large-scale domestic defense-industrial cooperation with Western and Ukrainian firms. If successful, this will reduce the defense industry's vulnerability to sanctions in the future. Furthermore, efforts to cultivate closer defense-industrial ties with non-Western powers might support a wider foreign policy shift toward building closer ties with the "non-West." In this respect, the potential of Russian adaptive measures is as much political as economic. As in the energy industry, the process of adjustment and adaptation has been state-led, with the leadership using its control over institutional, financial, and diplomatic levers to minimize the intended impact of Western sanctions.

The remainder of this chapter is organized as follows. First, I give a broad overview of the role that the defense industry plays in the Russian economy. This is followed by an assessment of the nature of the defense industry's relationship with the global economy. After this, the nature of the sanctions imposed on the Russian defense industry is described. I then examine how Russian government policies evolved in response to Western sanctions. The chapter concludes by examining how the adaptive measures initiated by the Russian government since 2014 have moderated the impact of Western and Ukrainian sanctions.

THE DEFENSE INDUSTRY AND THE RUSSIAN ECONOMY

During the Soviet era, the defense industry was one of the – if not *the* – highest priority sectors in the Soviet economy from the 1930s onward. It enjoyed preferential access to financial, physical, and human resources, at the expense both of other productive sectors of the economy and of the average Soviet consumer, who was forced to make do with a relatively limited variety of low-quality goods due to the priority assigned to defense-industrial production (Yaromenko 1981; Kontorovich and Wein 2009).[1] The huge importance assigned to the defense industry led to the Soviet Union being described as a "hyper militarized" economy (Gaddy 1996). This sobriquet was no exaggeration. Although estimates vary, it is likely that by 1990 the Soviet defense industry employed more than eight million people, nearly a quarter of whom were employed in research and development (R&D) activities (Cooper 2013). According to Julian Cooper, this

---

[1] However, defense-industrial enterprises also manufactured large quantities of "civilian" goods. As a result, Soviet consumers became aware that goods manufactured by defense industry enterprises tended to be of a much higher quality than those produced elsewhere in the economy.

Sanctions and the Defense Industry

accounted for nearly 20 percent of total industrial employment, with defense-industrial output amounting to around 12 percent of total industrial output (ibid, p. 99). Within Russia, the largest of the Soviet republics, nearly six million people were estimated to be in defense-industrial employment in 1985 (Gaddy 1996, p. 18). Such a large scale of defense-industrial production was only possible because of the enormous volume of state expenditure that supported it. Again, data constraints make it impossible to produce an estimate with any precision; however, midrange estimates suggest that defense expenditure accounted for around 15 percent of gross national product (GNP) in the late 1980s (Cooper 2013, p. 99).[2] What is certain is that the defense industry was of immense strategic, economic, and social importance, as shown by the degree of state support afforded to maintaining it.

This privileged status ended with the collapse of the Soviet Union in 1991. As state spending was cut dramatically in the early 1990s, the defense industry was forced to undergo a period of difficult and often slow adjustment and restructuring. Military expenditure in general was dramatically reduced, with state funding for procurement and R&D suffering the most. After all, the Soviet Union produced an excessive volume of military equipment, much of which was now surplus to requirements as military forces were reduced in number. This meant that the need for new equipment was much curtailed. As domestic demand was near enough eliminated, defense-industrial enterprises were forced to rely on either the sale of stockpiles of materials accumulated under the Soviet system of mobilization, or the commercial sale of armaments to foreign customers (Shlykov 1995). Within just five years of the collapse of the Soviet Union, defense-industrial output for military purposes had declined to less than one-tenth of its 1991 level (Cooper 2013). As a result, employment in the defense industry had reduced from around six million in 1990 to just under three million by 1997 (Cooper 2010, p. 156).

The brutal reduction in state demand for defense-industrial production was further exacerbated by institutional and administrative disintegration as the production associations and research production associations that underpinned defense-industrial activity in the Soviet period were dismantled. Reformist policymakers hoped they would be replaced by privatized firms that were expected to behave in a fashion more appropriate for a market economy, i.e. operating under hard budget constraints and without

[2] See Noren (1995) for a discussion of the different estimates of Soviet defense expenditure.

resort to the exorbitant privileges (i.e. access to the highest quality resources) that had so distorted the Soviet economy. It was envisaged that the privatization of defense-industrial assets would result in a smaller number of more efficient enterprises, with, in a serious departure from Soviet practice, scope for a role for foreign cooperation (Gaddy 1996). However, resistance by enterprise directors ensured that by the end of the 1990s only a quarter of defense-industrial enterprises were fully privatized (Cooper 2013, p. 102). Moreover, decentralization and a breakdown of state authority in those enterprises that remained under state control further aggravated the intractability of positive structural change within the industry (Sanchez-Andres 1998, 2000). Consequently, the desired efficiency gains were not realized and many firms focused their resources not on reorganization but instead on lobbying federal and local state structures to soften budget constraints (Gaddy and Ickes 2002). This left the Russian defense industry in a parlous state on the eve of the millennium (Shlykov 2004). Revenues were low, with exports proving vital in enabling important enterprises to survive; institutional change had proven intractable; and the sector as a whole was suffering from chronic under-investment, with little in the way of genuinely new, post-Soviet designs coming through the pipeline (Gonchar 2000; Zatspein 2012).

Vladimir Putin's appointment to the presidency on the eve of 2000, and his subsequent election that March, was accompanied by the resumption of rapid economic growth in the early 2000s (Hanson 2007; Appel 2008). This resulted in swelling federal government tax revenues, which in turn facilitated the rebuilding of state capacity (Popov 2014). As central authority was first restored and then strengthened, a concerted effort was made to reestablish control over the defense industry (Blank 2008). By the middle of the decade it was apparent that this reorganization would focus on merging the abundant and disparate enterprises scattered across the country into so-called "integrated structures" or state-owned holding companies. It was hoped that this process of consolidation and recentralization would help vertical management structures to generate greater efficiency and competitiveness among the kaleidoscope of profit- and loss-producing enterprises that had survived the tumultuous 1990s. Industrial giants such as United Aircraft Corporation (encompassing fixed-wing aircraft production), United Shipbuilding Corporation (bringing together most of the country's shipyards), and, most importantly, Rostec (overseeing thirteen holding companies and nearly 700 enterprises in both military and civilian production) emerged as the state reasserted its grip over this strategically important industry. By the end of 2013, it was estimated that around three-quarters of defense-industrial production took place within these consolidated industrial structures (Karavaev 2013).

This state-led effort to strengthen administrative capacity and operating efficiency to the industry did not result in the desired outcome. Instead of generating greater efficiency across the sector, consolidation in many instances led to the softening of budget constraints for poorly performing enterprises as the profits from healthy enterprises within the vast holding structures were used to cross-subsidize the loss-producing enterprises. Consequently, industrial consolidation suppressed already low levels of competition within subsectors of the defense industry, which in turn obviated any incentive to invest or innovate at firm level (Zatsepin 2012; Roffey 2013; Adamsky 2014). Centralization and consolidation was also unsuccessful in reducing the large number of relatively small enterprises in the defense industry, which pushed up costs as state resources were spread thinly across a large number of claimants.[3] These weaknesses meant that while state authority in the sector was certainly stronger than it was in the 1990s, it remained an area of the economy that, for the most part, was both controlled and supported by the state. Without access to soft loans, usually from state-owned banks, or to favorable (to defense industry enterprises) state procurement practices, it is difficult to imagine how large swathes of the industry could survive.

The defense industry's ability to extract resources from the state grew significantly after Russia's poor performance in the war with Georgia in the summer of 2008. This caused senior policymakers to recognize that ree-quipment of the military was necessary if it were to be transformed into a modern and capable fighting force (Bukkvoll 2009; Renz and Thornton 2012; Renz 2014; Trenin 2016; Hakvåg 2017). After accepting the strategic need to rearm, senior policymakers, led by the likes of Dmitri Rogozin and Vladimir Putin, embraced the idea that increased defense spending could serve as the locomotive of a wider breakthrough in high-technology and knowledge-intensive economic growth (Bukkvoll, Malmlöf, and Makienko 2017). While the defense industry was not elevated to quite the levels of the Soviet era, it did see its fortunes as a claimant on state resources improve dramatically, especially after a new ten-year state armament program to

---

[3] One other source of low productivity and high costs is that the extent of subcontracting and specialization in the production of components and other inputs within the OPK remains below average by international standards. This is a legacy of the Soviet-era practice of concentrating production within smaller units of production. I am grateful to Julian Cooper for pointing this out.

2020 (*gosudarstvennaia programma vooruzheniia*, hereafter the GPV-2020) was approved at the end of 2010 by then president Dmitri Medvedev (Cooper 2016a; Connolly and Senstad 2017).

GPV-2020 was designed to facilitate the partial reequipment and modernization of the Russian armed forces by 2020, through the large-scale procurement of a wide range of weapon systems. It was envisaged that at least 70 percent of the armed forces' equipment would be classed as modern by the time the GPV was completed – a sharp increase on the share of modern equipment in service in 2010, which was estimated to be just 15 percent. A total of 20.7 trillion rubles (or c. $700 billion at the average 2011 exchange rate) was reported to have been assigned to fulfill GPV-2020 and to help support the modernization of the wider defense-industrial base (Falichev 2011). The total funds allocated to the Ministry of Defense for rearmament can be disaggregated by service, with the Russian navy and air force reported to have been assigned nearly half of the total allocated funding (Centre for the Analysis of Strategy and Technology 2015, p. 23).

After rearmament moved to the top of the political agenda in the aftermath of the Georgia war, total Russian military expenditure grew from 3.8 percent of GDP in 2010 to nearly 5 percent in 2015 (IISS 2018, p. 176). Of this, the volume of spending allocated to defense procurement rose especially sharply, rising from 1 percent of GDP in 2010 to 2.4 percent of GDP in 2015. The funds allocated to the annual state defense order (*gosudarstevennyi oboronnyi zakaz*, or GOZ) were augmented with state guaranteed credits (SGCs), as well as additional funding for defense activities directed through other government departments, such as the Ministry of Industry and Trade, that included military components supporting defense research or production (Nikolsky 2015).[4] This caused a substantial redistribution of government spending. In 2010, military expenditure as a share of total federal government spending amounted to 15.9 percent. By 2015 it had grown to 25.8 percent. Indeed, by 2015, defense procurement (i.e. GOZ and SGCs) was the equivalent of around 12 percent of total federal government spending (Cooper 2016a).

By the end of 2015, this huge injection of funds into the defense industry meant that its footprint in the Russian economy was at a post-Soviet high. With total employment of around 2.5 million, defense industry employment

---

[4] A detailed explanation of other likely sources of federal government defense spending can be found in Cooper (2013).

stood at around 20 percent of total manufacturing employment.[5] While this figure no doubt includes R&D and other staff that would not otherwise be defined as in manufacturing employment, it is likely that defense industry manufacturing employment might be around 15 percent of total manufacturing employment. The defense industry's share of manufacturing value-added is estimated to be as high as 10 percent, which is again comparable to Soviet-era levels.[6] The fact that the industry's share of government spending and manufacturing output rose so sharply between 2011 and 2015 demonstrates the strong link between its performance and the federal government's willingness to fund it. Although some prominent Russian economists have described defense expenditure as "unproductive" (Kudrin and Knobel' 2017; Kudrin and Sokolov 2017), it is likely that the sharp increase in defense procurement that was necessitated by rearmament acted as a significant source of countercyclical state-led demand that helped moderate the recession of 2015 (Sharkovskiy 2016; Kubinowa 2017).

Thus, while the defense industry's fortunes have fluctuated considerably in the post-Soviet period, its strategic and economic importance at the point at which sanctions were imposed in 2014 was clear. It had, for one reason or another, emerged from its post-Soviet crisis, and once again occupied a position as one of the leading sectors in the Russian economy. However, its position as a prime recipient of revenues generated elsewhere in the economy, and its place within the state-centered network, meant that its success – notwithstanding its strong export performance, which is discussed later – was to a large degree shaped by the political leadership's willingness to provide it with large volumes of funding.[7]

THE RUSSIAN DEFENSE INDUSTRY AND THE GLOBAL ECONOMY

The relationship between the Russian defense industry and the global economy has, like that with the Soviet defense industry before it, a lopsided character (Pierre 1982; Krause 1992; Anthony 1998; Kirshin 1998). On the

---

[5] Defense industry employment figure from Putin (2017); total manufacturing employment from Rosstat "Russia in Figures in 2016."

[6] Kuboniwa (2016), Considerations on new Rosstat data on the contribution of Russia's military goods sector to GDP growth in recent years, Helsinki: Bank of Finland Institute for Transition.

[7] According to federal government spending projections until 2020, the peak of defense spending looked, at the time of writing, to have passed. See Cooper (2017).

one hand, the industry's consistently strong export performance means that it is one of the few technology-intensive areas of the Russian economy that is successful in global markets. On the other, the industry is only weakly integrated with global ownership structures and production networks, and before 2014 relied on imported components and final weapons systems in only a limited number of areas. This is, in many ways, a deliberate form of integration with the global economy. By reducing the industry's dependence on imported items, and by maintaining predominantly Russian ownership (usually by the state) of the means of defense-industrial production, the country's ability to preserve an independent capability to produce a wide spectrum of military equipment was sustained. The downside to this configuration, however, is that the industry's exposure to innovation – both organizational and technological – in other countries was dampened.

Russia as an Arms Exporter

Russia has, since 1991, been the world's second-largest exporter of weaponry. Only the United States has been able to export a larger volume of armaments.[8] Moreover, in recent years – i.e. since 2000 – Russia has been able to not only maintain its position in second place, but also increase the absolute volume of sales and its share of global arms sales (Figure 5.1). This competitiveness on global markets proved essential to the survival of many firms during the 1990s when domestic demand from the Ministry of Defense was negligible (Cooper 2013). However, Russian arms exports grew after 2000, reaching a peak in real terms (i.e. adjusted for inflation) in 2013. The share of arms exports in total exports (both goods and services) and of GDP peaked in 2015 (TASS 2016b). This was due to the fact that the recession, which began at the end of 2014 and lasted throughout 2015, caused both total exports and GDP to decline, while arms sales remained roughly stable. Because Russia's export basket, as illustrated in Chapter 2, is dominated by hydrocarbons and other natural resources,

---

[8] Measuring the precise value of arms sales is a challenging exercise. Essentially, there exist two main methods to measure arms sales across time and countries. The first involves estimating the material volume of arms transfers or the "military capability transfer." The second measures the financial value of arms transfers. Here, the former measure is used when comparing the volume of Russian arms exports with other countries, while the reported financial value is used when referring to the role of arms exports in Russia's domestic export (i.e. as a share of total exports). For a more comprehensive discussion of the relative merits and deficiencies of the two methods see Connolly and Senstad (2017).

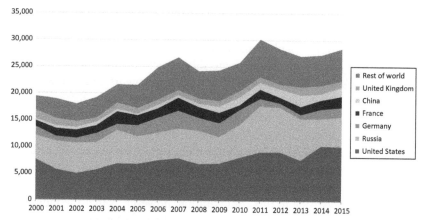

Figure 5.1 Value of arms exports by Russia and selected countries, 2000–2015 (TIV, constant 1990 USD, million)[9]
Source: SIPRI Arms Transfers Database (2017)

arms accounted for only around 3–4 percent share of total exports. However, the sale of weaponry represents a significant proportion of Russia's manufactured and technology-intensive exports (Koshovets and Ganichev 2015). In 2015, for example, exports of machinery and manufactured goods excluding weaponry amounted to around $25 billion. During the same year, armaments exports generated sales of around $14.5 billion.[10]

Russia's strong performance as an arms exporter was based on exports to a wide and growing range of countries in across the world.[11] While in the 1990s, Russian arms exports tended to be focused on the Chinese and Indian markets – at the time, among the largest importers of weaponry in the world – Russian producers have proven adept at opening new markets. Since 2000, new and important customers across Asia, Latin America, and the Middle East and North Africa have supplemented sales to China and India (Figure 5.2). Indeed, by the mid-2010s the array of countries importing Russian arms was more diverse than that of other major arms exporters such as the United Kingdom, Germany, France, and China.

---

[9] The Trend Indicator Value used by SIPRI is a measure of military capability transfer. According to SIPRI "[t]he TIV is based on the known unit production costs of a core set of weapons and is intended to represent the transfer of military resources rather than the financial value of the transfer."

[10] Calculated using export data for "machinery and transport equipment" (SITC Rev.3 category 7) and "other manufactured goods" (SITC Rev.3 categories 6 and 8). Data from UN Comtrade database, 2016, https://comtrade.un.org/data/ (accessed October 21, 2016).

[11] This is discussed in greater detail in Connolly and Senstad (2017).

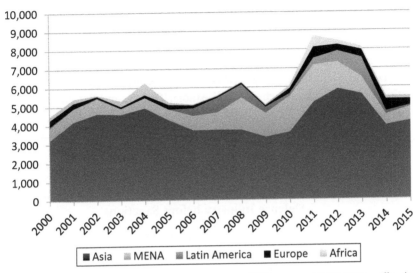

Figure 5.2 Russian arms sales by region, 2000–2015 (TIV, constant 1990 USD, million)
Source: SIPRI Arms Transfers Database (2017); author's calculations

To maintain their share in these markets, Russian producers have sold an increasingly varied range of weaponry, including some of the most technologically advanced equipment. For example, Russia has either agreed to sell, or is considering selling, the Su-35, an advanced fighter aircraft, to China (RIA Novosti 2016h) and Indonesia (RIA Novosti 2016), and the S-400 surface-to-air missile system to India, Turkey, and, apparently, Saudi Arabia. Russia has also agreed to lease nuclear-powered attack submarines (SSNs) to India (Nikolsky 2016a).

Russian arms sales also perform an important political function.[12] According to President Putin, the sale of weaponry is "an effective instrument for advancing [Russia's] national interests, both political and economic" (Putin 2012a). This sentiment was reinforced by the deputy prime minister for the defense industry, Dmitri Rogozin, who argued that the Federal Service for Military-Technical Cooperation – the government organization charged with coordinating arms exports – was "the country's second foreign policy agency." Arms exports, according to Rogozin, enabled Russia to "gain or increase [its] influence" in other countries (RIA Novosti 2013). This further illustrates that state-owned enterprises in strategically important sectors of the economy are valuable instruments

---

[12] The role of arms exports as an instrument of foreign policy is discussed in Krause (1992).

in promoting both the commercial and economic interests of the country. The relative importance of commercial or political interests varies across cases. For example, there is at least prima facie evidence that political concerns motivate the sale of Russian weaponry to the likes of Armenia, Syria, and Tajikistan. Indeed, Russian enthusiasm for carving out a position in new markets such as Saudi Arabia, Turkey, and the Philippines is likely to be caused as much by a desire to weaken ties between those countries and their traditional allies in the West as it is by a desire to generate revenue.

The Role of Foreign Technology and Capital in the Russian Defense Industry before Sanctions

Prior to the imposition of Western and Ukrainian sanctions in 2014, the role of foreign technology and capital was concentrated in a few specific areas of the production cycle. Broadly speaking, the highest degree of integration between Russian and foreign enterprises was evident with firms located in ex-Soviet republics, such as Ukraine and Belarus. Here, the existence of integrated supply chains was a legacy of the Soviet-era distribution of production rather than a result of any post-Soviet design. Crucial intermediate components, such as helicopter engines, vehicles designed to transport ballistic missiles, guidance systems for missiles, and power units for large warships, were often produced in ex-Soviet republics. After the disintegration of the planned economy in 1991, these production networks continued to function, with what was once a matter of intra-industry trade becoming a matter of international trade.

Close relationships such as this did not tend to occur with enterprises located outside the former Soviet Union. To be sure, Western and Chinese components – especially electronic components – were increasingly used in the production of Russian military equipment, especially as domestic capabilities in this area weakened sharply (Cooper 2016a, pp. 37–38). However, imports from outside the former Soviet space tended to be off-the-shelf purchases, rather than a result of any closely integrated production network. While components were imported on a considerable scale, Russia tended not to import final weapons systems, at least until Anatoly Serdyukov became Defense Minister in 2007. Serdyukov, in an effort to expose domestic producers to greater competition, made the decision to import several important types of weapons systems from Western countries. From 2010 until November 2012, Serdyukov's openness to closer ties with Western defense suppliers threatened to presage a shift in the nature of the Russian defense industry's integration with the wider global economy (Klein 2012; Renz and Thornton 2012).

Imports from Former Soviet States

The most important foreign supplier of components and subsystems used in the Russian defense industry was Ukraine. This was due to the dense links that existed between the two industries during the Soviet era, when the Ukrainian defense industry was second in size and technological importance to Russia (Malmlöf 2016, p. 4). Ukrainian firms were particularly important in the production of some intercontinental ballistic missiles and space rockets, large warships and their power units, heavy transport aircraft, guidance and control systems for air-to-air missiles and torpedoes, and helicopter engines (Voronov 2016). Large and economically and socially important enterprises in Ukraine, such as Motor Sich (aircraft and helicopter engines), Antonov (transport aircraft), Arsenal (optics and electronics), Dnepropetrovsk Aggregate Plant (components used in aircraft), Yuzhmash (missiles), and Zorya-Mashproekt (gas turbines), were closely integrated within Russian defense-industrial production chains. Indeed, some of these enterprises were assigned an important role in the implementation of GPV-2020. Antonov, in particular, was expected to jointly develop the An-70 transport aircraft, as well as to help develop a modernized version of the larger, Soviet-era An-124 (Cooper 2016a, p. 36). Thus, while the overall scale of Ukranian defense-industrial exports to Russia was not enormous – 3.5 percent of all inputs used in Russian defense-industrial production, according to one estimate – the fact that they were concentrated in subsectors of the defense industry meant they were important (ibid).

Belarus was also an important supplier of components and subsystems to Russia, especially in optical equipment, electronics and vehicles (Faltsman 2015). Prior to the conflict with Ukraine in 2014, numerous senior officials expressed a desire to reduce Russia's dependence on foreign-supplied components, including from Ukraine and Belarus (Frolov 2016). However, inertia and cost constraints prevented any serious action to reduce this dependence.

Imports from Outside the Former Soviet Union

Because of the absence of any meaningful procurement of conventional weapons in the 1990s and early 2000s, and because the Russian defense industry was able to produce most of the weapons used by its armed forces, very few final weapons systems were imported from any countries outside the former Soviet Union, with the exception of some very small-scale imports from the Czech Republic, Israel, Italy, and Turkey. However, this looked set to change when, in 2010 – and in the face of considerable criticism from the Russian defense industry – the Ministry of Defense decided to purchase armaments on a significant scale as part of GPV-2020. It was hoped that the procurement of foreign military equipment would help fill technology gaps exposed by the Russian military's experience in Georgia (e.g. the need for unmanned aerial vehicles, or UAVs) and, by threatening the Russian defense industry's near monopoly over arms deliveries to the Ministry of Defense, help introduce competition that would lower costs and boost efficiency.

As illustrated in Table 5.1, the decision to begin acquiring weapons systems from abroad resulted in a number of significant deals being signed around 2010–2011. The decision to acquire the Mistral-class amphibious landing ship was the most lucrative and high-profile deal. But all shared in common an effort to localize production within Russia and, as a result, to boost Russian capabilities in defense-industrial production in areas where the Russian industry was considered to be lagging behind global competitors. Taken together, these deals represented only a small fraction of the procurement that was envisaged as part of GPV-2020. Nevertheless, the very fact that the Russian military was acquiring systems from abroad signaled a significant shift in defense procurement practice. These deals were later supplemented by further joint ventures, including that between Uralvagonzavod and the French manufacturer Renault to develop the heavy 8×8-wheeled "Atom" infantry fighting vehicle.

If the move toward greater cooperation and joint ventures with firms located outside Russia's traditional suppliers in the former Soviet Union was a relatively new and controversial development, importing components used to produce final weapons systems was more deeply established and, in financial terms, occurring on a much larger scale. While the Soviet Union was largely self-sufficient in the production of electronic components, these capabilities diminished dramatically with the disintegration of the Soviet Union in 1991 (Faltsman 2015). A large proportion of production took place in Belarus, from which Russian firms continued to source components. But imports from outside Belarus also increased significantly. Western countries – many of which were NATO members – as well as Asian suppliers in the likes of China, Taiwan, and South Korea began to establish themselves as crucial suppliers of dual-use electronic components

Table 5.1 *Procurement of foreign military equipment, 2009–2011*

	Supplier	System	Value	Details
2009	Israel	Bird-Eye 400 UAVs; Searcher II UAVs; I-View Mk 150 UAVs	$53 million	12 UAV systems
2010	Israel	Heron TP UAVs	c. $400 million	A joint venture between OPK Oboronprom and Israel Aerospace Industries to build up to 36 UAVs. Training of Russian personnel also included.
2010	Italy	Iveco M65 armored vehicles	c. $1 billion	Initial small-scale procurement followed by local production of up to 1,700 vehicles.
2011	France	Mistral-class amphibious assault ship	c. $2 billion	Two ships were to be acquired from French producers with some Russian participation. There was also an option for a further two ships to be built in Russia.
2011	Germany	Diesel power units for Gremyashchy-class corvette and Buyan-M small missile ship.	Unknown	German firm, MTU, contracted to supply diesel engines for use in new naval vessels.
2011	Germany	Military training center	c. $150 million	German firm, Rheinmetall, established a joint venture with JSC Oboronservis to build military training facility.

Source: Author's assessment

used to manufacture armaments. It is difficult to establish the precise scale of the role that imported electronic components play in the defense industry, but fragments of information give some idea. First, the fact that the industry was set a target in 2015 of increasing the share of Russian production in the domestic electronics market to 20 percent reveals that the share of Russian producers was already much lower than this

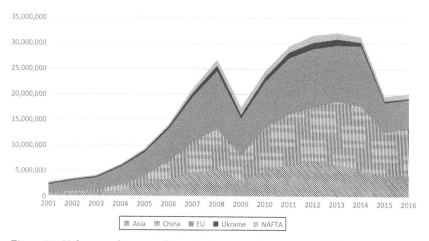

Figure 5.3 Volume and source of Russian imports: all categories of electronic
equipment and components, 2001–2016 (current USD, thousand)
Sources: International Trade Centre (ITC); United Nations Comtrade database; author's
calculations

(Cooper 2016b, p. 135). Second, the scale and range of electronic components imported annually for use across the Russian economy is large,
again suggesting that defense industry dependence on imported electronic equipment was high (Figure 5.3).

In Figure 5.3, data are presented for Russian imports of all categories of
electronic equipment and components (HS, or harmonized system, codes
85-). While this includes some finished consumer electrical items, such
as mobile telephones, it also includes the types of electronic equipment
and components that are used in the production of defense-industrial
equipment. Typically, these finished electronic items account for around
25 percent of the total volume of imported equipment; the remaining
75 percent comprises components and machinery used in the production
of other goods.

A clear shift away from imports from the EU, North America, and
Ukraine was apparent from the turn of the century. In 2001, this group
accounted for 75 percent of Russian imports in this trade category. By
2013, their share had declined to 42 percent. However, while the economic
slowdown caused imports to drop sharply in the second half of 2014,
imports from the EU, North America, and Ukraine fell much more sharply
than imports from China and other countries of East Asia. As a result,
their share of Russian imports fell to just 33 percent in 2016. Meanwhile,
the Chinese share rose from 39 percent in in 2013 to 45 percent in 2016.

Over the same period, the other countries of East Asia, led by Vietnam and South Korea, saw their share rise from 19 percent in 2013 to 22 percent in 2016. A similar trend is evident within certain subcategories, such as parts and transformers (HS-8504), which are likely to include items covered by Western and Ukrainian sanctions. Here, China's share grew from 20 percent of all imports in 2013 to more than 30 percent in 2016. China was the not only beneficiary, either. Over the same period, Indonesia saw its share in Russia's imports of electronic parts and transformers rise from less than 1 percent to nearly 10 percent, becoming Russia's second largest supplier. This took place at the expense of traditional suppliers such as Germany, France, and Italy, who experienced a 55–60 percent reduction in the volume of their sales to Russia. Thus, while a shift toward Asia was already evident in imports of this type of equipment before sanctions, it does appear to have accelerated considerably since 2014.

Russian dependence on imported equipment was not limited to electronic components. Another area of weakness – or one of Russia's two "Achilles' heels," as they were described by the deputy prime minister for the defense industry, Dmitri Rogozin (the other being electronic components) – is that of machine tools and advanced equipment used to produce military equipment (Gordeev 2015). Indeed, this is a problem for Russian industry in general, with a recent study suggesting that the import dependency ratio was highest in precisely this area (Vedev and Berezinskaya 2015). This is supported by official estimates which indicate that more than 70 percent of the machinery required for upgrading defense-industrial capital stock would have to be imported (Faltsman 2015, p. 119). This weakness is likely to be a matter of considerable concern to Russian policymakers, as the serial production of advanced new weaponry – and, indeed, of existing weapons systems – is predicated on the existence of high-precision machine tools. Although efforts were already underway to consolidate domestic production under the aegis of Stankoprom, a holding company established in 2013 to integrate Russia's existing machine tool enterprises, it is indicative that pre-2014 plans to develop the industry envisaged an important role for cooperation with foreign enterprises to boost technology transfer (Cooper 2016b, p. 135).

It is therefore clear that before 2014, the Russian defense industry exhibited a rather unbalanced pattern of integration with the global economy. Russia was, on the one hand, the world's second-largest exporter of armaments. On the other, however, it was only weakly integrated within global production networks, with much of the domestic industry insulated from technological and organizational transfer through cooperation with other countries. What did exist tended to be a result of the legacy of Soviet-era production networks, or to arise where enterprises imported components or advanced production equipment that Russian enterprises had proven unable to supply on a large and reliable scale. Nevertheless, while this general pattern characterized most of the post-Soviet period, it is also the case that at the beginning of the 2010s the defense industry was being pushed toward placing greater emphasis on internationalization, including interaction with firms from Western countries such as Italy, Germany, and France. The impulse for what has been described as a "cautious, but steady, move towards more active participation in global defense and high technology networks, [and] an international-ization of a formerly rather closed system" came from a recognition on the part of some senior defense officials that the defense industry would, through closer cooperation with foreign enterprises, be able to better weapons systems in a more efficient manner (Cooper 2016b, p. 136). As will be discussed presently, Western and Ukrainian sanctions caused this nascent reorientation toward the global economy to be quickly reversed.

SANCTIONS AND THE RUSSIAN DEFENSE INDUSTRY

The trajectory toward closer integration with the global defense industry was halted by the sanctions imposed in 2014. Following the Russian annexation of Crimea, a series of increasingly stringent sanctions were imposed both on specific firms within the Russian defense industry and, in principle, on all firms that might be involved in defense-industrial production. While Western countries were at the forefront of the energy sanctions discussed in the previous chapter, the role of Ukrainian sanctions in the defense industry was equally, if not more, important than those applied by the United States, the EU, and their allies.

As with the sanctions targeted at the energy industry, sanctions against the Russian defense industry were introduced in several phases. On March 20, President Obama signed an executive order that placed restrictions on activities involving enterprises in a range of industries, including defense and related industries (US Treasury 2014b). A month later, the United States expanded the scope of restrictions on the export of defense-related technologies and services to Russia so that the list of prohibited items encompassed a broader range of defense and dual-use equipment. The EU sanctions regime against the Russian defense industry moved in parallel with US legislation, although, crucially, considerable leeway was afforded to member state governments as to whether contracts concluded before March 2014 could be executed.[13]

As the sanctions regime was gradually expanded, the scope of items whose sale was prohibited grew. Following the imposition of sector-wide sanctions in the summer of 2014, the United States, the EU, and their allies had imposed comprehensive restrictions on the sale of military hardware to Russia. They also identified specific firms that were to be denied access to technology, capital, and services, including United Aircraft Corporation, Uralvagonzavod, and Almaz-Antey. In addition to the embargo on the provision of arms and related material, an embargo was also placed on the sale of dual-use (i.e. items that can be used in both civilian and military production) goods and technology that might be intended for military use or for a military end-user. This meant that dual-use items, such as electronic components or machine tools used to produce military equipment, also fell within the purview of the restrictions. Sender countries also imposed a ban on imports of arms and related items, although this was in most cases a symbolic gesture as the United States, the EU, and their allies imported only a very small volume of restricted equipment from Russia.

Western sanctions were buttressed by a moratorium on the export of military equipment to Russia issued by the Ukrainian government at the end of March 2014. Initially, this moratorium was not comprehensive; some dual-use items, such as helicopter engines, were not covered by the moratorium and continued to be supplied to Russian customers (Malmlöf 2016, p. 10). Some Ukrainian enterprises, such as Yuzhmash, failed to observe the moratorium and attempted to honor existing contracts (ibid). However, over the course of the summer of 2014, the newly elected Ukrainian president, Petro Poroshenko, endorsed legislation that prohibited nearly all defense cooperation between the two countries (TASS 2014). This included dual-use items as well as final weapons systems, but did permit exports of technology used in space exploration (Malmlöf 2016, p. 6).

While the combined sanctions regime (i.e. encompassing both Western sanctions and the Ukrainian embargo) was comprehensive in scope, there

---

[13] The relevant legislative framework can be found in Council Decision 2014/512/CFSP, 2014/659/CFSP, 2014/872/CFSP, Council Decision (CFSP) 2015/1764, Council Decision (CFSP) 2016/1071, Council Regulation (EU) No. 833/2014, Council Regulation (EU) No 960/2014, Council Regulation (EU) No 1290/2014, Council Regulation (EU) 2015/1797. European Union: Restrictive Measures (Sanctions) in force, updated July 7, 2016, http://eeas.europa.eu/archives/docs/cfsp/sanctions/docs/measures_en.pdf.

were several critical differences in the sanctions legislation that would affect how sanctions worked in practice. As with energy sanctions, the EU utilized a preapproval procedure for deals involving the supply of defense and dual-use equipment to Russia. This gave considerable discretion to authorized government bodies of the countries in which the exporting companies were registered to decide whether approval for the sale of such equipment would be granted. The so-called grandfather provision was also applied to defense trade. This meant that authorities in EU member states could issue permits for the delivery of equipment if it was deemed to be related to a commitment arising from a contract or agreement executed before EU sanctions were imposed. Ukrainian firms could still supply equipment for civilian use, which allowed Motor Sich to continue supplying helicopter engines to Russian customers (Frolov 2016).

Sanctions caused most of the joint projects between Russian and foreign firms – whether from Ukraine or from the United States, EU, and allied countries – to come to a halt. The German firm MTU decided to halt the delivery of engines for use in Russian naval vessels, and Rheinmetall also cancelled its deal to build a military training center. Perhaps most importantly, the French government decided, after some deliberation, to cancel the delivery of two Mistral warships to Russia. Instead, the Russian Ministry of Defense received compensation for the breach of contract, and the ships were later sold to the Egyptian armed forces (Kirk 2015). However, not all deals were affected by sanctions. For instance, the Italian firm Iveco fulfilled the terms of its deal to supply armored vehicles (Korolkov 2016).

THE RUSSIAN RESPONSE TO SANCTIONS

As in the energy industry, the Russian government was quick to formulate a response to the restrictions placed on its strategically important defense industry. The Russian response included a determined policy of: (1) drawing down existing stocks of military and related equipment to prevent the short-term emergence of bottlenecks in the production cycle of military equipment; (2) substituting Western and Ukrainian technology with Russian-produced equipment, or if not, acquiring analogues from non-Western alliance countries with whom Russia continued to enjoy normal trade relations; and (3) undertaking diplomatic and commercial initiatives to develop closer defense-industrial relations with non-Western countries, such as China and India. Thus, as with the energy industry, the policy response consisted of a mix of Russification (i.e. import substitution) and reorientation of Russia's foreign economic relations. Again, Russia's leaders used the state and its position at the apex of the country's system of political economy to achieve these objectives.

The Use of Industrial Reserves

Defense-industrial firms' most immediate response to restrictions on accessing components was to use existing stockpiles (Frolov 2016). These industrial reserves tended to be substantial due to the Soviet-era practice of hoarding items provided by foreign countries (Cooper 2016a, p. 35). As a result, most firms were in a position to avoid the emergence of bottlenecks, at least in the short term. Moreover, the fact that electronic imports rose as a share of total imports in 2014 also suggests that Russian firms – both within the defense industry and from other sectors of the economy – responded to sanctions by increasing their acquisition of prohibited items. While the data presented in Figure 5.3 do not prove that this was the case, the fact that the share of imports rose does provide at least circumstantial evidence that Russian firms sought to stockpile those components to which access had become restricted. This was not, though, considered to be an adequate long-term solution to the problem, for several reasons.[14] First, the components produced by alternative suppliers – such as China – were not always considered to be equal to those produced by Western suppliers (Istomin 2016). Second, the use of items used in more technically demanding production processes – such as the installation of power units on warships – required trained personnel as well as components that were often no longer available. Finally, military and defense-industrial officials were reluctant to tolerate any dependence on foreign suppliers – whether in the West or anywhere else – for strategically important items. Consequently, Russian policymakers, seeking a longer-term solution to restricted access to strategically important items that would reduce Russia's vulnerability to sanctions in the future, formulated a larger-scale and more sophisticated response, in the form of an import substitution program to produce defense-industrial equipment.

---

[14] I am grateful to Maxim Shapovalenko of the Moscow-based Centre for Analysis of Strategic Technologies (CAST) for describing to me the problems encountered by defense-industrial firms after restrictions on technology transfer were imposed.

The Russification of Defense-Industrial Production

Sanctions provided added impetus to an already strong current of support within Russian defense-industrial circles to promote the Russification of production within the industry. To be sure, this was not a new sentiment. Some officials and industry representatives had been arguing since the 1990s that all stages of defense-industrial production should take place within Russia (Voronov 2016, p. 1). Indeed, several legislative measures intended to support domestic production were put in place long before sanctions were imposed. For instance, legislation concerning public procurement in defense contracts was put in place between 2005 and 2013 granting the state permission to impose "prohibitions and restrictions" on goods originating from foreign countries.[15] However, for as long as high-quality inputs were available from foreign suppliers, and while the geopolitical environment remained favorable, Russian enterprises tended to favor imports over domestic analogues. This changed quickly after March 2014. Within a year, government officials had crafted an elaborate and well-financed effort to shift the production of a large volume of defense-industrial equipment and components to within Russia.

The first steps toward creating a fully fledged import substitution plan began in the weeks after the annexation of Crimea, as President Putin discussed the challenge of producing substitutes for items used in defense-industrial production previously supplied by Ukraine at meetings held on April 9–10, 2014 (Kremlin.ru 2014). As would become normal when talking about measures designed to overcome sanctions, Putin presented import substitution as an investment "in developing our own manufacturing" that would "be to the benefit of Russian industry and the economy" (Kremlin.ru 2014). Over the course of the next year, two main import substitution programs were developed. First, President Putin sanctioned a program to develop substitute items produced in Ukraine (Vzglyad 2015). It was initially estimated that the cost of this program would reach around 50 billion rubles, with federal funds used in conjunction with financial resources of defense-industry firms. Six months later, a program to produce defense-industrial and dual-use items previously supplied by Western suppliers was approved, although the estimated cost of this program was not made public (Mukhin 2015).

---

[15] 94-FZ, July 21, 2005; updated with 44-FZ, April 5, 2013. Reinforced by Resolution of Government of the Russian Federation No. 1275, December 26, 2013.

These programs were later brought under the aegis of the Government Commission on Import Substitution, which was formed in August 2015. The commission, chaired by the Prime Minister, Dmitri Medvedev, was charged with coordinating, monitoring and implementing import substitution across the economy. It comprised two sub-commissions: one, chaired by Arkady Dvorkovich, was tasked with overseeing import substitution in the non-military (i.e. civilian) sectors of the economy; the second, chaired by Deputy Prime Minister for the Defense Industry, Dmitri Rogozin, was given the brief of developing domestic production of items for the defense industry. This included not just military equipment, but also dual-use items, such as components and machinery used in defense-industrial production (Government of the Russian Federation 2015a).

The stated objectives of import substitution in the defense industry were ambitious. As far as the plan for replacing Ukrainian production was concerned, Rogozin declared that Russian firms should produce 95 percent of what was previously imported by as soon as 2016 (Vzglyad 2015). Russian production of the remaining 5 percent of items was intended to take place by 2018 (TASS 2015b). It is difficult to ascertain precisely how many components the import substitution program was intended to replace. Estimates from different sources place the number of components and products that were to be substituted at anywhere between 700 and 3,000.[16] In any case, given Ukraine's role as the largest single supplier of defense-industrial equipment before 2014, the list was undoubtedly long, ranging from small electronic components to much larger gas turbine power units used in the Project 11356 (Admiral Grigorovich-class) and Project 22350 (Admiral Gorshkov-class) frigates.

The program to replace Western-produced defense-industrial and dual-use items was similarly grand in scale. Again, estimates of the volume of items that were planned to be replaced vary. In July 2015, Dmitri Rogozin, stated that 640 items of Russian military equipment required components, mainly optical and electronic components, that were imported from NATO and EU countries. Of these, he declared that "we will have to replace [components used in the production of] 571 items [i.e. c.90 per cent] by 2018" (Rosbalt.ru 2015). Later that month Deputy Defense Minister Yuri Borisov suggested that the number of items of military equipment reliant on imported products was 826 (VPK-news.ru 2015). Whether these differing figures reflect different methods of calculation or

---

[16] The lower bound of the estimate is taken from Frolov (2016) while the upper bound was reported in Umnoye Proizvodstvo (2014).

different sources of information is unclear. What is clear, however, is that the import substitution objectives to replace items previously supplied by both NATO/EU countries and Ukraine were large in scale and no doubt in complexity. Plans to replace the vast majority (90 percent) of these items by 2018, with full substitution envisaged by 2021, illustrated the urgency attached to import substitution in the defense industry.

While the volume of federal government funding allocated to supporting import substitution in the defense industry has not been revealed, it is likely to be substantial and far in excess of that allocated to, for example, the energy industry. Direct federal funding would be supplemented by capital from enterprises (most of which are state-owned) involved in the program. Moreover, additional means of finance were made available. Defense expenditure covered by the "national defense" chapter of the federal budget rose significantly over 2014–2015 and was further supplemented by the use of state guaranteed credits (SGCs) channeled via state-owned banks, as well as additional indirect funding directed via other ministries, such as the Ministry of Industry and Trade, which funded the development of industrial projects with military applications (Nikolsky 2015).

While the use of SGCs was intended to support production for the annual state defense order (GOZ), the fact that they alleviated any financial pressures faced by defense enterprises at the time can only have helped those enterprises that were also involved in import substitution activities. More substantial funding for import substitution was likely to have been supplied from 2016 onward through the "Stimulating the Development of the Defense-Industrial Complex" subprogram of the wider state program for the Development of the OPK, No. 425–8 (Government of the Russian Federation 2016b). According to Julian Cooper, the subprogram provides resources to support R&D, the development of human capital, and direct financial support for enterprises engaged in in import substitution activities (Cooper 2016a, p. 41). Given that the total value – spread over five years – of the state program for the Development of the OPK is likely to be around 1 trillion rubles, it is likely that the funds allocated to the subprogram supporting import substitution are of a considerable magnitude (Zatsepin 2016, p. 62).

Building new capacity to supply components and other defense-industrial equipment on such a large scale clearly represented an enormous challenge. Even with the allocation of significant additional funding – through the various sources of capital available to defense enterprises – it was likely that there would be delays in investing in new capital stock and then in successfully integrating new facilities with existing production cycles (Zatsepin 2016, p. 64). Nevertheless, steps were quickly put in place to ensure that delays in the production of the most important items were minimized. Within a month of the annexation of Crimea, the St Petersburg-based Klimov enterprise accelerated efforts that were already underway to produce helicopter engines, previously supplied by the Ukrainian firm Motor Sich. A stable supply of these engines was needed to ensure that the procurement of military helicopters was uninterrupted. Similar weaknesses threatened naval modernization. Plans were quickly drawn up to switch the production of maritime gas turbine engines previously produced by Zorya-Mashproekt to the Saturn enterprise in Rybinsk.[17] It was hoped that Saturn would be able to supply engines used in the Gorshkov-class frigates. Elsewhere in the shipbuilding industry, the Kolomna plant was tasked with producing substitutes for the German-made MTU diesel engines, which had been intended to be used on Gremyashchiy-class corvettes (Project 20835) in their initial design (Voyenno-promyshlennyy kur'yer 2015). Similar efforts were made to stimulate local production of electronic components – including large-scale production of inertial navigation systems, based on laser gyroscopes, for combat and civil aircraft and missile systems – which shifted away from Ukrainian and French suppliers to production clusters in Tambov that were assigned additional funding after 2015 (RIA Novosti 2016g). Policymakers were not, however, ignorant to some of the difficulties inherent to producing like-for-like replacements for previously imported items. Consequently, the localization of production was emphasized where straightforward substitution proved difficult.

Diversification of Foreign Defense-Industrial Relations

While the primary emphasis in Russia's response to sanctions in the defense-industrial sphere has been on substituting domestically produced analogues for foreign-supplied products, there was also a concerted effort to source imported equipment from more politically reliable partners, overwhelmingly located in east Asia, and to cement closer defense-industrial ties with enterprises in China and India. Thus, while

---

[17] Although this did not proceed as smoothly as was initially hoped (Soyustov 2015). Doubts have also been expressed as to whether Russian producers possess the technological capabilities to perform all the tasks associated with replacing Ukrainian components (Khodarenok 2016).

Russification was considered desirable, this should not be conflated with a move toward autarky. Instead, closer economic ties with the "non-West" were viewed as a useful supplement to strengthening domestic defense-industrial capabilities.

The trend toward importing increasingly large volumes of electronic components from east Asian economies – especially China – was evident before 2014, as shown in Figure 5.3. However, this trend accelerated after 2014, with Asian economies seeing their share of Russian imports of electronic equipment rising sharply. In some instances, imported electronic components and equipment – often from China, where producers often supply equipment without certification – were presented as being of Russian origin by local producers keen to extol their own credentials as pioneers in import substitution (Dmitriyenko 2016). Imports of nonelectronic items also rose. For instance, as well as developing domestic capabilities in the sphere of marine diesel engines for use on naval vessels, diesel engines for Russia's Project 21631 (Buyan M-class) and Project 21980 (Grachonok-class) vessels were brought from China to replace engines that were originally intended to be imported from Germany (Frolov 2016). Switching suppliers from Europe to China was not, however, always a smooth process, with some new suppliers unable to provide the same high-quality products (Istomin 2016).

In addition to importing greater volumes of electronics and machinery from Asian economies, increasing attention was paid by senior Russian policymakers to establishing closer defense-industrial cooperation between Russian firms and those in strategically important partner countries such as China and India. Particular attention was given to establishing closer ties with Chinese conglomerates. This is because the Chinese defense-industrial base is much better at producing the types of civilian and dual-use equipment – such as industrial and consumer electronics, software, telecommunication equipment, and machine tools – with regard to which Russian firms have struggled to remain competitive since the disintegration of the Soviet Union (Kashin 2016). Unlike in the case of Russian enterprises, the majority of output from Chinese conglomerates involved in defense-industrial activities is concentrated in the area of nonmilitary output.[18] This means that there is scope for synergies between the two countries' defense enterprises, with Russian firms retaining significant advantages in certain segments of defense-industrial

---

[18] Russian firms have been encouraged to rectify this by the president (Vedomosti 2016).

production, while Chinese firms have clear advantages in the production of machinery and electronic equipment.

Within weeks of the annexation of Crimea, military-technical cooperation between Russia and China intensified. Several deals to purchase advanced weaponry – including Su-35 aircraft, S-400 air-defense systems, and Saturn AL-31 aircraft engines – were agreed over the following year, which caused China to reemerge as a major importer of Russian weaponry. In total, these amounted to around $8 billion worth of orders (Nikolsky 2016b). Perhaps more importantly, military-technical cooperation between the two countries accelerated, signaling a serious attempt to move beyond the simple licensed production of Russian equipment in China toward a more collaborative relationship. Cooperation between the two countries is institutionalized through periodic meetings of the Russian–Chinese intergovernmental commission on military-technical cooperation, with Russian and Chinese firms agreeing to work jointly on the development of, inter alia, an advanced heavy lift helicopter (RIA Novosti 2016b), helicopter engines (RIA Novosti 2016c), engines for large transport aircraft (Khodarenok 2017), and the integration of Chinese cockpit electronic equipment into the Su-35 aircraft (TASS 2016c). Officials from the two governments were also considering enhanced cooperation in naval production (TASS 2016). It is also possible that China may prove to be a useful source of knowhow for Russia in the production of ship engines and UAV technology.

More broadly, the development of closer defense-industrial ties between the two countries is considered an integral component in cementing a strategic relationship between the two countries, as explicitly stated by President Putin shortly after the annexation of Crimea (RIA Novosti 2014). In this respect, the forging of a genuinely cooperative relationship in the defense sphere, based on the two countries' comparative advantages, has the potential to draw Russia and China together at the larger geopolitical level.

THE IMPACT OF SANCTIONS ON THE DEFENSE INDUSTRY

As was the case in the energy industry, sanctions – imposed by both the West and, especially, Ukraine – caused significant disruption, at least in the short term, and specifically in several areas of defense-industrial production where Russian domestic capabilities were at their weakest. However, the focused and relatively timely response coordinated by the Russian state enabled the defense industry not just to maintain output, but

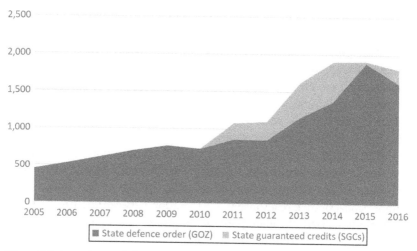

Figure 5.4 Annual state defense order (GOZ) and state-guaranteed credits (SGCs), 2005–2016 (constant 2015 rubles, billion)
Sources: Ruble prices deflated using consumer price index; CAST (2016a); Cooper (2016); author's calculations

in fact to grow rapidly. Furthermore, by investing in new productive capabilities, the Russian defense industry became even more self-sufficient than it was before 2014.

Financial Support

Financial sanctions targeted at defense-industrial firms did not cause any significant problems, largely because the Russian state sharply increased the volume of financial support given to the industry. This process had already been underway since 2011, but accelerated in 2014. As illustrated in Figure 5.4, state expenditure on defense procurement rose over 2014–2015, even as the wider economy entered a severe recession. This resulted in a substantial reorientation in the composition of federal government spending. In 2010, total military expenditure – as defined according to the SIPRI convention – as a share of total federal government spending was 15.9 percent. By 2015 it had grown to 25.8 percent. The volume of SGCs provided to support enterprises in the execution of the annual GOZ also rose in 2014, which proved to be a significant source of financial resources to defense-industrial firms. In principle, the nature of the financial support extended to the defense industry was similar to that channeled toward the energy industry. Both made use of federal government resources or borrowing from state-owned banks; however, the volume of state resources allocated to the defense industry was an order of magnitude greater than it was for the energy industry.

Production

Because defense expenditure continued to rise after 2014, aggregate output in the defense industry did not appear to be unduly affected by sanctions. Indeed, aggregate output grew rapidly over the course of 2014–2015, and remained close to post-Soviet-high levels in 2016–2017. Indeed, in 2014, defense industry output grew by 15.5 percent, compared to overall industrial output growth of 1.7 percent (Cooper 2016a, p. 26). This strong performance occurred alongside a recession that caused output to fall across most other sectors of the economy. The fact that state demand for defense-industrial equipment rose, even as federal government spending on health and education declined, was a function of the leadership's determination to modernize the Russian armed forces. It is reasonable to assume that the conflict in Ukraine, and the rise in geopolitical tensions with Western countries, only heightened this determination to ensure that Russia's armed forces were well-armed and adequately trained. As such, the political decision to continue channeling large volumes of financial resources toward defense-industrial production met relatively little in the way of serious resistance, either from within the policy elite or from society more broadly.

As a result, Russian officials expressed satisfaction with the progress that had been made in increasing the share of modern weapon systems and other equipment in the inventory of the armed forces. At the end of 2017, Defense Minister Sergei Shoigu declared that most of the annual targets for military modernization had been exceeded, and that more than 95 percent of the state defense order had been fulfilled according to schedule (Kremlin.ru 2017). For example, over the course of 2014–2015, around a hundred new or modernized fixed-wing combat aircraft were delivered to Russia's armed forces, along with around a hundred land-based or submarine-launched intercontinental ballistic missiles (Connolly and Senstad 2017). Similar performance levels were reported across most subsectors of the defense industry for 2016. Indeed, even in the context of sanctions, the Russian defense industry proved capable of producing a wide range of established weapons systems in large quantities. This in turn made a significant contribution toward achieving the political objective of military modernization by 2020 (Cooper 2016a).

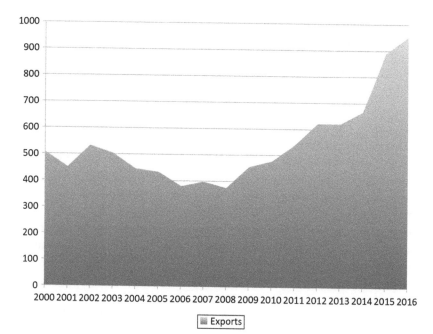

Figure 5.5 Value of Russia's arms exports, 2000–2016 (constant 2015 rubles, billion)
Note: Annual average dollar/ruble exchange rates used for each year to convert dollar export prices reported by CAST into domestic currency. Ruble prices deflated using consumer price index.
Source: CAST (2017); authors' calculations

Russian defense-industrial enterprises' ability to perform export contracts also appeared to be unhindered by sanctions (Connolly and Senstad 2017). According to Aleksandr Mikheev, the Director General of Rosoboronexport – the Russian organization tasked with coordinating foreign military cooperation and trade – sanctions, and in particular interruptions to the supply of components, had caused some disruption to production cycles (RIA Novosti 2017a). However, deliveries of armaments continued the precrisis trend of robust growth in ruble terms (Figure 5.5). Demand for Russian defense-industrial products continued at around the levels observed before sanctions were imposed because Western counties tended to engage only in small-scale arms trade with Russia before 2014. As a result, the arms embargo did not materially affect Russian arms exports (Connolly and Senstad 2017). Traditionally, the highest demand for Russian weaponry came from Asia and the Middle East, a pattern that continued after 2014.

However, while aggregate performance was impressive, and at first glance may appear to have been unaffected by sanctions, the breakdown of relations with Ukrainian enterprises and the imposition of Western sanctions did have an observable and significant impact on the delivery of certain subcategories of defense-industrial equipment. Deliveries of naval vessels were most affected. Perhaps the most high-profile deal to fall foul of Western sanctions was the contract to acquire two Mistral-class helicopter carriers from France.[19] However, the cessation of deliveries of power units for naval vessels was of even greater importance. The two largest classes of ship scheduled to be built during GPV-2020 were the Admiral Gorshkov-class (Project 22350) and Admiral Grigorovich-class (Project 11356R) frigates. It was originally envisaged that the navy would acquire six ships from each class, but the construction of ships from both classes was impeded because deliveries from the Ukrainian firm Zorya-Mashproekt of gas turbine engines that were used for both types of ship were halted, causing severe delays (VPK.ru 2014). By the end of 2017, only one Admiral Gorshkov-class and two Admiral Grigorovich-class vessels had been delivered to the navy. Replacement engines were required to complete construction of four of the Admiral Gorshkov-class and three Admiral Grigorovich-class vessels.[20]

Sanctions also affected the supply of German-made engines for the Gremyashchiy-class corvettes (Project 20835), which had been earmarked to form the core of a modernized corvette fleet (VPK.ru 2015). As a result, the Ministry of Defense introduced a plan to produce the engines in Russia. As a stop-gap measure, orders of the older Steregushchiy-class vessels (Project 20380) were scaled up to compensate for these delays (VPK-news.ru 2016). These delays meant that the modernization of the larger surface combat vessels proceeded much more slowly than originally planned (Connolly 2017). However, construction of submarines and other vessels (including smaller landing craft, artillery, minesweeping, intelligence, and other auxiliary ships), in which dependence on imported components was much lower, occurred in greater quantities (Ministry of Defence of the Russian Federation 2016). Moreover, some foreign-supplied components continued to be used. For instance, the Swedish company, Volvo-Penta, continued to supply engines used in the construction of the

---

[19] There was an option to build a further two ships in Russia.
[20] An agreement was reached in late 2016 to sell the three incomplete Admiral-Grigorovich-class vessels, with the engines supplied separately by Ukrainian enterprises, to the Indian navy (Nikolsky 2016a).

Chibis-class coast guard small patrol ships used by the FSB Border Service (Project 21850) despite restrictions (Frolov 2016).

It was not only the navy that suffered because of sanctions. The original rearmament plans envisaged the construction of around 175 modern cargo aircraft, a figure that was subsequently revised up to 300 (VPK.ru 2013). However, by the end of 2015, only thirty-five new transport aircraft had been delivered (Connolly and Senstad 2017). This was in part caused by the fact that Russia had planned to procure An-70 (jointly developed with Kazan Aircraft Production Association) and An-124 aircraft from the Ukraine-based aircraft producer Antonov, with deliveries initially scheduled to commence in 2015. However, the Ukrainian moratorium on arms sales caused orders for Ukrainian aircraft to be canceled, which in turn disrupted the procurement of military cargo aircraft.

Import Substitution in the Defense Industry

By the end of 2017, significant progress had been made in Russifying defense-industrial production, especially in replacing items previously supplied by Ukrainian enterprises. One of the most challenging areas identified in 2014 was power plants for naval ships, especially gas turbines used in larger vessels, such as the Admiral Gorshkov- and Admiral Grigorovich-class frigates. Initially, delivery and installation of engines for the third and fourth ships of the Admiral Gorshkov class was not expected to take place until 2018 at the very earliest. However, work on a replacement engine by NPO Saturn was accelerated and it was reported that the first ship (the Admiral Golovko) equipped with Russian-made engines was expected to be launched by the end of 2017, with serial production of engines expected to begin in 2018 (RIA Novosti 2016a). In June 2017 it was also announced that United Shipbuilding Corporation was planning to resume construction of the remaining three Admiral Grigorovich-class ships because of the successful development of new engines, again developed and produced by NPO Saturn (TASS 2017).[21] Similar progress was made in developing diesel engines used in smaller vessels, leading to plans for the construction of a larger quantity of Karakurt-class small missile ships (*malyy raketnyy korabl'*) in place of the Buyan-M class corvettes that were equipped with German engines (VPK-news.ru 2016). Russian officials also hoped that deliveries of

---

[21] One of these vessels – the Admiral Butakov – was at the time of writing scheduled to be delivered to the Russian Navy's Black Sea Fleet, with the remaining two vessels expected to be sold to the Indian Navy (RIA Novosti 2016a).

the Gremyashchiy class would begin in 2018, although whether Russian manufacturers would be able to overcome serious engineering challenges in this area remained unclear (TASS 2016e).

Considerable progress also appeared to have been made outside the shipbuilding industry. The Klimov enterprise was able to produce sixty engines by 2016, and planned to more than double production in 2017 (Lenta.ru 2017). While this was a slower rate of production than had been envisaged in 2014, the fact that serial production had begun was considered an important success. Elsewhere, electronic and optical equipment used in fighter aircraft and helicopters, as well as guidance and navigation systems used in missile systems – all of which were previously sourced from France and Belarus – were in production in Russian enterprises by the end of 2015 (Frolov 2016). Similar advances were reported in the production of components used in ICBMs (Gazeta.ru 2017), cruise missile engines (Soyustov 2015), and radiation-resistant integrated circuits used in the GLONASS-K satellites (Shadrina 2016).

Such was the success achieved in import substitution that by the middle of 2017, senior officials were declaring the program a success. In August, Sergei Chemezov, CEO of the defense and technology state corporation Rostec, stated that all items previously supplied by Ukraine would be in production in Russia by the end of 2018, claiming that 90 percent of that process had already been completed (Rostec.ru 2017). He also claimed that many items previously supplied by EU countries were now imported from South East Asia, and that the Russification of remaining prohibited items would be complete by 2020. These sentiments were echoed later by Denis Manturov, the Minister for Industry and Trade, who confidently declared that by 2017, Russian defense-industrial firms had "adapted" to sanctions (RIA Novosti 2017b).

Despite such bullish pronouncements, it was nevertheless clear that progress, while impressive, had not been quite as smooth as some officials were prepared to admit. While Chemezov had claimed that 90 percent of items previously supplied by Ukraine had been replaced, Manturov presented a less favorable assessment, instead claiming that only around half of these items were produced in Russia and that the full replacement of Ukrainian items would not take place before 2019 (Nikitin 2017). Indeed, the slippage in meeting admittedly ambitious targets was admitted by President Putin in April of 2017 when he revised a previously stated target of substituting 90 percent of all sanctioned equipment by 2018 to the less onerous one of replacing 85 percent by 2020. While this still represented an ambitious target, it was clear that Russian producers were experiencing delays in replacing more complicated items, such as components for satellites (Nikolsky 2017). Some of these problems can be explained by the reduced availability of high-precision machine tools used to produce advanced components. Indeed, problems were not limited to machinery and technology; according to Maxim Shapovalenko, a Moscow-based expert on the Russian arms industry, shortages of highly skilled labor slowed progress in producing engineers in the required quantities.

CONCLUSION

It is clear that Russia's defense industry certainly experienced significant disruption as a result of Western and Ukrainian sanctions. While the overall program of military modernization initiated in 2010 continued to proceed in a broadly positive fashion, the impact of reduced access to Western and Ukrainian components and defense-industrial equipment caused progress to slow in the procurement of surface ships for the navy and transport aircraft for the air force. However, as proved the case in the energy industry, the sanctions' impact on the Russian defense industry was not as bad as some may have initially feared. Moreover, adaptive measures taken by Russian policymakers after March 2014 created the conditions for gaps in supply to be filled and appeared to have reduced the industry's vulnerability to sanctions in the future. That defense-industrial production continued to grow was largely because the state's response to sanctions was comprehensive in scope, institutionally sophisticated, and utilized considerable financial resources.

Sanctions and the Russian response also looked to have irrevocably altered the trajectory of the industry's integration with the wider global economy, which before 2014 had undergone some small but important changes. While the Russian defense industry's links with the global economy were always uneven – focused more on exporting large volumes of final weapons systems than on cooperation with foreign firms – signs had emerged that both policymakers and industry officials were beginning to see the benefit of a more open relationship with foreign firms. However, the imposition of sanctions from March 2014 onward halted this process, instigating a renewed emphasis on import substitution and self-sufficiency in the production of both final weapons systems and components used in arms production. To the extent that cooperation with foreign firms in the production of weapons systems is still a feature of the OPK's future plans, it is now largely confined to collaboration with firms from non-Western countries such as China and India.

From the Russian perspective, significant progress was made in the first three years after sanctions were put in place. Although delays had been experienced in the construction of large surface vessels for the navy, the crash import substitution program initiated in 2014 generated sufficient capacity to begin construction of new engines by 2016. It was expected that ships of the Admiral Gorshkov class would be equipped with domestically produced engines by 2018. If this proves to be the case, it will be an impressive feat given the poor state of naval engine production in Russia prior to 2014. The replacement of imported helicopter engines with domestically produced analogues from the Klimov factory near St Petersburg further demonstrated the ability of Russian policymakers to generate robust solutions to the challenges posed by sanctions. Alongside the concerted effort to boost domestic production capabilities, continued growth in the share of imported electronics from non-Western countries, especially China, reinforced the trend toward increasing reliance on Asian sources of equipment. Finally, a determined effort by leading Russian officials to strengthen defense-industrial cooperation with China and India has the potential – albeit still unfulfilled – to take advantage of each country's comparative advantages in defense production to build advanced new weapons systems.

To be sure, despite the scale of support extended to the OPK since sanctions were imposed, progress in adapting to sanctions has not always proven to be smooth. The prospects for military transport aircraft production, for instance, continued to look bleak. The fact that the quantitative objectives issued by Russian officials have become progressively less ambitious, especially in relation to the Russification of production of equipment previously imported from Western countries, also suggests that obstacles were encountered. Nevertheless, and in slight contrast to the oil and gas equipment industry, it is clear that there is a firm commitment on the part of the Russian leadership to pursue import substitution, even if the exchange rate strengthens in the future. This, it would appear, particularly applies to the replacement of equipment previously supplied by Ukrainian enterprises.

The defense industry may also encounter difficult challenges in the future. For example, the increased emphasis on Russification of defense-industrial production may further reduce competition and efficiency in an industry where these are already in short supply. This may augur ill for innovation in the industry and impede the development of a new generation of weapons to replace designs that still trace their roots to the late Soviet period. Whether the OPK can avoid the pitfalls of sectoral autarky will probably be contingent on the nature of future relations with the

Chinese defense industry. If relations between the two defense industries become closer, the transfer and diffusion of technology and ideas between them could boost both countries. Strengthening defense-industrial cooperation with China is an "unconditional priority," according to Defense Minister Sergei Shoigu (RIA Novosti 2017c). On the Russian side, the prospect of gaining access to Chinese dual-use products on a more systematic and integrated scale would surely be attractive. However, if the potential for closer relations does not yield concrete results, the OPK could find itself in a position where the government's commitment to security of supply in the sphere of defense-industrial products could lead to the emergence of a sellers' market in which producer prices rise but product quality and innovation decline.

Nevertheless, the trajectory for the Russian defense industry is obvious: It is rapidly moving away from its previous reliance on technology and equipment from both Ukraine and Western countries. This should alleviate Russia's vulnerability to any Western sanctions that target the defense industry in the future, although, as in the energy industry, the logical corollary of Russia's turn away from the West is that new sources of vulnerability vis-à-vis Asian countries – especially China – are emerging. This, of course, is a natural outcome of closer economic relations with any country. Policymakers in Russia will only hope that political relations with China continue to remain warm and cooperative.

To sum up: As was observed in the energy industry, the Russian response to sanctions in the defense industry offers a vivid illustration of how target countries can use the resources at their disposal to adapt to sanctions and, in doing so, moderate the impact that was intended by sender countries and use the opportunity to channel support to what policymakers consider strategically important industries. In this instance, a country that possessed one of the largest defense-industrial complexes in the world, and which had a proven track record of producing a wide range of weapons to a relatively high standard, was able to adjust to sanctions and continue to pursue an ambitious program of military modernization. The key features of Russia's system of political economy made this possible. Enterprises either owned by, or close to, the state were at the forefront of nearly all the instances where adaptation has taken place. Moreover, a clear political commitment on the part of the country's leadership – essentially unchallenged by other social groups – toward strengthening the military and maintaining an independent and secure industrial base certainly helped justify the sizable transfer of resources toward the OPK that formed part of the response to sanctions (RIA Novosti 2016g).

6

Sanctions and the Financial System

INTRODUCTION

As in most countries, in Russia the financial sector is an integral part of the system of political economy. The various organizations that make up the financial sector – banks, investment funds, insurance companies, and other organizations involved in the allocation of capital – collectively manage the flow of money between different sectors of the economy. In the simplest sense, financial sector organizations act as intermediaries between savings and investment. However, the reality is more complicated than this. Savings in Russia tend to be generated by specific sectors of the economy, most notably by enterprises in the natural resources sector of the economy, or Sector A, as it is called in this book, while capital flows tend to be managed by state-owned or state-influenced organizations. This means that the allocation of capital often favors politically or socially important activities rather than those that might be expected to generate a profitable return on investment. This has resulted in a specific pattern of investment in Russia, with certain sectors of the economy (i.e. Sector B) tending to enjoy more success in accessing capital than others (i.e. Sector C).

Moreover, the financial sector is embedded in a wider financial system, which is defined by the institutions – i.e. the rules and regulations – that shape the environment in which financial sector organizations interact with other economic organizations, not only within Russia – both in the financial sector and in the so-called real economy – but also with financial and nonfinancial organizations outside Russia. Ultimately, the architecture of the financial system is chosen by state officials. Policies formulated by different government organizations – e.g. by the central bank in charge of monetary policy, or by the Ministry of Finance, the coordinator of fiscal policy – establish the parameters that govern how prices are set (both domestic prices and the exchange rate) and whether and in what quantity capital can move in and out of the country, and between sectors of the domestic economy. The state, though, is often constrained in how these choices are made, not least by structural features of the economy (e.g. whether a country exports natural resources or capital-intensive manufactured goods), which in turn shape the leadership's political calculus due to the distributional consequences of the choices made.

The relationship between the financial sector in Russia, on the one hand, and the country's financial institutional landscape, on the other, exhibited a peculiar pattern of development over the post-Soviet period. First, it is worth noting that the Russian financial system remains comparatively young. After emerging almost from nowhere during the tumultuous late 1980s and early 1990s, the institutional landscape was, for much of the post-Soviet period, in a state of flux, and what existed in 2014 had been forged in the crucible of several severe financial crises. Second, the financial system is, by international standards, relatively small and centered on a banking sector that came to be increasingly dominated by the state. This has limited access to capital across the Russian economy to a relatively small group of politically and socially important enterprises. Third, like the defense industry, the financial sector has an uneven relationship with the global economy. Foreign ownership of banks and other financial organizations is comparatively modest in scale. For many countries, this might dampen the importance of global financial flows. However, this was not the case in Russia. Because of the importance of natural resource exports – especially oil – to the Russian economy, the volume and direction of capital flows, and with them the country's economic fortunes, were heavily conditioned by fluctuations in the price of oil and other commodities. It is no accident that all three of the major post-Soviet financial crises were preceded by a sharp decline in the price of oil. Each time this occurred, Russia experienced a "sudden stop" in capital inflows, usually followed by large outflows of capital that rapidly reduced the availability of capital to the wider economy (Calvo 1998). The availability or otherwise of foreign capital, therefore, has proven to be one of the single most important variables in shaping economic performance in Russia. The fact that the availability of foreign capital is so heavily influenced by movements on global commodity markets is one of the most important characteristics of the Russian political economy, and a structural constraint that policy-makers have struggled with since the Soviet period.

These features made the financial sector another obvious and, in many ways, extremely vulnerable target for Western sanctions. Reducing the availability of capital to Russian firms – a de facto, artificially induced sudden stop of capital inflows – carried enormous destructive potential. When, in the summer of 2014, some of Russia's most important financial organizations were restricted from accessing capital from Western countries, a sudden stop was exactly what occurred, although the role of sanctions should not be overplayed due to the much more important sharp decline in oil prices that took place at almost the same time.

As was the case in the energy and defense industries, the Russian policy response to financial sanctions comprised a mixture of measures intended to promote the simultaneous Russification and diversification of financial flows. In the financial sector, Russification encompassed a wide range of policies, some of which are difficult to separate from the response to the downturn in oil prices that began at the same time that sanctions were imposed, and which caused a sharp outflow of capital in late 2014 and early 2015. Several key features were evident. First, domestic, state-controlled sources of capital were used to fill the gap created by the sudden stop of foreign capital inflows. Second, informal capital controls were put in place to encourage private and quasi-public organizations to repatriate foreign currency. Third, after the immediate panic at the end of 2014 had subsided, the government took action to strengthen the financial system and to insulate it from the threat of further sanctions, including the potentially damaging move of excluding Russia from the use of international electronic payments systems. Moves to reduce the domestic financial system's vulnerability to external pressure were accompanied by efforts to seek out alternative sources of foreign capital, both through the cultivation of closer links with a number of non-Western economies and through state participation in the creation of new multilateral financial organizations with non-Western powers that might be used to finance investment in the future. As was the case in the other two sectors discussed previously, the process of adaptation to sanctions was overwhelmingly state-led, with the leadership utilizing a range of institutional, financial, and diplomatic instruments to minimize the intended impact of Western sanctions and to begin the process of forging a new relationship with the global economy.

The remainder of this chapter is organized as follows. First, I give a brief overview of the key characteristics of the Russian financial system and the role that it performs in Russia's political economy. Then, the broad contours of the financial system's relationship with the global economy are presented. I go on to describe the financial sanctions imposed in the summer of 2014.

Then I trace the evolution of the Russian government policy response, and finally I consider how the adaptive measures initiated by the Russian government since 2014 helped reduce the impact of sanctions.

THE FINANCIAL SECTOR AND THE RUSSIAN ECONOMY

The modern Russian financial system was born in the chaos of the late Soviet period. Prior to the late 1980s, the Soviet financial system was a servant to the requirements of the planned economy. Money was "passive" in the sense that monetary values (i.e. the price of goods and services) were assigned not in a decentralized manner – as is the case in most market economies, where the independent choices made by households and enterprises convey information about quality and the balance between supply and demand in different product markets – but instead centrally, by bureaucrats charged with administering the planned economy (Kornai 1992). Essentially, bureaucrats and their political leaders made choices concerning the broad direction of production; a plan to achieve these objectives was then formulated, and instructions on how to carry out these plans were given to ministries and enterprises.[1] The role of money in this process was thus intended only to be passive and to facilitate accounting and monitoring (Sutela 2012, p. 152). Prices often deviated considerably from international prices, with thousands of commodity-specific exchange rates existing alongside a more general, arbitrary official exchange rate. These exchange rates also differed considerably from unofficial exchange rates obtained on the black market.

Capital flows, both within the Soviet Union and with other countries, were tightly managed by state organizations. Current and capital account convertibility did not exist. As a result, the functions performed by the state banking system were limited in scope. The state monobank, Gosbank, which controlled three subsidiary banks – Stroibank (the All-Union Bank for the Financing of Investments of the USSR), Vneshtorgbank (the Foreign Trade Bank), and Sberbank (the Savings Bank) – was directly subordinate to the Council of Ministers. Its primary function was to ensure that sufficient money was available to support the economic exchange between different sectors of the economy. Moreover, a crucial feature of the Soviet financial system lay in the separation of cash money (*nalichnye*) and

---

[1] This is a deliberate simplification. In practice, there was significant bargaining and negotiation between different layers of the centrally planned economy. For a fuller discussion, see Rutland (1985).

noncash money (*beznalichnye*) into a dual monetary circuit (Johnson 2000, p. 28). The state's allocation of *beznalichnye* – which could not be converted into cash that could be used outside the state enterprises sector – to enterprises was one mechanism used by state planners to soften budget constraints without generating open inflation.[2]

This primitive financial landscape was altered dramatically by Mikhail Gorbachev's attempt to restructure (*perestroika*) and democratize (*demokratizatsiya*) the Soviet economic system from 1987 onward (Aslund 1989; Hewett and Winston 1991; Hanson 2003). In 1988, Gosbank was broken up as a new two-tier financial system was created. On the top tier, Gosbank began to perform the function of a central bank, shifting its focus from the provision of credits to the formulation of monetary policy and interest rates. While it retained control of the newly named Vnesheconombank (the erstwhile Vneshtorgbank) and Sberbank, its remaining functions were split among three specialized banks, or *spetsbanks* (Johnson 2000, p. 30). The creation of the spetsbanks presaged the rapid decentralization and de facto liberalization of the banking system. Later in 1988, the Law on Cooperatives created the conditions for the emergence of a slew of new commercial banks, many of which were founded by state enterprises and other state structures, often as a way of breaking the separation between *nalichnye* and *beznalichnye*. As the financial environment became more permissive as *perestroika* gathered momentum, the number of banks mushroomed. As described by Juliet Johnson, "[b]y the end of 1988, the USSR had registered 77 commercial and cooperative banks, and by August 1990 it had registered 358 new banks" (ibid, p. 34). By the end of 1991, more than a thousand banks were in existence (Sutela 2012, p. 169). As state capacity weakened, little real monetary or banking supervision took place. Most new banks did not act as intermediaries between savings and investment but instead functioned as parasites, sucking resources from the weakening state and using their ill-gotten gains to facilitate the acquisition, or "spontaneous privatization," of state property (Solnick 1998).

After the disintegration of the Soviet Union at the end of 1991, the chaotic and unregulated banking sector of the newly independent Russia grew quickly. The reformist government led by Yegor Gaider embarked on an ambitious plan to construct a market economy from the ruins of the failed Soviet planned system (Aslund 1995). However, the ambitions of reformers were compromised from the outset by the Russian state's

---

[2] Of course, repressed inflation in the form of shortages, queues, and poor quality was rampant.

weakness (Hedlund 1999; Robinson 1999, 2001). The uncontrolled spiral of decentralization and liberalization that led to the disintegration of the Soviet economy continued into the early post-Soviet period. In conjunction with an institutional environment that tended to subvert the intentions that underpinned the formal changes enacted by policymakers, the Russian state found itself unable to perform many of the roles expected of a functioning state. Taxes were not collected, control over the money supply evaporated, and the enforcement of the new legislation put in place by market reformers was weak (Shliefer and Treisman 2000; Taylor 2011; Popov 2014).

Against this unfavorable backdrop, the state found itself unable to exert any significant control over the development of the financial system. Although hundreds of banks were formed each year, the institutional architecture incentivized banks to engage in currency speculation, arbitrage in conditions of high inflation, and money laundering. Banks were also used as vehicles to facilitate the privatization of state assets by the Soviet-era *nomenklatura* and unscrupulous criminal groups (Johnson 2000). Very little in the way of meaningful intermediation between savings and investment took place. As some semblance of macroeconomic stabilization was achieved in the mid-1990s, and as the process of privatization lost momentum, the opportunities for banks to make money from inflation, exchange rate instability and privatization subsided (Aslund 2007). But this did not mean that banks came to be any more occupied with the more conventional side of financial intermediation. Instead, after 1996, banks shifted their focus toward lending to the weak Russian state. After proving unable to raise sufficient taxes to cover expenditure, the state began to rely on high-interest short-term state bonds (GKOs) to fund expenditure in a noninflationary fashion. Banks reaped enormous profits as they exploited the government's weakness by monopolizing the domestic government bond market. Ultimately, these profits were short-lived. In an attempt to reduce the cost of borrowing and decouple the state from its dependence on powerful domestic banks and their owners, the Russian government opened up its debt market to foreign investors, generating a sharp influx of capital inflows (Robinson 1999). However, when oil prices fell due to the Asian financial crisis, which unfolded over 1997 and 1998, and as doubts accumulated over the size of the Russian budget and current account deficits, Russia was plunged into crisis in August 1998 as the state defaulted on much of its domestic debt to the banking sector, leading to a full-blown financial crisis that in turn resulted in the failure of large swathes of the domestic financial system (ibid).

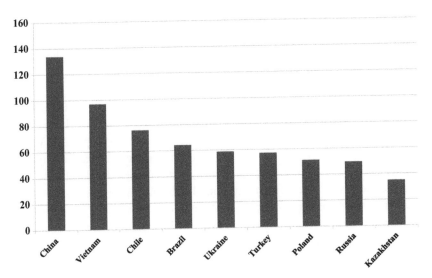

Figure 6.1 The relative size of the Russian banking sector, 2013 (domestic credit provided by the banking sector to the private sector as a percentage of GDP)
Source: World Bank (2017)

The August crisis represented the nadir of the financial system's development. After that, measures were put in place to strengthen the institutional foundations of the financial system. In some respects, these changes reflected broader institutional development. For instance, the fact that a Land Code was signed into law in 2001 helped strengthen property rights, which in turn facilitated easier access to finance (Karas, Pyle, and Schoors 2015). This was further buttressed by the sharp stabilization of the macroeconomic environment that took place after 1999 as growth accelerated (Merlevede, Schoors, and Van Aarle 2009). At the end of 2003, a deposit insurance law was passed, quickly followed by creation of the Deposit Insurance Agency (Tompson 2004). Bank regulation and supervision was also improved. While this did not solve all the banking system's weaknesses – too many banks remained too systemically important to fail, for instance – it did result in an improvement in capital and liquidity standards (Claeys and Schoors 2007).

By 2014, the domestic financial system had become more stable than was the case in the 1990s. Nevertheless, significant weaknesses remained. As described in Chapter 2, the Russian financial sector was small by international standards (Figure 6.1). It was also a system that remained overwhelmingly bank-centric, with very few alternative sources of finance available to prospective borrowers. Moreover, not only was the financial system comparatively small, but it was also dominated by state-owned or state-controlled banks, with only a modest role played by foreign banks (Sutela 2012, p. 151). In 2014, 55–60 percent of all assets and liabilities in the Russian banking system were held by state-controlled banks. State ownership rose as a result of the 2008–2009 global financial crisis, when state-owned banks absorbed several medium-sized private banks that had failed (Vernikov 2010; Sutela 2012, p. 172). While not necessarily inefficient in their allocation of capital, at least compared to domestically-owned private banks, state-owned banks tended to restrict access to credit for many households and firms (Vernikov 2013). Outside the banking sector, Russia's financial markets – primarily the Moscow Exchange, comprising the Moscow Interbank Currency Exchange (MICEX) and the Russian Trading System (RTS), which were merged in 2011 – tended to be dominated by state-controlled entities, largely operating in either banking or natural resources. However, perhaps the principal weakness of the domestic financial system was the dependence on foreign capital. A failure to generate trust in the domestic financial system meant that aggregate lending consistently outstripped aggregate domestic deposits.

Taken together, the core characteristics of the Russian financial system describe above amounted to what Pekka Sutela has described as a "dual financial system" (Sutela 2012, p. 218). In this system, two tiers existed. The first tier comprised the largest state-controlled or resource-focused enterprises (both publicly and privately owned). These approximate Sector A described in Chapter 2, and include the likes of Sberbank, Rosneft, Gazprom, and Norilsk Nickel. They were able to tap international financial markets for supplies of financial capital for equity, Eurobonds, and syndicated loans. Under normal circumstances, foreign sources of capital were preferred to domestic sources of capital. By contrast, the second tier of this financial system relied primarily on domestic capital and services. This included most Russian firms located outside the globally significant segment of financial and industrial behemoths from Sector A. It also included Russian households. Because the available pool of domestic capital was so small, credit was rationed, meaning that it was often comparatively expensive and available only to politically well-connected enterprises. This dual structure could exist for as long as Sector A firms were able to access international capital markets. In periods when international capital was scarce – in 1998 and 2008–2009, for instance – the demand for domestic capital tended to rise sharply, causing the price of capital to rise and its availability to decline for all but the most well-connected or socially important of firms.

One of the most important consequences of the chronic weakness of Russia's financial system was that investment was lower than was needed to fuel structural transformation (Connolly 2011). Since 1991, the investment share of GDP in Russia had consistently been lower than that of most other middle-income economies. This was an important factor in preventing the emergence of a sizable new class of strong and independent property owners. Before 2014, Russia's annual average investment-to-GDP ratio of less than 20 percent was among the lowest of the major middle-income countries. In the years preceding the global recession of 2008–2009, the annual rate of investment growth had ranged between 10 and 22 percent. After 2009, however, investment growth failed to return to precrisis rates, averaging around 6 percent per year in 2010–2012. After 2012, investment began to contract – the annual rate was −0.3 percent in 2013 – and this trend accelerated until 2017. While there were no doubt numerous sources of this decline in investment, the weakness of the financial system was undoubtedly an important factor (Zamaraev et al. 2013). Moreover, because of the fact that the vast majority of assets and deposits were in the hands of state-controlled or state-influenced entities, capital tended to flow to politically favored enterprises in Sector B. Enterprises operating outside this nexus were forced to rely on retained earnings.

Overall, the financial sector in Russia developed in an extremely distorted fashion. As was the case in the other "commanding heights" of the Russian economy, a period of freedom and excessive liberalization in the 1990s was followed by a period of Thermidorian reaction as the state reasserted its control (Mau and Starodubrovskaya 2001). While this no doubt reduced some of the risks associated with the financial system of the 1990s, the state's grip on the financial sector meant that the scope for releasing capital to new or innovative parts of the economy was much curtailed. Instead, the financial sector acted as a glue that bound the state to the politically important sectors of the economy (A and B). However, although the state occupied a dominant role in terms of ownership of the financial sector, it was the global economy that provided much of the capital that flowed from the banks to the wider economy. It is to this relationship of dependency between the Russian financial system and the global economy that I turn next.

THE RUSSIAN FINANCIAL SYSTEM AND THE
GLOBAL ECONOMY

The Russian banking system, and the financial system more widely, has been highly dependent on inflows of foreign capital since the mid-1990s. This was to some degree a consequence of the underdevelopment of the banking system just described. Domestic deposit growth was lower than growth in lending, and very few sources of genuinely long-term finance emerged. As a result, external capital was required to fill the gap. But perhaps just as importantly, this dependence on capital inflows was also a corollary of Russia's economic structure. As an exporter of huge volumes of natural resources – primarily crude oil and oil products – capital flows were conditioned by both the global price of oil and the volume of domestic production. This led to a highly volatile macroeconomic environment in which capital tended to flow toward the country when natural resources prices were high, but leave the country when prices declined. In this respect, the macroeconomic consequences of Russia's economic structure are crucial to understanding the forces that have shaped the financial sector in Russia over the course of the past quarter of a century. In turn, the Russian government has resorted to a variety of monetary and fiscal instruments over the years to mitigate the problems associated with wild fluctuations in natural resource prices and capital flows.

As shown in Table 6.1, since 1994 there have been only been two years – 2006 and 2007 – in which the private sector in Russia has registered net inflows of capital. The tendency toward capital outflows has been driven primarily by capital outflows from outside the banking sector. By contrast, the banking sector relied more on external finance, especially when confidence in the Russian economy was high, usually due to rising oil prices (Figure 6.2). Both the 1998 and 2008–2009 crises were preceded by a sustained increase in the five-year average net capital inflows to the banking sector. In both instances, these inflows turned quickly into large capital outflows after financial crises that were either preceded or accompanied by a sharp decline in oil prices, first as a result of the Asian financial crisis of 1997–1998, and then as a result of the global financial crisis of 2008–2009 (Johnson and Woodruff 2017). This demonstrated the link between Russian banks' ability to access external finance, on the one hand, and fluctuations on the global oil market, on the other. This linkage between natural resource exports – driven by oil – and capital flows also explained why global finance had proven to be so important to Russian economic performance despite the relatively modest role played by foreign

Table 6.1 *Private sector net capital inflows and outflows, 1994–2016 (USD billion)*

	Total private sector net capital inflows	Net capital inflows by banks	Net capital inflows by other sectors
1994	−12.7	1.0	−13.7
1995	−7.8	5.5	−13.3
1996	−22.4	2.7	−25.1
1997	−18.4	7.6	−26.0
1998	−22.6	−6.4	−16.2
1999	−19.6	−4.5	−15.1
2000	−23.1	−1.7	−21.4
2001	−13.6	−4.0	−9.6
2002	−7.0	−3.0	−4.0
2003	−0.3	12.8	−13.1
2004	−8.6	−0.7	−7.9
2005	−0.3	−3.7	3.4
2006	43.7	27.9	15.8
2007	87.8	50.5	37.3
2008	−133.6	−84.5	−49.1
2009	−57.5	−32.4	−25.1
2010	−30.8	22.8	−53.6
2011	−81.4	−27.6	−53.8
2012	−53.9	7.9	−61.8
2013	−60.3	−17.3	−43.0
2014	−152.1	−86.0	−66.1
2015	−58.1	−34.1	−24.0
2016	−19.8	1.1	−20.9

Note: Exports are denoted by negative values; imports are denoted by positive values.
Source: Bank of Russia (2017); author's calculations.

banks in the domestic financial sector. Quite simply, because the domestic deposit base remained so small, foreign capital was of vital importance.

The Russian financial system and its relationship with the global economy evolved in several other important respects before 2014, showing clear signs of becoming progressively more intertwined.

First, as a logical corollary of the dual financial system just described, both financial and nonfinancial entities from Sector A accumulated a growing stock of external debt. This represented a significant change in the sectoral distribution of external debt in the 1990s. In the 1990s, the fiscally weak Russian state borrowed on international markets, as well as from official agencies such as the IMF, to plug the gap between expenditure and revenues. During the 1990s, the government was the only significant

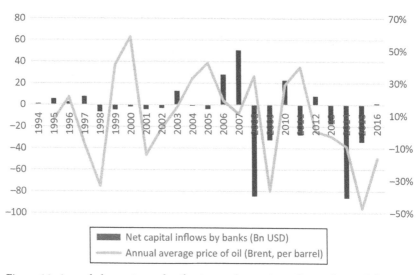

Figure 6.2 Annual change in crude oil prices and net private financial capital flows, 1994–2016 (net capital inflows by banks, billion USD on left axis; annual percentage change in annual average price of oil on right axis)

Source: Bank of Russia (2017); BP Statistical Review of World Energy (2017); author's calculations

Russian borrower on international markets. External debt rose until the 1998 financial crisis and declined thereafter (Figure 6.3). In an effort to strengthen Russia's financial sovereignty, the Russian leadership accelerated its repayments of external debt so that it had declined to only modest levels by the mid-2000s, both in absolute terms and as a proportion of Russia's overall external debt and international reserves (Gaddy and Ickes 2009). As oil prices rose after 2000, and as the decline in government external debt resulted in an improvement in Russia's credit ratings, Sector A enterprises began to rely on international markets for capital. The majority of this external debt was accumulated in nonfinancial firms, including privately owned metals and mining companies, and in quasi-public entities such as Gazprom and Rosneft (Hanson 2007). Even the global financial crisis of 2008–2009 failed to stem the rapid growth in external debt: after registering a modest decline in total external debt in 2009, it grew from just over $460 billion to a peak of over $725 billion in 2013.

Second, as a result of a twin-pronged approach toward monetary policy that saw the monetary authorities attempt to reduce inflation and nominal exchange rate volatility simultaneously, the Central Bank's stock of international reserves rose sharply throughout the 2000s (Figure 6.4). In the

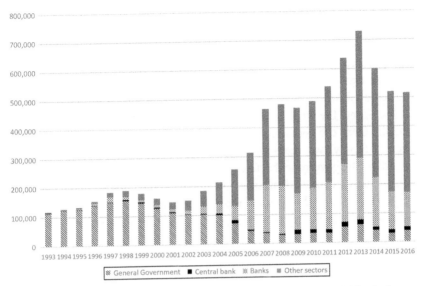

Figure 6.3 External debt by public and private sector sectors, 1993–2016 (end of year; million USD)
Source: Bank of Russia (2017)

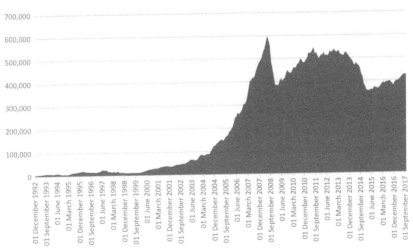

Figure 6.4 Russia's international reserves, 1992–2017 (million USD)
Note: Total international reserves comprise foreign exchange reserves, SDRs and gold
Source: Bank of Russia (2017)

immediate aftermath of the 1998 financial crisis, the Central Bank sold rubles (i.e. it acquired foreign exchange reserves) to prevent an excessively rapid appreciation of the nominal exchange rate (Ulyukaev 2009). As oil prices rose, and with them the volume of production of oil in Russia, surging export revenues caused capital inflows to rise further. This was exacerbated when full capital account convertibility was introduced in 2006, lifting the final constraints on capital movements in and out of Russia. Over the course of 2006–2007, capital inflows rose sharply; these were the only two years since 1991 in which total capital inflows were positive. The government acted to prevent the economy from overheating – i.e. to exert downward pressure on inflation and nominal exchange rate appreciation – by the accumulation of foreign exchange reserves, some of which was "sterilized" by being placed in a sovereign stabilization fund creation created in 2004. The monetary authorities were never fully successful in either achieving a low rate of inflation or preventing nominal appreciation of the ruble. Both occurred, albeit at a slower rate than would have occurred had the authorities not intervened at all. This resulted in the steady appreciation of the real effective exchange rate between 2000 and 2008 (Figure 6.5). After 2009, however, central bank intervention in foreign exchange markets became more infrequent as the bank moved toward the adoption of a purely inflation-targeting monetary policy. Under this strategy, the exchange rate was increasingly left to "float" without support from the central bank.

Fluctuations in the level of international reserves mirrored movements in the volume of natural resource revenues. This was no coincidence: the vast majority of export earnings by Russian oil companies were heavily taxed by the state (Gaddy and Ickes 2009). Although the authorities sold more than $200 billion of reserves during the 2008–2009 crisis, primarily to prevent what they saw as a disorderly depreciation of the ruble, foreign exchange reserves grew again as oil prices increased after the crisis subsided. The magnitude of Russia's stock of international reserves was especially noteworthy. For the duration of the 1990s, Russia's reserves were tiny, and always dwarfed by its external debt. By 2007, Russia was among the world's largest holders of foreign exchange reserves. It was only in 2012 that reserves were smaller than the country's consolidated stock of external debt. The size of Russia's reserves was thus an important component of Russia's much improved financial health.

Third, the deficiencies within the domestic financial system led to the acquisition of substantial assets abroad. A significant proportion of the outflows of capital that occurred before 2006 and after 2008 was used to

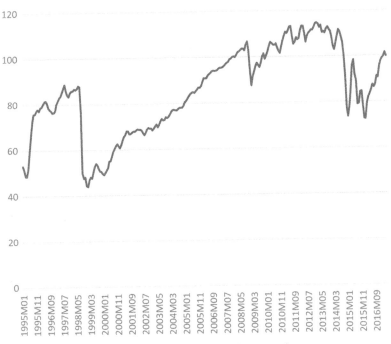

Figure 6.5 Real effective exchange rate, 1995–2017 (2007=100)
Source: Bruegel (2017)

acquire foreign assets. For the government, this took the form of reserve accumulation, which tended to account for around a third of Russia's total assets held abroad. For other sectors of the economy, this took the form of either direct investment (around a third of total assets held abroad), deposits in foreign bank accounts (10–15 percent), or loans to foreign customers (10–15 percent). As illustrated in Figure 6.6, foreign assets tended to exceed liabilities for most of the period after 2000. This again shows how the links between Russia and the wider global financial system were becoming stronger despite – and in some cases because of – the obvious weaknesses of the domestic financial system.

To sum up: Over the course of the post-Soviet period, Russia enjoyed a mixed relationship with global finance. On the one hand, when oil prices were rising or high, inflows of capital from abroad filled the gap vacated by Russia's comparatively small financial system. Although these inflows tended to benefit either state-controlled entities or natural resource export-ers most, the fact that they were able to access funds from abroad – whether that be in the form of portfolio investment, direct investment,

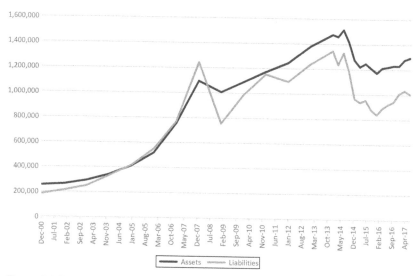

Figure 6.6 International investment position of Russia, 2000–2017 (billion USD)
Source: Bank of Russia (2017)

or loans – released scarce capital for the rest of the economy. On the other hand, when oil prices declined or were low, capital inflows quickly became outflows, causing the number of claimants on Russia's small domestic savings pool to grow, in turn raising the cost and reducing the availability of capital to all but the most well-connected of enterprises. It is no surprise, therefore, that all three recessions in Russia since the mid-1990s have been preceded by a simultaneous decline in commodity prices and contraction in access to international capital. The Russian authorities revealed themselves to be cognizant of the need to create a firmer domestic deposit base to fuel investment and modernize the country's economy. Immediately after the 2008–2009 crisis, officials declared a desire to turn Moscow into a regional, if not global, financial center (Ministry of Economic Development 2009). The idea expressed here was to generate much more stable sources of domestically based finance so that Russia would be less vulnerable to the vicissitudes of global finance in the future. However, there was very little progress in making these aspirations become a reality, so that by 2013, as total external debt exceeded the country's foreign exchange reserves for the first time since 2007, signs were again emerging that Russian firms were fast developing financial vulnerabilities that might harm the country's economy again in the future.

SANCTIONS AND THE FINANCIAL SECTOR

Because the Russian economy was so dependent on inflows of foreign capital before 2014, it was no surprise that as the conflict in Ukraine escalated, Western governments and their allies decided to impose restrictions on access to external finance for Russian firms. As was the case in the defense and energy industries, sanctions that limited Russian access to external capital were gradually put in place over the course of the summer of 2014. In addition to restricting the ability of key Russian defense and energy firms to access external capital, Western sanctions imposed restrictions on a number of banks. These banks were either state-owned banks (i.e. banks in which the state's equity share was higher than 50 percent) or banks owned by, or otherwise linked with, individuals deemed to be close to the Russian leadership.

The first financial sanctions were imposed almost immediately after the annexation of Crimea. On March 18, both the United States and the EU imposed restrictions on individuals and legal entities that were deemed to constitute the leadership's "inner circle," and who had been judged to have been involved in undermining the territorial integrity, sovereignty, and independence of Ukraine (Council Regulation 269/2014) (Executive Order 13660). These individuals included Gennady Timchenko, Arkady Rotenberg, Boris Rotenberg, and Yuri Kovalchuk, as well as Bank Rossiya, which was controlled by Kovalchuk and was considered to function as a bank that carried out financial services for members of the inner circle (US Treasury 2014). At this early stage, financial sanctions did not affect the wider sector, although this began to change in the summer.

In July, both the EU and the United States widened financial sanctions to include prohibitions that prevented individuals and entities from the EU and United States from trading bonds, equities, and related brokering services for products with a maturity period of over ninety days for several state-owned financial organizations and their subsidiaries. The EU included Sberbank, VTB, VEB, Gazprombank, and Rosselkhozbank (Council Regulation 833/2014). The United States initially included Gazprombank and VEB on July 15, although the list was quickly expanded on July 29 to include VTB, Rosselkhozbank, and, in a move that was not replicated by the EU, Bank of Moscow. Sberbank was finally included in the US list on September 12. In September, the debt financing restrictions were tightened by reducing the maturity period for new debt issued by the targeted banks from ninety days to thirty days (Council Regulation 960/2014). Japan,

Norway, Switzerland, Australia, and a number of other allies of the EU and the United States adopted similar restrictions.

Together, the four banks affected by both EU and US sanctions (i.e. excluding Bank of Moscow, which was only targeted by the United States, and VEB, which is a development bank), accounted for around half of total banking assets in Russia in 2014. Thus, while sanctions targeting the energy industry were intended to have an impact on Russian oil production over the long term, those affecting the financial sector were clearly designed to exert an immediate effect on the Russian economy. By stimulating what was in effect an artificially induced "sudden stop" on foreign capital flows to Russia, the United States, EU, and their allies employed what might have been one of their most potent weapons. Indeed, the destructive potential of financial sanctions was compounded by the indirect effects that accompanied the immediate impact on the targeted banks. For example, other Russian banks that were not explicitly targeted by sanctions found themselves experiencing "soft" sanctions. These manifested themselves in the form of increased transactions costs as nonsanctioned Russian banks faced stricter scrutiny when accessing foreign capital (Orlova and Egiev 2015). Uncertainty rose, and with it the risk premium paid by nonsanctioned financial and nonfinancial firms when seeking to access capital, both from abroad and from within Russia. This resulted in an increase in the cost of long-term capital for both sanctioned and nonsanctioned entities alike (Orlova 2014). The intended and actual impact of sanctions targeting the financial sector was, therefore, felt by a considerably larger section of the economy than just the small number of state-owned banks contained in the official sanctions lists.

THE RUSSIAN RESPONSE

As in the other sectors targeted by sanctions, the Russian government developed a multifaceted response that was intended to both reduce the impact that sanctions had upon the economy in the short run, and raise the resilience of the economy to similar measures in the future. In the financial sector, the response again took the form of Russification of certain financial flows and services alongside efforts to seek out alternative external sources of capital and financial services. In parallel, the issue of financial security – i.e. of the security of access to capital – became increasingly important. As a result, after 2014, official statements and documents stressed the importance of increasing Russia's financial security. Almost immediately after sectoral sanctions were applied in the summer of 2014, the price of oil plummeted from more than $115 per barrel in June to just under $50 per barrel by the end of January 2015. This fact alone complicates any analysis of the impact of financial sanctions, because of the strong link between oil price movements and capital flows previously described. As with the other targeted sectors of the Russian economy, the Russian state was able to use the considerable tools at its disposal – institutional and financial – to act in a reasonably quick fashion.

The Securitization of Financial Sector Development

Because of the Russian financial sector's role as one of the "commanding heights" of the economy, and because it represents a crucial component of Russia's national system of political economy, policymakers in Russia viewed Western sanctions targeted at the sector as a serious threat. As a result, the issue of the country's financial security – i.e. the ability of Russian firms and households, as well as the Russian state, to access capital – was quickly transformed into an issue of national security. The rapid depreciation of the ruble that occurred at the end of 2014 and in early 2015, alongside the "sudden stop" of external capital that reemerged as oil prices declined and sanctions were put in place, once again focused policymakers' attention on the deficiencies of Russia's financial system, especially its dependence on external capital. This unfavorable turn of events led policymakers to develop an array of new measures that were designed to reduce the impact of sanctions and to insulate Russia from any potential future expansion of financial sanctions in the future.

This rising awareness of the threat posed by vulnerabilities connected to the financial sector was explicitly articulated in the National Security Strategy published in 2015 (Security Council of the Russian Federation 2015, Section V). The "vulnerability of the national financial system to actions of non-residents" was highlighted as one of the most important dangers facing the Russian economy (Security Council of the Russian Federation 2015, Section IV.56). This was particularly notable because the previous iteration of the National Security Strategy, published in 2009 – drafted immediately after the global financial crisis had laid bare Russia's dependence on external capital – did not mention this as a threat to Russia. Economic sanctions targeting Russia's financial sector were also explicitly cited as a threat to the country's economic development (Security Council of the Russian Federation 2015, Section IV.57). To deal with the threats posed to its national security, the authors of the strategy stated the urgent need to enhance "the security of the financial system to ensure its stable functioning and development" by "strengthening [the] financial system" and bolstering Russia's financial "sovereignty" (Security Council of the Russian Federation 2015, IV.62).

These sentiments were repeated once again in 2017 with the publication of the Economic Security Strategy, which, echoing the National Security Strategy, highlights the threat posed by restrictions on "access to foreign financial resources and modern technologies" (Ukaz prezidenta 2017, Section II.12), as well as the excessively close links "between global commodity and financial markets" (ibid). This was reinforced by warnings of the exposure of the Russian financial system to the "information infrastructure" of the global financial system (ibid). To deal with these threats, the authors of the document emphasize the need to develop domestically based, long-term sources of capital, to reduce the Russian financial system's exposure to fluctuations in global commodity and financial markets, to improve the functioning of the domestic banking system, and to develop an independent Russian information and payment infrastructure for the financial sector (ibid, Section III.19). In practical terms, achieving these objectives would reduce the dependence of the domestic financial system on both external finance and external financial infrastructure. As shown in the following section, it was with precisely these objectives in mind that policymakers developed the response to Western sanctions.

The Russification of Capital and Financial Services

At the same time as securitizing the issue of financial sector development, different branches of the state engaged in a collective effort to "decouple the domestic financial system from the international one" (Johnson and Woodruff 2017, p. 630). This endeavor was multifaceted in nature, addressing different aspects of financial sector development, and took place over an extended period of time. The response to sanctions was also complicated by the fact that the sharp drop in oil prices that occurred toward the end of 2014 prompted an emergency policy response from the monetary authorities. As a result, separating some of the measures undertaken to deal with the macroeconomic consequences of the decline in oil prices – including rising capital outflows, inflation, and a sharp depreciation of the ruble – overlapped with the measures developed to deal with sanctions. In some ways, this is not surprising given that sanctions were intended to effect much the same outcome that the decline in oil prices achieved: a sudden stop of capital flows to Russia. Taken together, the response to low oil prices and sanctions coincided well, reflecting the "judgement that international sanctions and low oil prices were likely to persist, and that Russia would need a financial system capable of operating more autarkically" (ibid).

The immediate challenge for the authorities at the end of 2014 was to achieve some degree of macroeconomic stabilization. Oil prices reached an annual peak in June 2014 and declined thereafter. This corresponded almost exactly with the imposition of sectoral sanctions at the end of July. As those Russian firms and banks that had relied on Western finance began to experience difficulties in refinancing existing debt and in accessing new loans, they hoarded foreign exchange reserves in the expectation that existing loans would need to be repaid. Further pressure on the ruble came as foreign capital left the country and as Russian firms sold rubles to purchase foreign currency that would be needed to service foreign currency denominated debt. When the decline in oil prices accelerated toward the end of the year, the ruble fell in line with it, causing a growing sense of panic to engulf Russian financial markets (Figure 6.7). This panic intensified in December when the Central Bank (Bank of Russia) employed opaque measures to help state-owned Rosneft raise nearly $15 billion to meet its scheduled foreign debt repayments (Kuztensov 2014). This resulted in the ruble losing nearly 20 percent of its value in just one day.

Prior to the onset of panic in December, the monetary authorities and the government had adopted much the same policy as they had done before sanctions and the oil price collapse (Mau 2016, p. 330). This was centered on moving toward an inflation-targeting regime based on a floating exchange rate and the use of the "key interest rate" as the main policy instrument to influence financial markets. Between January 2014 and the end of November, the central bank raised interest rates from 5 percent to 10.5 percent. However, as the oil price declined and capital outflows accelerated, it became clear that the use of interest rates alone was insufficient to maintain even an orderly depreciation, let alone exchange rate stability. As a result, nearly $100 billion of reserves were sold in an effort to moderate the depreciation of the ruble. Moreover, after the turbulence caused by the central bank's support of Rosneft, which prompted the worst one-day fall since the August 1998 financial crisis, the bank was forced to increase the key interest rate from 10.5 percent to 17 percent in an emergency move designed to halt the ongoing collapse of the ruble (Farchy and Hille 2014). This was the largest single interest rate rise since the 1998 crisis, yet it proved insufficient to halt exchange rate turbulence.

Figure 6.7 Ruble–dollar exchange rate and oil price (Brent, USD), 2010–2017
Source: Bank of Russia (2017); author's calculations

Despite taking these emergency measures, the authorities realized that a combination of interest rate policy and moderate intervention on foreign exchange markets was not enough to arrest the depreciation of the ruble. As a result, these actions were buttressed by the imposition of informal capital controls in December. Several personnel changes facilitated this move. The deputy governor, Ksenia Yudaeva, with responsibility for monetary policy, was replaced by Dmitri Tulin (Bershidsky 2015). It was rumored that Russia's Security Council, a body not known for its tendency to involve itself in economic affairs, encouraged his nomination. This was followed by the appointment of Alexander Torshin to the post of deputy governor in charge of relations with the government and parliament. These appointments were made to improve the flow of communication surrounding central bank actions and to help coordinate the authorities' response to the mounting currency and banking crises. This coordination quickly resulted in export-oriented firms being "encouraged" to exchange their foreign currency for rubles provided by the central bank and then instructed to coordinate their sales of foreign currency with the bank.[3] In the same month, President Putin also used his annual address to the Federation Council to announce an amnesty for all capital repatriated to Russia from abroad (Putin 2014b).[4]

This combination of high interest rates, targeted intervention on currency markets, and informal capital controls helped restore some order to Russian financial markets at the beginning of 2015. However, the price of oil began to decline again, falling from $63 per barrel at the beginning of May to nearly $40 per barrel in June. This triggered a corresponding depreciation of the ruble (Figure 6.7). However, the central bank resisted calls to sell foreign exchange reserves in an attempt to prop up the ruble (Mau 2017, pp. 198–199). Instead, the governor of the bank, Elvira Nabiullina, reaffirmed the bank's commitment to focusing on inflation rather than the value of the ruble, preferring to use interest rates rather than intervention on currency markets as the instrument of choice to achieve official policy objectives (Kuvshinova 2015).

The move toward inflation targeting was accompanied by measures to strengthen the domestic banking sector to make it more resilient in the face of the turbulence caused by the decline in oil prices and the Western sanctions. In early 2015, the Russian government developed an anticrisis package, an important part of which included a focus on recapitalizing the most important state-owned banks through the provision of around 1.4 trillion rubles (around $22 billion at the exchange rate of early 2015). Over the course of 2015, the capital of state-owned or state-linked banks grew by nearly 900 billion rubles, compared with less than 100 billion rubles for other banks (Mau 2017, p. 198). In turn, these banks were expected to ensure that Russia's most important enterprises – primarily from Sectors A and B – would enjoy access to credit that was, due to capital outflows, sanctions, and the growing economic downturn, increasingly scarce. By fortifying the domestic financial system at a time when it was effectively cut off from external capital, the authorities were as much enhancing Russia's capacity

---

[3] Letter from Central Bank, available at www.cbr.ru/analytics/standart_acts/bank_supervision/423.pdf.

[4] The wording of the law was changed in mid-2015 so that the law promoted not an "amnesty" on the repatriation of capital, but instead the "simplification of the declaration of assets." See Lenta.ru (2015).

for self-reliance as they were dealing with impending recession. By 2017, proposals emerged to formalize restrictions on capital convertibility during periods of economic turbulence like that experienced over the course of 2014–2015 (Bazanova, Papchenkova, and Lomskaya 2017).

The central bank also continued the process of cleaning up – or "sanitizing" – the domestic banking system (Movchan 2017). This process had been underway since well before the imposition of sanctions and the decline in oil prices, and was intended to ensure that smaller banks that were either close to bankruptcy or were engaging in excessively risky activities were merged with larger banks, which in turn were provided with capital injections from the central bank. However, the turbulence that struck the financial system in 2014–2015 was not used as an excuse to postpone this policy. Instead, the central bank strengthened regulatory and macroprudential requirements. According to Ksenia Yudaeva, around 350 banks were removed from the market between 2013 and 2017 (IMF 2017). While these measures were not a response to Western sanctions per se, the fact that the central bank persisted in this course of action even as the financial sector was put under serious pressure in 2014–2015 demonstrated the resolve of supervisory authorities to ensure a cleaner and more effective banking sector. One consequence of this, however, was that as the number of smaller private banks declined, the share of state-owned banks in Russia's banking sector rose – to what one analyst suggested was around 80 percent of total banking sector assets (Movchan 2017).

In addition to taking steps to improve the health of the domestic banking system, the Russian authorities also acted to further insulate the domestic financial system from actual or potential threats from outside Russia. In 2015, one such threat that was looming large in the mind of policymakers was that of Russian banks being excluded from the SWIFT international bank communications system. Previously, Iranian banks had been excluded from the system, causing considerable distress in the Iranian economy (Recknagel 2012). The Russian leadership was keen to avoid a similar fate. Indeed, Andrei Kostin, the chief executive of VTB – the country's second largest bank – declared that excluding Russia from the SWIFT system would be tantamount to a "declaration of war" (Vaseykina 2014). As a result, the authorities acted quickly to develop a new national electronic payment system that replicated the functions of the SWIFT payments system. In addition, new domestic credit ratings agencies were created to supplant Western companies that were previously dominant in providing credit rating assessment services in Russia. And as a further measure to ensure the smooth functioning of domestic payments, a newly developed national card payment system, functionally equivalent to Visa and MasterCard, was also rolled out. Both MasterCard and Visa were required to clear their transactions in Russia through this system.

These measures attracted some criticism at the time, primarily on the grounds that they were likely to prove economically inefficient, i.e. they were considered likely to raise costs for economic activity in Russia rather than reduce them (Shestopal 2015a). The new Mir payment card, for instance, was reported to cost banks 50 percent more than international cards (Shestopal 2015b). And the fact that Visa and MasterCard were obliged to use the CBR's settlement system raised their costs of operation in Russia (Bank of Finland 2016). However, the purpose of these measures was not to enhance economic efficiency, but instead to make the Russian financial system more durable and less vulnerable to pressure from foreign powers. This was not a transient objective, either. In autumn 2017, Deputy Foreign Minister Sergei Ryabkov reiterated Russia's commitment to reducing its dependence on US-dominated payment systems (Vzglyad 2017).

Diversification of Foreign Sources of Capital and Financial Services

In the short run, Russification of financial capital and services accounted for the bulk of the Russian response to financial sanctions. This is because it would have been very difficult to have quickly replaced the "lost" inflows of capital with capital from non-Western sources. Nevertheless, the Russian government, state agencies, and firms – both state-owned or -controlled and private – accelerated efforts to seek out new sources of capital that were already underway. In Chapters 4 and 5 I discussed how measures were taken by the Russian state and several large state-owned enterprises to tap non-Western sources of capital in the energy and defense industries. But attention was also paid to attracting capital beyond these industries. To be sure, this was complicated by the uncertainty in the investment environment generated by sanctions, something that was not helped by the fact that additional banks and nonfinancial enterprises were added to the list of sanctioned entities over the course of 2014–2016. Those foreign companies that were not deterred by risk created by sanctions were prompted to insert "sanctions clauses" into new investment contracts, especially when it was possible that the ultimate beneficiaries of foreign investment may have in fact been sanctioned entities.

Notwithstanding the desire to promote import substitution, Russian officials devised new incentives to attract investment in selected sectors of the economy. This was done under the guise of "localization," with inducements offered to foreign investors to encourage them to ensure that significant portions of the production process would take place within Russia's borders. These inducements were offered across a range of sectors, including the pharmaceutical and automotive industries and even the agricultural sector, where Russian "countersanctions" might have created the impression that foreign investment was unwelcome. One state-backed initiative in particular was used as a vehicle to attract foreign investment. The Russian Direct Investment Fund (RDIF), an organization created in 2011 to support strategic partnerships between Russian and foreign firms by providing matching funding to investment projects, continued to be used as an instrument to promote investment in Russia despite the fact that it was the subject of US sanctions. After 2014, the RDIF announced a number of large-scale investments from the likes of China, Saudi Arabia, India, Qatar, Kuwait, and even Japan. These were complemented by efforts to secure debt financing on international markets with Eurobonds placed by Norilsk Nickel and Gazprom within less than a year of sanctions being put in place. Russian officials also spoke about selling yuan-denominated bonds, which would give the Russian government access to onshore Chinese investors. In December 2017 it was rumored that this would finally take place, with the Ministry of Finance reported to have hired banks to arrange the placement in a way that made use of Russian financial and legal infrastructure.

In a more long-term perspective, the Russian state also accelerated its participation in multilateral financial organizations where Russian influence would be greater and where Western sanctions would not undermine its access to capital. In 2015, Russia became one of the founding members of the China-led Asian Infrastructure Investment Bank (AIIB), with the Russian government supplying the third-largest injection of capital into the venture. This gave Russian firms easier access to capital to participate in jointly financed infrastructure projects across Eurasia and the Asia-Pacific region. It also meant that Russian firms could tap an alternative source of foreign investment. In July 2014, Russia also became a founder member of the BRICS Development Bank, a multilateral development bank established by Brazil, Russia, India, China, and South Africa. Headquartered in Shanghai, the BRICS bank was designed to support public and private projects through loans, equity participation, and other financial instruments. Russia holds equal shares and voting rights in the bank, with Russian firms and the state possessing the right to apply for capital to support projects focused on infrastructure and the environment. Taken together, Russia's participation in these multilateral institutions that are not dominated by Western countries constituted an important component of both opening up new sources of capital and building non-Western institutional structures (Stuenkel 2016, chapter 4). These sources of funding also have the potential to provide a more stable, less volatile source of foreign capital that is not as highly correlated with oil prices as Western capital proved to be.

Overall, the Russian response to sanctions imposed on the financial sector was similar in nature to the responses developed in the energy and defense sectors. The state – which occupied an important place in the Russian financial system, both through its official monetary authorities and considerable assets on the one hand, and through its presence in the banking sector on the other – moved quickly to insulate the country's financial sector from the sudden stop of external capital that emerged as a result of sanctions and the precipitous drop in oil prices. It was able to use its financial and institutional instruments – both formal and informal – to cushion the Russian financial system from the most adverse consequences of the reversal of capital flows in late 2014 and early 2015. While capital certainly became scarcer, the country did not experience a contraction in investment on the scale of either the 1998 financial crisis or the 2008–2009 global financial crisis. Over time, measures were put in place to make the Russian banking system more resilient, both to the threat of international financial sanctions and to movements in global commodity prices. In doing so, the state's role in the financial system – already strong to begin with – grew. This was not a trivial change in emphasis. Prior to 2014, the Russian financial system had become closely integrated with the global financial system, with most of this integration taking place with Western-dominated banks and financial organizations. Sanctions changed this. Within three years, concrete steps had been taken both to ensure that the Russian financial system was more resilient and, where external capital was used, to make greater use of non-Western sources of capital.

IMPACT OF SANCTIONS ON RUSSIA'S FINANCIAL SECTOR

The impact of Western sanctions on Russia's financial was certainly moderated by the Russian response. However, these measures were not enough to prevent considerable disruption to the Russian financial system. Again, this was at least partially – if not primarily – due to the fact that the decline in oil prices had the same impact on Russia that it exerted in 1998 and 2008–2009, in that it generated a sudden stop of Russian access to external finance. Sanctions merely exacerbated what would already have been a severe contraction in the availability of external finance. As a result, the impact of sanctions, in so far as it can be separated from the decline in oil prices, contributed to a significant sense of financial panic, especially at the end of 2014 and early 2015. This took the form of what might be called direct effects, as Russian entities dealt with the sudden unavailability of capital, and also indirect effects, as the general sense of political uncertainty caused foreign investors on aggregate to reduce their direct investment in Russia. I describe the latter as an indirect effect because the impact of sanctions was felt well beyond those sectors and individuals specifically targeted by sanctions. However, as the Russian response began to take shape, the adverse impact of sanctions moderated. By 2017, as oil prices began to stabilize and then to creep up slowly, the impact of financial sanctions had diminished significantly.

Direct Effects

The most immediate effects of sanctions and the decline in oil prices were observed from the final quarter of 2014 and the first quarter of 2015 (Figure 6.8). Gross private sector capital inflows fell dramatically, as they had during the 2008–2009 financial crisis. In this respect, capital inflows fluctuated in exactly the same way as they previously had during periods in which oil prices had declined sharply. Between 2010 and 2013 the average quarterly private sector capital inflow was $18.6 billion. But between

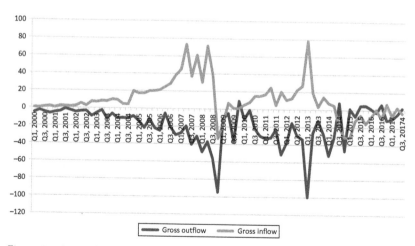

Figure 6.8 Quarterly gross private sector capital flows, 2000–2017
Source: Bank of Russia (2017)

Q3 2014 and Q3 2015, gross inflows became negative, averaging −$23.6 billion over the year. Moreover, gross inflows did not return sharply, as they did after the 2008–2009 crisis. Instead, gross inflows averaged just $4.2 billion between Q4 2015 and Q3 2017. This was because foreigners were reducing their holdings of Russian assets, thereby disinvesting in the Russian economy. Russian borrowers found it difficult both to refinance existing debt and to secure additional loans to finance investment. Banks were hit harder than nonfinancial-sector borrowers, primarily due to the fact that the largest banks in Russia were subject to sanctions. The decline in oil prices in late 2014 and early 2015 would certainly have explained a good proportion of the short-term sharp reduction in foreign holdings over this period (Gurvich and Prilepskiy 2015, p. 368). However, as the Russian economy began to stabilize over 2016–2017, foreigners continued to reduce their holdings of Russian assets. The monetary authorities' decision to adopt an inflation-targeting strategy based on a floating exchange rate also discouraged a return of capital inflows, as it introduced greater uncertainty over the likely direction of the ruble (ibid, p. 370). Sanctions would have exacerbated this tendency, while Russian efforts to secure alternative sources of capital were clearly not replacing the disinvestment by Western investors as quickly as policymakers would have hoped.

Nevertheless, the impact of the sudden stop of foreign capital was at least partially mitigated by the official policy response that began in late 2014. The imposition of informal capital controls, alongside efforts to encourage the repatriation of Russian capital from abroad, caused gross outflows of capital to decline significantly. In simple terms, this meant that Russian entities reduced their holdings of foreign assets. Capital – including holdings of foreign currency abroad – was moved back to Russia. This boosted the availability of foreign currency to meet debt repayment obligations, which peaked over late 2014 and early 2014, especially for some large state-owned firms such as Rosneft. In the final quarter of 2014, gross private sector capital outflows reached $46.6 billion. This was not an unusually high amount. For example, gross outflows in excess of $50 billion were observed. Indeed, between 2010 and 2013, gross outflows – i.e. the increase in foreign assets held by Russians – rose by an average of just over $30 billion per quarter. However, while gross outflows declined briefly during the 2008–2009 crisis and then returned from 2010 onward, gross outflows failed to follow the same pattern after 2014. Instead, gross outflows of private capital reached an average of just over $1 billion per quarter from 2015 onward, indicating that official efforts to maintain greater control over the acquisition of foreign assets (i.e. to move Russian capital abroad) were having the desired effect.

Another important consequence of financial sanctions and the fall in oil prices was that the aggregate external debt owed by Russian entities – including the state as well as banks and nonfinancial firms – fell sharply after 2014 (Figure 6.3). Due to difficulties encountered in refinancing existing debt, Russian firms found themselves obliged to repay their debts on schedule. Consequently, Russia's total external debt fell from around $728 billion in January 2014 – i.e. before sanctions were imposed – to $597 billion at the end of 2014. By the end of 2016, total external debt had fallen to just over £500 billion. This reduction of nearly $200 billion in the stock of external debt was caused by a combination of repayments (primarily to Western banks) and a reduction in the dollar value of ruble-denominated debt. The sharp increase in net private sector capital outflows that generated panic and a rapid depreciation of the ruble at the end of 2014 was at least partially caused by these forced external debt repayments. In turn, this contributed to the reduction in Russia's foreign exchange reserves, as rubles were exchanged for foreign currency to service external debt obligations. As a result, Russia's international reserves fell from $510 billion at the beginning of 2014 to $388 billion at the end of the year.

This sharp increase in debt repayments did not help investment demand in Russia. Onerous debt repayments further exacerbated the unavailability of capital to domestic borrowers. However, the sudden repayment of external debt did mean that Russia's overall financial vulnerabilities were reduced, thus increasing the resilience of the domestic financial system, which before 2014 had shown signs of rising to worrying levels. Before sanctions were imposed, total external debt exceeded Russia's international reserves by around $200 billion. However, as oil prices began to stabilize and then rise slowly over the course of 2016 and 2017, the gap between official international reserves and total external debt had narrowed to around $100 billion. Moreover, much of Russia's scheduled external debt repayments consisted of obligations to banks or other corporate entities that either own or are linked with Russian debtors. The existence of large volumes of "intragroup" debt, where Russian firms borrowed from entities registered offshore for the purpose of "tax efficiency," and to which they were often linked through common ownership structures, meant that a significant portion of the external debt owed was relatively easy to reschedule. As a result, the overall stock of debt indicated in official data overstated the extent of Russia's real "hard" debt obligation. This helped Russian firms manage debt repayments after 2014. By the end of 2017, "intragroup" debt

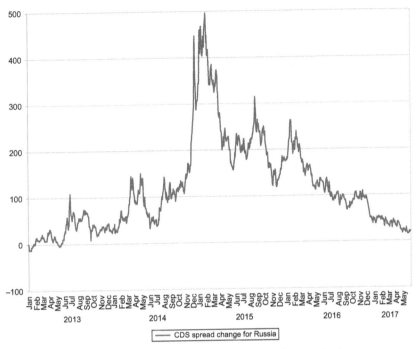

Figure 6.9 Change in risk premium in Russia, 2013–2017 (basis points)
Source: Bank of Russia (2017)

accounted for around 27 percent of Russia's total external obligations, or around $150 billion. Foreign holders' share of Russian sovereign debt also declined by half during this period (Pashutinskaya 2017).

The deployment of state instruments – both formal and informal – in response to the dual threat of sanctions and low oil prices helped to reduce the impact of the sudden stop of external capital inflows. By 2017, this was helping to generate a greater sense of financial stability in Russia. Credit default spreads – a commonly used measure of risk associated with lending to Russian entities – declined to presanctions levels, indicating that foreign perceptions of Russian entities' ability to service existing debt burdens were more sanguine and less driven by fear of the potential impact of sanctions (Figure 6.9). Although capital inflows were not as supportive of growth as they had been in 2006–2007 and after the global financial crisis, the fact that capital inflows had declined so sharply ceased to generate too much in the way of concern for policymakers. This was helped by the sustained reduction in gross capital outflows.

Alongside efforts to reduce the domestic financial sector's vulnerability to the restrictions in access to external capital, policymakers also continued to focus on strengthening the domestic banking sector. As stated previously, the number of private banks – many of which were considered to be weak and a threat to overall banking sector stability – declined. In parallel, additional and significant state support was extended to state banks (Astapenko, Voronova, and Yeremina 2017). According to estimates by the ratings agency Fitch, somewhere in the region of two trillion rubles of state assistance was extended to state-owned banks between 2014 and 2017 (approximately 2.5 percent of 2014 GDP). This support took the form of direct transfers from the federal budget (c. 260 billion rubles), support from the National Welfare Fund (c. 850 billion rubles), and state bonds issued to finance the recapitalization of banks. According to the ratings agency, a large proportion of the capital held by VTB, VEB, Gazprombank, and Rosselkhozbank – all subject to sanctions – was provided by the state after sanctions were imposed. By contrast, Russia's largest bank, Sberbank, was not forced to rely on state support, largely because it continued to attract the largest share of domestic deposits.

If the support of the state helped Russian state-owned banks survive the twin dangers of sanctions and declining oil prices, then efforts to increase the Russian financial system's resilience to any potential future expansion of sanctions also proceeded apace. The Mir payment card system – promoted under the banner "Your card is free from external factors. Created in Russia" – had been issued to nearly twenty-five million users by November 2017, although a large proportion of these users – ten million – were so-called *byudzhetniki*, or people dependent on the state for income (Zubkov 2017). Around 380 banks operating in Russia accepted the new card, with around 120 banks able to issue the cards (RFE/RL 2017). In line with wider efforts to develop closer ties with non-Western economies, Prime Minister Dmitri Medvedev also stated that Russian officials were attempting to integrate the Mir system with the Chinese analogue Union Pay (Soldatkin 2016). The development of the national system also proved more compatible with the SWIFT international electronic payments that Mir was developed to replace: by 2017, SWIFT had reduced the price of clearing payments using the Mir system (Prime.ru 2017).

Indirect Effects

Sanctions also affected the financial system and the availability of capital to the domestic economy through indirect channels. Thus, despite the fact that sanctions were targeted at specific sectors and individuals, many nonsanctioned entities also experienced problems in accessing capital. As just discussed, refinancing of existing loans, or access to new ones, was increasingly difficult to obtain. As a result, the available pool of capital within Russia was reduced, pushing the cost of capital higher. This contributed to a reduction in overall investment, although this reduction in investment was also caused by a reduction in demand for investment capital, especially at the end of 2014 and early 2015 (CBR Monetary Policy Report 2017, p. 84). In this respect, sanctions had clearly observable indirect effects. Furthermore, indirect effects were observed elsewhere. Flows of inward foreign investment also declined after the imposition of sanctions. That this occurred alongside the reduction in oil prices was to be expected. After all, IFDI flows also declined after the 1998 and 2008–2009 crises. However, unlike previous crises, IFDI flows did not recover strongly when oil prices began to grow again.

As discussed in Chapter 2, investment in fixed capital in Russia at around 20 percent of GDP, was, by the standards of many other middle-income countries, relatively low (Connolly 2011; Gaddy and Ickes 2014). Moreover, the rate of investment growth slowed after resuming growth after the 2008–2009 recession (Figure 6.10). Around a third of aggregate fixed capital formation in Russia tends to be focused on the extraction of metals and hydrocarbons. Thus, when confidence in those areas of the economy declines – as it did in 2008–2009, and again in the final quarter of 2014 – aggregate investment also tends to fall. This is often exacerbated by the fact that a large proportion of the capital goods and equipment used in investment activities is imported (Berezinskaya and Vedev 2015). As a result, sudden exchange rate depreciation of the sort observed when oil prices fall tends to increase the cost of investment, causing many firms to cancel or defer investment. After the imposition of sanctions and the fall in oil prices, investment in Russia fell for five consecutive quarters. Even when growth did resume in early 2016, its pace was anemic. A scarcity of capital is likely to have contributed significantly to this. Indeed, according to surveys of investment sentiment carried out by the central bank, the demand for capital amongst large firms rose after the second quarter of 2015 (CBR Monetary Policy Report 2017, p. 84). The fact that investment continued to fall suggests that insufficient capital was available to satisfy demand. Of course, some large enterprises continued to access capital. As shown in previous chapters, politically important firms in the energy and defense industry, as well as no doubt well-connected firms in the construction sector, were able to fund investment, largely due to their close links

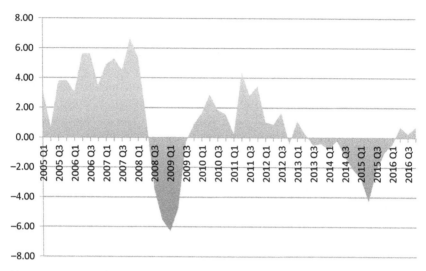

Figure 6.10 Quarterly growth rates of fixed capital formation, 2005–2017
(percent quarter-on-quarter growth, seasonally adjusted)
Source: OECD (2017)

with the state. However, this meant that the composition of investment shifted. Investment in the fuel and energy complex grew as the share of investment in nondefense manufacturing fell (Figure 4.4). This occurred despite the high-profile state campaign to support domestic production through import substitution. A perpetuation of these trends would cause Russia's economic structure to become even more dependent on energy extraction and exports, a characteristic that policymakers had identified as a threat to Russia's economic security ('O strategii' 2017).

As shown in Figure 6.11, net inflows of FDI fell sharply in 2014, albeit following a trend that was evident before sanctions were put in place. Again, separating this from the decline in oil prices is difficult. After all, similar proportional falls in IFDI flows were observed after the 1998 and 2008–2009 crises. However, while net IFDI resumed after those two crises, the return of growth took longer – occurring at the end of 2015 – and, when it did occur, was both modest in volume and short-lived. However, this does not necessarily mean that Russia's attractiveness as a destination for direct investment fell dramatically; rather, gross outflows of direct investment were rising faster than gross inflows. Gross inflows of FDI did not, after 2014, follow a different trajectory to that observed before sanctions. Official efforts to attract alternative sources of IFDI helped. In the postsanctions period, the volume of non-Western IFDI rose as deals

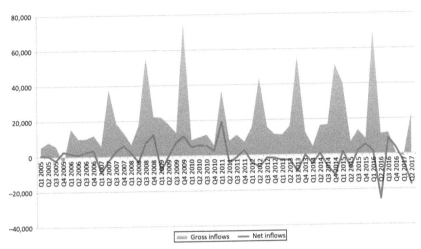

Figure 6.11 Quarterly flows of net and gross inward foreign direct investment, 2005–2017 (million, USD)
Source: Bank of Russia (2017)

were struck to secure investment from the likes of China, Saudi Arabia, Qatar, Japan, and India (Szakonyi 2017). Indeed, Western direct investment was not wholly deterred, either. Significant investment from the United States and Europe was announced in the retail and pharmaceutical industries, suggesting that nonsanctioned sectors remained attractive to Western firms (ibid). Nevertheless, the majority of gross FDI inflows continued to come from the likes of the British Virgin Islands, Cyprus, and the Bahamas – i.e. the usual destinations associated with Russian "round-tripping" operations – suggesting that real foreign direct investment was lower than policymakers would have hoped. This was important because non-Russian direct investment is where most of the gains of direct investment – transfer of technology and knowhow – would come from. Simple repatriation of Russian capital would not bring these gains with it.

Overall, the impact of financial sanctions was far from trivial. In the short term – i.e. during the second half of 2014 and early 2015 – sanctions certainly exacerbated the sharp fall in oil prices and contributed to the sudden stop of external capital. The indirect impact of sanctions was also significant. However, due to official measures taken to insulate Russia from both the impact of sanctions and the withdrawal of capital that accompanied a decline in oil prices, the negative consequences of the sudden stop were offset by efforts to reduce the gross outflow of capital from Russia (Gurvich and Prilepskiy 2016). In turn, this meant that the intended impact of sanctions was diluted relatively quickly. The resources of the state were deployed to reasonably good effect, both reducing the impact in the short term and helping lay the foundations for a more resilient financial system in the future.

CONCLUSION

Prior to the imposition of sanctions, Russia's financial system had become progressively more integrated with the Western-dominated sections of the global financial system. Russian banks, in particular, relied on Western capital to finance their activities, as did a number of the large firms from Sector A of the economy. While the relationship between foreign capital and the Russian economy was often turbulent – the structure of the Russian economy caused capital inflows to be highly correlated with developments in the global oil market – it is fair to say that finance was one of the most globally integrated sectors of the Russian economy. Sanctions changed this. By contributing to the sudden stop of capital that generated a considerable economic shock at the end of 2014, sanctions forced Russian policymakers to develop adaptive measures that changed the nature of the financial system's integration with the global economy.

As was observed in the energy and defense industries, the Russian policy response to financial sanctions comprised a mixture of measures intended to promote the simultaneous Russification and diversification of financial flows. In the financial sector, Russification involved a number of initiatives, many of which are difficult to separate analytically from the response to the simultaneous decline in oil prices. Most notably, domestic, state-controlled sources of capital were used to fill the void created by the sudden stop of foreign capital inflows. Informal capital controls were also implemented to boost the repatriation of foreign currency from private and quasi-public entities and to reduce gross outflows of capital. With a view to the longer term, the authorities reduced the financial system's vulnerability to the threat of further sanctions by creating a new national electronic payments system and by continuing to bolster the domestic banking system. The latter involved the removal of weak and financially risky banks while simultaneously providing capital to state-owned banks. One outcome of this process was that the state's influence over the domestic banking system rose. Moves to reduce the domestic financial system's vulnerability to external pressure were accompanied by efforts to seek out alternative sources of foreign capital, both through the cultivation of closer links with a number of non-Western economies, and through state participation in the creation of new multilateral financial organizations with non-Western powers that might be used to finance investment in the future.

As was the case in the other two sectors discussed previously, the process of adaptation to sanctions was overwhelmingly state-led, with the leadership utilizing a range of institutional, financial, and diplomatic tools to minimize the intended impact of Western sanctions and to begin the process of forging a new relationship with the global economy. While it would be an exaggeration to state that Russia's response created anything like absolute immunity from developments in the global financial system, it was true that the Russian financial system was less vulnerable than it was in early 2014. Indeed, by the end of 2017, Elvira Nabiullina felt emboldened enough to state that "in general, [the] immunity of the financial system to various negative decisions that could be made is now higher than, say, it was three years ago" (Vesti.ru 2017).

The impact of sanctions on the financial system was considerable, albeit difficult to estimate in precise terms due to the complicating effect of the sudden and sharp fall in oil prices that occurred alongside sanctions. In the short term, at least, financial sanctions appeared to generate the most pain. However, as in the energy and defense industries, the Russian policy response moderated the impact of sanctions. Adaptive measures taken by policymakers after 2014 created the conditions for a more self-reliant financial system. In doing so, they seemed to have reduced the financial system's vulnerability to any expansion of sanctions in the future. To be sure, the Russian financial system continued to exhibit many of the problems identified as existing before sanctions were put in place. The banking system remained dominated by state-owned entities, and sources of long-term capital were few and far between. Moreover, relatively scarce capital continued to be allocated to entities with closer links to the state. Nevertheless, Russia did not experience a full-blown credit crunch. Through the deployment of focused state resources, politically and socially important firms from Sectors A and B continued to access capital. The fact that Sector C firms did not was nothing new: They relied on their own resources before 2014 and continued to do so after 2014. The fact that this occurred without accessing significant new sources of external capital from non-Western sources was also noteworthy.

Whether this process of adaptation created a more efficient financial system is unclear. The state's role in allocating capital has certainly grown, and the country's vulnerability to a debt-induced financial crisis has been reduced. However, the price paid for greater stability may prove to be lower credit growth and an exacerbation of politically driven allocation of credit. As in many countries, there is a tradeoff between financial stability and economic dynamism. By emphasizing stability and control, the newly emerging financial system may reduce further the emergence of new economic actors and dampen already low levels of competition. However, for a country that has experienced several severe financial crises over the post-Soviet period, this may well prove an acceptable price to pay, especially if it also means that the country's vulnerability to Western economic statecraft is also reduced.

Conclusion

> Russia does not yield to concessions under pressure and generally does not do anything under orders ... It is quite customary in our history and it is a typical method to derive pluses from minuses.
> Sergei Ryabkov, Russian Deputy Foreign Minister, in Vlasova 2017

The sanctions imposed by Western powers and their allies in the spring and summer of 2014 exerted a powerful influence over the subsequent evolution of political economy in Russia. After nearly two and half decades of ever closer integration with the global economy – especially with Western countries – sanctions caused policymakers in Russia to reassess the nature of the country's relationship with the global economy. They did not, however, turn to Soviet-era aspirations to autarky. Instead, significant efforts were made to build a more secure and durable system of political economy based on the development of domestic capabilities in strategic (as defined by Russian policymakers) industries, as well as by cultivating closer ties with alternative sources of technology and capital from outside the West and its allies. In formulating this response, policymakers reduced the impact of sanctions upon the functioning and performance of the Russian economy, which in turn alleviated the economic and political pressure that Western powers hoped might cause Russia to modify its policies toward Crimea and Ukraine.

The longer-term impact of the Russian strategic response to sanctions – for better or worse – remains to be seen. What does seem almost certain, however, is that political economy in Russia has been significantly reshaped. Throughout this book, I have sought to understand precisely how sanctions affected Russia, and how the Russian authorities crafted a strategic response that facilitated a relatively prompt process of adaptation. To do this, I focused on how the trajectory of development in the domestic system of political economy and the country's integration with the wider global economy was altered in the three sectors of the Russian economy that were targeted by Western sanctions. In this final chapter I consider two questions. First, what was the overall impact of sanctions on political economy in Russia? What is this likely to mean for Russia's relationship with the global economy? And what might these changes mean for the future of Russia? Second, what does the evidence presented in this book mean for the study of sanctions as a tool of statecraft?

THE IMPACT OF SANCTIONS ON RUSSIAN POLITICAL ECONOMY

The most important finding in this book is that while sanctions caused some initial disruption – especially at the end of 2014 and in early 2015 – the impact on targeted sectors subsided after a relatively short period of time. In the energy industry, sanctions limiting Russian firms' access to technology did not exert any discernably negative impact on oil and gas production. Instead, oil production rose, at least until Russia concluded a deal with OPEC to limit production as a means to push up prices. While Rosneft experienced problems meeting its external debt obligations, the use of public resources and access to alternative sources of foreign capital enabled it not only to survive, but also to embark on an unprecedented investment and acquisition program. In the defense industry, sanctions – most notably Ukrainian sanctions – certainly disrupted the Ministry of Defense's plans for naval rearmament, with severe shortages of power systems delaying the production of several classes of warship. However, most other areas of defense-industrial production proceeded largely as planned, allowing Russia to continue making considerable progress with its ambitious domestic military modernization agenda and to fulfill its export obligations. That it could so was in no small part due to the adaptive measures taken by the defense-industrial complex in conjunction with the authorities. The financial system also experienced significant disruption, not least because it had always proven vulnerable to sudden stops of external capital whenever oil prices dropped, as they did in the winter of 2014–2015. However, the monetary authorities' decision to move toward a floating exchange rate helped mitigate the impact of the reduced availability of foreign capital. Additional adaptive measures taken by policymakers after 2014, such as the imposition of informal capital controls, the provision of ample liquidity, and a concerted effort to "sanitize" the banking system, all created the conditions for a more self-reliant financial system.

The second key finding is that it was only possible for the Russian authorities to put in place the adaptive measures that they did because they had access to a wide range of tools and resources. This was achievable only because of the role played by the state in Russia's system of political economy, which enabled it to craft a prompt and coordinated response to sanctions that cushioned the targeted sectors from their intended effects. The strategic response in all three targeted sectors was similar in form. First, state officials moved quickly to securitize policy in each sector. It was made clear that Western sanctions were a threat to national security and that this justified a reshaping of the role of the state in directing energy, defense-industrial, and financial sector development. To be sure, the state was involved, to some degree, in each of these sectors before sanctions were put in place. But the events of 2014 caused a rising share of the policy elite to accept that security concerns justified the implementation of special measures to reduce each sector's vulnerability to external pressure. Second, a process of Russification took place in each sector. This was carried out primarily through import substitution, which in the energy and defense-industrial sectors took the form of increasing the domestic production of goods and technology. In the financial sector, this resulted in greater use being made of domestic sources of capital. Third, there was evidence of a concerted effort to seek out alternative foreign sources of goods, technology, and capital in all three sectors to supplement domestic technology and capital. Progress across each of these dimensions was uneven. The energy industry, for example, appeared to be more successful in sourcing new sources of foreign capital and, to a lesser extent, technology, while the defense industry made reasonably swift progress in shifting the production of certain components to within Russia's borders. Nevertheless, there was evidence of both Russification and diversification in all three sectors, with the Russian state usually leading the way in promoting both processes. Thus, the state's position at the apex of Russia's system of political economy, which was often considered by observers to be the biggest source of economic weakness in Russia during normal times, became a source of durability during a period of conflict.

The third significant finding is that the Russian response reduced both the economic pain inflicted by Western sanctions and Russia's vulnerability to any possible expansion of sanctions in the future. By promoting greater reliance on domestic resources in key sectors, on the one hand, and working toward a more pluridirectional foreign economic policy that emphasizes closer relations with non-Western countries, on the other, any future sanctions imposed on Russia will meet a target that is adept at shifting resources within the domestic economy to reduce the impact of external pressure. This process is, at the time of writing, far from complete. Obstacles to developing domestic industrial capabilities and alternative trading partners and sources of external capital were encountered between 2014 and 2017, and new ones will no doubt emerge in the future. But the direction of travel is clear. If, as I have argued, the changes that took place in Russia after 2014 are both significant and likely to shape the future configuration of political economy in Russia and its relationship with the global economy, what are the implications for the future development of the Russian economy?

Perhaps a good starting point is to consider what, on the eve of sanctions, were considered to be the most significant weaknesses of the Russian economy. For many observers, the slowdown in economic growth that preceded sanctions suggested that the model of political economy that delivered such good results between 2000 and 2012 had run out of steam. This meant that certain challenges needed to be addressed if economic growth was to be reignited. Writing in 2014, I outlined these challenges as follows (Connolly 2015, pp. 17–18):

Sector A should be managed more efficiently to ensure that oil and gas production volumes do not drop and, consequently, that rents continue to be generated well into the future. Because of the large share of government income derived from taxation of the energy industry, the health of the public finances will depend significantly on this condition being met. This will entail reform of the regulatory and legal frameworks for the energy industry, in order to encourage the innovation and entrepreneurship required to boost future production. Efforts should be made, at the very minimum, to ensure that Sector B grows more slowly than the other two sectors. This would ensure that its share of GDP diminishes over time, even if the sector does not decrease in absolute size. This cannot happen immediately because of the financial hardship it would create for a large proportion of the politically important labour force. Nevertheless, a number of policies can usefully be attempted. These include reform of the pension and welfare systems, a reduction of subsidies to 'dinosaur' enterprises, measures to increase competition across markets and a reduction in military spending ... Efforts should [also] be made to ensure Sector C grows faster than the other two sectors. This would reduce stress on the federal budget, and boost competition across the economy. Because competition is more intense in Sector C ... faster growth here would raise the overall level of total factor productivity. In doing so, it would advance the goal of modernization in a less obvious but arguably more effective way than any prevailing initiatives based on state direction. Obvious areas for improvement include financial reforms that broaden access to capital ... [and] establishing property rights that are not conditional on good relations with state officials.

The rough outline of the challenges facing the Russian economy presented here was not original. Very similar proposals were put forward by ex-finance minister Alexei Kudrin and by the authors of the "Strategiya 2020" published in 2012 (Ministry of Economic Development of the Russian Federation 2012). Indeed, at the time of writing, similar proposals were again put forward by Kudrin, this time in his capacity as director of the Centre for Strategic Research (Centre for Strategic Research 2017). Taken together, such proposals might be considered to constitute a "liberal" economic reform agenda. However, if the likelihood of implementing some variation of the liberal economic reform agenda was low before 2014, sanctions and the Russian response pushed economic policy in the opposite direction. After all, the strategic policy response documented in this book emphasized state-driven economic policy at the expense of the decentralized (i.e. market-based) allocation of resources. Securitization justified greater state involvement; Russification took place primarily through either state-owned firms or privately owned firms utilizing public resources; and a large proportion of the new ties formed with non-Western countries came about through state-owned firms with the assistance of state officials. Indeed, writing in 2014, Igor Yurgens, a high-profile member of the management board of the Russian Union of Industrialists and Entrepreneurs (one of Russia's largest business associations), stated that Western sanctions and the Russian response served to "weaken the modernizers" in Russia (Yurgens 2014). By modernizers, Yurgens was referring to those who wanted to promote innovation and private entrepreneurship. By contrast, elements within the policy elite who desired a more active role for the state in the name of enhancing Russia's security saw the emergence of a policy response that contained many, although by no means all, of their prescriptions put forward in early 2014 (Papchenkova and Biryukova 2014).

In this sense, the Russian response to sanctions described in this book appeared to reinforce the prevailing system of political economy rather than change it in any meaningful sense. Revenues from Sector A continued to shape the prospects for economic performance, while the expansion of defense and security expenditure that took place after 2014, along with the rise in pecuniary and nonpecuniary support given to "strategic" areas of the economy and the rising share of state-owned banks in the banking sector, all pointed to the rising share of rent-dependent entities in Russia's political economy. Sector C remained beleaguered by the weakness of property rights and an investment environment that seemed to favor those with strong links to the authorities.[1] The intensity of competition declined in all three sectors examined in this book, while capital and ownership became more concentrated. All of which made structural change – whether seen in terms of the diversification of the economic structure or as "modernization" – appear even less likely than was the case before sanctions were put in place. In this respect, the argument presented in this book – that the strategic response weakened the immediate economic impact of sanctions – may prove to be of little comfort if longer-term economic development is hampered.

Of course, those who prioritize Russia's security might suggest that all of this is to miss the point. The Russian response was primarily concerned with enhancing the country's security, not with fostering economic efficiency. Paying a higher price for goods and services, or paying more to access capital, may well have been suboptimal from an economic point of view. But these considerations were secondary to the country's security, durability, and flexibility as a geopolitical actor. The facts that oil firms might have to pay more for goods and technology of a lower quality than before sanctions, that defense-industrial firms might have to make do with lower quality machine tools, or that the price of capital might be higher and its availability lower, all showed that there was an economic cost to pay. But this, according to those fixated on security, was a price worth paying for preserving Russia's political sovereignty, especially when it is considered that maintaining and, where possible, enhancing this sovereignty was one of the most – if not *the* most – important accomplishments of Vladimir Putin's leadership (Gaddy and Ickes 2009b).

But the argument in favor of security neglects the fact that the likes of import substitution and higher military expenditure were presented not only as the means to make Russia more secure, but also as a way to promote economic modernization. The leadership – at least if President Putin is to be believed – wanted to deliver greater security *and* economic modernization. After all, Russia's longer-term security will not be helped if the country slips further behind those countries it considers to be peer competitors, both in terms of its rate of economic growth and in its level of technological development. As such, it is unlikely that what Clifford Gaddy and Barry Ickes described as a "Kalashnikov economy" – that is, a system

---

[1] The argument that the weakness of property rights could be the most important factor holding back investment is Russia is presented in Hanson (2014). Property rights in Russia are also discussed in extensive detail and with the aid of considerable empirical evidence in Frye (2017).

that is durable yet unsophisticated – is really what the leadership envisaged for Russia's future (Gaddy and Ickes 2014). In principle, a state-directed modernization agenda is not necessarily bound to failure. It has, after all, worked for Russia at several times during the past. A hybrid economic system based on state direction of the "commanding heights" and private initiative elsewhere delivered strong growth and structural change in China, although whether state direction of economic development is appropriate for countries seeking to make the journey from middle-income status to high-income is an open question. However, what is clear is that establishing a policy recipe that would ignite the single most important source of growth and structural change in Russia – investment – appeared, at the time of writing, to remain beyond the reach of the Russian policy elite. If, as some would argue, there is a tradeoff between allocative efficiency on the one hand and security on the other, there remains the distinct danger that by erring too much toward security, little is done to improve the investment environment. Ultimately, the economic verdict on the policy response described in this book will depend on whether it stimulates a rapid and sustained rise in investment, whether that be by the state, private sector, Russians, or foreigners.

While the domestic configuration of Russia's political economy will be of immense importance to Russia's future economic prospects, the nature of its relationship with the global economy will be equally important. As I have argued throughout the book, the extent of Russia's openness to trade and capital flows, not to mention people, in the post-Soviet period should not be underestimated. It is also noteworthy that the policy response to sanctions was not to dust off the Soviet playbook and move toward another variation on the Soviet-era form of autarky. Ever since sanctions were put in place, Russian officials have reiterated their desire for Russia to continue to enjoy the benefits of closer integration with the global economy. Instead, what emerged were moves toward not "deglobalization," as argued by Sergei Guriev, but "reglobalization" (Guriev 2015). Not only did the authorities continue to encourage inward foreign investment, albeit under the condition that firms agreed to "localize" certain stages of the production process, but they also made strenuous efforts to attract capital from non-Western sources. This was reinforced by attempts to carve out positions in new markets outside the West. This process of diversifying Russia's foreign economic relations – or, as Dmitri Trenin described it, "maximizing connectivity" – was evident both in the sectors targeted by sanctions and across the wider economy (Trenin 2017). Whether this proves successful over the longer term will be a key question for the country's economic future. Even if it proves possible to generate a higher rate of investment at home, there will still be a need to acquire capital (to finance that investment) and technology and knowhow (to make that investment more effective) from abroad.

Finally, it is also worth noting that integration with the global economy takes place not only through people, capital, and trade; rules and the governing structures that shape a country's interaction with the global economy are also important. For Russia, the postsanctions period has seen it participate more enthusiastically in new non-Western structures that are being built in parallel to the Western-dominated order (Stuenkel 2016). If this trend persists, it is unlikely that Russia will fully turn away from the West. A more likely course of action is that Russia will seek to use its place in both orders to maximize its bargaining position vis-à-vis both the West and the non-West.

IMPLICATIONS FOR THE STUDY OF SANCTIONS

There are two main findings of relevance to those interested in the study of sanctions beyond the case of Russia.

First, the system of political economy of a target country is an extremely important mediating factor when considering how sanctions affect the target country. This goes well beyond simple categorizations of regime type. The type of social order that exists in a target country is of crucial importance to understanding how sanctions might unfold in a target country. In limited-access orders, such as Russia, states can find themselves well placed to use their position in ensuring differential access for individuals or organizations to goods, services and resources to ensure they are distributed according to the preferences of the ruling elite. Consequently, states in target countries can divert resources to socially and politically important groups in a way that bolsters the ruling coalition and cushions targeted entities or social groups from the worst effects of sanctions. Furthermore, understanding the nature of a country's economic structure, the relative balance between social and economic forces, and the pattern of integration between the target country and the global economy is essential to understanding the opportunities and constraints that face target country policymakers when they are formulating a strategic response to sanctions. As I have shown in this book, the specific context in which Russian policymakers crafted their response to sanctions helps explain how they were able to adjust to sanctions. Such adaptation might only be possible under conditions; understanding which conditions facilitate adaption and which make it less likely is an important area for future research.

Second, as I noted at the beginning of this book, there are relatively few scholarly works that provide in-depth analyses of sanctions' impact on target countries. This, I believe, is a serious weakness, as without single-country studies of this kind, it is difficult to test hypotheses and probe causal mechanisms in a rigorous fashion. I hope that this book has shown the value of undertaking such a study, and also that it may prompt others to write in more detail about how sanctions have affected other target countries. Nevertheless, equally as important as devoting sufficient time and attention to one case is doing so with the aid of an Area Studies background. Understanding the context in which sanctions play out in a target country requires an understanding of the way in which that country's political economy functions, including the institutional framework, the economic structure, the main actors and organizations, the relationship between state and market, the relationship of the target country and the global economy, and so on – all of which can be difficult to determine if English-language secondary sources serve as the primary base of evidence. Thus, a more careful and rigorous analysis of the impact of sanctions surely requires closer collaboration between disciplines.

***

To conclude: The sanctions imposed by the West in 2014 exerted a powerful influence over the development of political economy in Russia. However, this influence manifested itself in a fashion that was probably not intended by Western policymakers. After a period of economic turbulence caused primarily by the decline in oil prices rather than by sanctions, Russian policymakers were able to formulate a rapid and sophisticated response that altered both the domestic system of political economy and the country's relationship with the global economy. While it is by no means clear that this response will lay the foundations for a more dynamic and competitive economy in the future, it is nevertheless true that the Russian system of political economy is a more robust target than it was before sanctions were imposed. Given the wider state of geopolitical conflict in which the West and Russia find themselves today, this has important implications for the future. If, as I have argued, Russia has built a system that is less vulnerable to external pressure, it is possible that persisting in the use of sanctions will not help Western policymakers achieve any of their publicly stated primary objectives. Instead, only the secondary and tertiary objectives might be achieved, and even then in only a superficial sense. After all, if a target country is able to adapt to sanctions relatively quickly and at a modest cost, the signal sent to both the domestic constituencies and the international community might serve only to highlight the weakness of sender states. However, unless and until a political solution to the emerging political conflict between Russia and the West is found, sanctions are likely to continue to be used as the preferred tool of statecraft, in the absence of anything better. The fact that they generate very little in the way of meaningful economic pain is unlikely to act as a barrier to their continued use.

Bibliography

Abramov, Alexander, Maria Radygin, Alexander Chernova, and Revold Entov. 2017. "Gosudarstvennaya sobstvennost' i kharakteristiki effektivnosti." *Voprosy Ekonomiki* (4): 5–37.

Abramov, Andrey, Andrey Radygin, and Maria Chernova. 2016. "Kompanii s gosudarstvennym uchastiyem na rossiyskom rynke: struktura sobstvennosti i rol' v ekonomike." *Voprosy Ekonomiki* (12): 61–87.

Adamsky, Dmitri. 2014. *Defense Innovation in Russia: The Current State and Prospects for Revival*. IGCC Defense Innovation Briefs, January.

Agenstvo Neftegazovoi Informatsii. 2016. *Schetnaya palata RF sochla nedostatochnymi prinyatyye Minenergo mery po importozameshcheniyu*. March 16. www.angi.ru/news.shtml?oid=2835240.

Aghion, Phillipe, and Elena Bessanova. 2006. "On Entry and Growth: Theory and Evidence." *Revue de l'OFCE*.

Aghion, Philippe, Richard Blundell, Rachel Griffith, Peter Howitt, and Susanne Prantl. 2009. "The Effects of Entry on Incumbent Innovation and Productivity." *The Review of Economics and Statistics* 91 (1): 20–32.

Aghion, Philippe, and Rachel Griffith. 2008. *Competition and Growth: Reconciling Theory and Evidence*. Cambridge: MIT Press.

Ahrend, Rudiger. 2005. "Can Russia Break the 'Resource Curse'?" *Eurasian Geography and Economics* 46 (8): 584–609.

Allen, Susan. 2008. "The Domestic Political Costs of Economic Sanctions." *Journal of Conflict Resolution* 52 (6): 916–944.

Andreas, Peter. 2005. "Criminalizing Consequences of Sanctions: Embargo Busting and Its Legacy." *International Studies Quarterly* 49 (2): 335–360.

Anthony, Ian. 1998. "Economic Dimensions of Soviet and Russian Arms Exports." In *Russia and the Arms Trade*, by Ian Anthony, 71–79. Stockholm: SIPRI.

Appel, Hilary. 2008. "Is It Putin or Is It Oil? Explaining Russia's Fiscal Recovery." *Post-Soviet Affairs* 24 (4): 301–323.

Ardaev, Vladimir. 2016. "Perspektivnyye proyekty i "deshevyye" den'gi." *RIA Novosti*, March 14.

Askari, Hossein, John Forrer, Hildy Teegen, and Jiawen Yang. 2003. *Economic Sanctions: Examining Their Philosophy and Efficacy*. London: Praeger.

Aslund, Anders. 1989. *Gorbachev's Struggle for Economic Reform*. Ithaca: Cornell University Press.

———. 1995. *How Russia Became a Market Economy*. Washington, DC: Brookings Institution Press.

———. 2007. *Russia's Capitalist Revolution: Why Market Reform Succeeded and Democracy Failed*. Washington, DC: Peterson Institute.

Astapenko, Aleksandra, Tat'yana Voronova, and Anna Yeremina. 2017. *Gosudarstvu prikhoditsya spasat' svoi banki*. September 27. www.vedomosti.ru/finance/articles/2017/09/27/735465-gosudarstvu-spasat-banki.

Bacon, Ed, and Bettina Renz. 2006. *Securitising Russia: The Domestic Politics of Russia*. Manchester: Manchester University Press.

Baker, Peter, Alan Cowell, and James Kanter. 2014. "Coordinated Sanctions Aim at Russia's Ability to Tap Its Oil Reserves." *New York Times*, July 24.

Baldwin, David. 1985. *Economic Statecraft*. Princeton: Princeton University Press.

Baldwin, David, and Robert Pape. 1998. "Evaluating Economic Sanctions." *International Security* 23 (2): 189–198.

Bank of Finland. 2016. "Russia's National Payments Card System Moves Ahead." *BOFIT Weekly*, January 8.

Barber, James. 1979. "Economic Sanctions as a Policy Instrument." *International Affairs* 55 (3): 367–384.

Bardhan, A., and C. Kroll. 2006. "Competitiveness and an Emerging Sector: The Russian Software Industry and Its Global Linkages." *Industry and Innovation* 13 (1): 69–95.

Barsukov, Yuri. 2014. "'Rosneft' provela sekretnoye razmeshcheniye." *Kommersant*, December 12.

Bazanova, Yelizaveta, Margarita Papchenkova, and Tat'yana Lomskaya. 2017. "V krizis konvertiruyemost' rublya mozhet byt' ogranichena." *Vedomosti*, October 23.

Berezinskaya, Olga, and Alexey Vedev. 2015. "Proizvodstvennaya zavisimost' rossiyskoy promyshlennosti ot importa i mekhanizm strategicheskogo importozameshcheniya." *Voprosy Ekonomiki* (1): 103–114.

Bershidsky, Leonid. 2015. *New Mr. Ruble Is Mr. Fixit of Russian Banks*. January 15. www.bloomberg.com/view/articles/2015-01-15/new-mr-ruble-is-dr-doom-for-russian-banks.

Bessanova, Elena. 2010. "Vliyaniye vnutrenney konkurentsii i inostrannykh investitsiy na effektivnost' rossiyskikh promyshlennykh predpriyatiy." *Prikladnaya ekonometrika* (1): 106–127.

Biersteker, Thomas, and Peter van Bergeijk. 2016. "How and When Do Sanctions Work? The Evidence." In *On Target? EU Sanctions as Security Policy Tools*, by Iana Dreyer and José Luengo-Cabrera, 17–29. Paris: EU ISS.

Blackwill, Robert, and Jennifer Harris. 2016. *War by Other Means*. Harvard: Harvard University Press.

Blanchard, Jean Marc, and Norrin Ripsman. 1999. "Asking the Right Question: When Do Economic Sanctions Work Best?" *Security Studies* 9 (1): 219–253.

———. 2008. "A Political Theory of Economic Statecraft." *Foreign Policy Analysis* 4 (4): 371–398.

Blank, Stephen. 2008. "Ivanov, Chemezov, and State Capture of the Russian Defense Sector." *Problems of Post-Communism* 55 (1): 49–60.

Bloomberg. 2013. *Varco to Honghua Vying for $9 Billion of Russia Oil Rigs.* May 23. www.bloomberg.com/news/articles/2013-05-28/varco-to-honghua-vying-for-9-billion-of-russia-oil-rigs-energy.

BOFIT. 2017. "Russia Statistics." *Bank of Finland Institute for Transition Economies.* www.bofit.fi/en/monitoring/statistics/russia-statistics/.

Boussena, Sadek, and Catherine Locatelli. 2017. "Gazprom and the Complexity of the EU Gas Market: A Strategy to Define." *Post-Communist Economies* 29 (4): 549–564.

Bradshaw, Michael, and Richard Connolly. 2016. "Russia's Natural Resources in the World Economy: History, Review and Reassessment." *Eurasian Geography and Economics* 57 (6): 700–726.

Bradshaw, Michael, and Elena Shadrina. 2013. "Russia's Energy Governance Transitions and Implications for Enhanced Cooperation with China, Japan and South Korea." *Post-Soviet Affairs* 29 (6): 461–499.

British Petroleum. 2016. *BP Statistical Review of World Energy 2015.* www.bp.com/content/dam/bp/pdf/energy-economics/statistical-review-2016/bp-statistical-review-of-world-energy-2016-full-report.pdf.

Brooks, Risa. 2002. "Sanctions and Regime Type: What Works, and When?" *Security Studies* 11 (4): 1–50.

Bruegel. 2017. *Real Effective Exchange Rates for 178 Countries: A New Database.* June 2017. http://bruegel.org/publications/datasets/real-effective-exchange-rates-for-178-countries-a-new-database/.

Bukkvoll, Tor. 2009. "Russia's Military Performance in Georgia." *Military Review* 89 (6): 57–62.

Bukkvoll, Tor, Tomas Malmlöf, and Konstantin Makienko. 2017. "The Defence Industry as a Locomotive for Technological Renewal in Russia: are the Conditions in Place?" *Post-Communist Economies* 29 (2): 232–249.

Bureau of Industry and Security. 2014. *Commerce Department Announces Expansion of Export Restrictions on Russia.* Washington, DC: Office of Congressional and Public Affairs.

Burmistrova, Svetlana. 2017. *RFPI i kitayskiy fond proinvestiruyut v Eurasia Drilliing.* June 1. www.rbc.ru/business/01/06/2017/59303d519a79473bed6c6d4e.

Calvo, Guillermo. 1998. "Capital Flows and Capital-Market Crises: The Simple Economics of Sudden Stops." *Journal of Applied Economics* 1 (1): 35–54.

Campbell, Robert. 1980. *Soviet Energy Technologies.* Bloomington: Indiana University Press.

Centre for Political Technologies. 2008. "Reiderstvo kak sotsial'no- ekonomicheskii i politicheskii fenomenon sovremennoi Rossii: Otchet o kachestvennom sotsiologicheskom issledovanii." Moscow: Centre for Political Technologies.

Centre for Strategic Research. 2017. *Ustoychivyy ekonomicheskiy rost: model' dlya Rossii.* Moscow: Centre for Strategic Research.

Centre for the Analysis of Strategy and Technology. 2015. *Gosudarstvennye programmy vooruzheniia Rossiiskoi Federatsii: problemy ispolneniia i potentsial optimizatsii.* Moscow: Tsentr analiza strategii i tekhnologii.

Charap, Samuel, and Timothy Colton. 2017. *Everyone Loses: The Ukraine Crisis and the Ruinous Contest for Post-Soviet Eurasia.* London and New York: Routledge/International Institute for Strategic Studies.

Claeys, Sophie, and Koen Schoors. 2007. "Bank Supervision Russian Style: Evidence of Conflicts between Micro- and Macro-Prudential Concerns." *Journal of Comparative Economics* 35 (3): 630–657.

Connolly, Richard. 2008. "The Structure of Russian Industrial Exports in Comparative Perspective." *Eurasian Geography and Economics* 49 (5): 586–603.

———. 2011. "Financial Constraints on the Modernisation of the Russian Economy." *Eurasian Geography and Economics* 52 (3): 428–459.

———. 2012a. "Climbing the Ladder? High-Technology Export Performance in Emerging Europe." *Eurasian Geography and Economics* 53 (3): 356–379.

———. 2012b. *The Economic Sources of Social Order Development in Post-Socialist Europe.* London and New York: Routledge.

———. 2013. "State Industrial Policy in Russia: The Nanotechnology Industry." *Post-Soviet Affairs* 29 (1): 2013.

———. 2015a. *Troubled Times: Stagnation, Sanctions and the Prospects for Economic Reform in Russia.* Chatham House Russia and Eurasian Programme Research Paper. London: Royal Institute for International Affairs.

———. 2015b. "Economic Modernisation in Russia: The Role of the World Trade Organization." *European Politics and Society* 16 (1): 27–44.

———. 2017. *Towards a Dual Fleet? Industrial Capabilities and the Russian Maritime Doctrine.* NATO Russian Studies Research Review, Rome: NATO Defence College.

Connolly, Richard, and Cecilie Senstad. 2016. "Russian Rearmament an Assessment of Defense-Industrial Performance." *Problems of Post-Communism.*

———. 2017. *Russia's Role as an Arms Exporter the Strategic and Economic Importance of Arms Exports for Russia.* Russia and Eurasia Programme. London: Chatham House.

Connolly, Richard, and Philip Hanson. 2016. *Import Substitution and Economic Sovereignty in Russia.* Russia and Eurasia Programme. London: Chatham House.

Cooper, Julian. 1991. *The Soviet Defence Industry: Conversion and Reform.* London: Royal Institute for International Affairs.

———. 2006a. "Can Russia Compete in the Global Economy?" *Eurasian Geography and Economics* 47 (4): 407–425.

———. 2006b. "The Economy." In *Securitising Russia: The Domestic Politics of Russia,* by Edwin Bacon and Bettina Renz. Manchester: Manchester University Press.

———. 2010. "The Security Economy." In *The Politics of Security in Modern Russia,* by Mark Galeotti, 145–170. Farnham: Ashgate.

———. 2013. "From USSR to Russia: The Fate of the Military Economy." In *Handbook of the Economics and Political Economy of Transition,* by Paul Hare and Gerard Turley, 98–107. London and New York: Routledge.

———. 2016a. *Russia's State Armament Program to 2020: A Quantitative Assessment of Implementation 2011–2015.* Stockholm: FOI/Ministry of Defense.

———. 2016b. "The Military Dimension of a More Militant Russia." *Russian Journal of Economics* 2 (2): 129–145.

Coser, L. 1956. *The Function of Social Conflict.* New York: Free Press.

Council Decision 2014/119/CFSP. 2014. "Council Decision 2014/119/CFSP of 5 March 2014 Concerning Restrictive Measures Directed against Certain Persons, Entities and Bodies in View of the Situation in Ukraine." Brussels.

Council Decision 2014/145/CFSP. 2014. "Council Decision 2014/145/CFSP of 17 March 2014 Concerning Restrictive Measures in Respect of Actions Undermining or Threatening the Territorial Integrity, Sovereignty and Independence of Ukraine." Brussels.

Council Decision 2014/386. n.d. "Council Decision 2014/386."

Council Decision 2014/512/CFSP. 2014. "Council Decision 2014/512/CFSP of 31 July 2014 Concerning Restrictive Measures in View of Russia's Actions Destabilising the Situation in Ukraine." Brussels.

Crane, K., and A. Usanov. 2010. "Role of High-Technology Industries." In *Russia after the Global Economic Crisis*, by Anders Aslund, Sergey Guriev, and Andrew Kuchins, 95–124. Washington, DC: Peterson Institute for International Economics.

Crooks, Ed, and Henry Foy. 2017. "Russia Sanctions Freeze Out US Groups." *Financial Times*, June 20.

Davidson, Jason, and George Shambaugh. 2000. "Who's Afraid of Economic Incentives? The Efficacy-Externality Tradeoff." In *Sanctions as Economic Statecraft*, by Steve Chan and A. Cooper Drury, 37–64. London and New York: Palgrave Macmillan.

Deloitte. 2015. *Russian Oilfield Services Market: Current State and Trends*. October. www2.deloitte.com/content/dam/Deloitte/ru/Documents/energy-resources/2015-russian-oilfield-service-market-current-trends.pdf.

Director of the Office of Foreign Assets Control. 2014. "Directive 4 Under Executive Order 13662 – Blocking Property of Additional Persons Contributing to the Situation in Ukraine." Washington, DC, September 12.

Dmitriyenko, Ivan. 2016. *Rodina nachinayetsya s upakovki*. November 7. www.profile.ru/economics/item/112333-rodina-nachinaetsya-s-upakovki.

Downs, George, and David Rocke. 1994. "Conflict, Agency, and Gambling for Resurrection: The Principal-Agent Problem Goes to War." *American Journal of Political Science* 38 (2): 362–380.

Drezner, Daniel. 1999. *The Sanctions Paradox*. Cambridge: Cambridge University Press.

———. 2015. "Targeted Sanctions in a World of Global Finance." *International Interactions* 41 (4): 755–764.

Drury, A. Cooper. 1998. "Revisiting Economic Sanctions Reconsidered." *Journal of Peace Research* 35 (4): 497–509.

Dzis'-Voynarovskii, Nikolay. 2015. "ZAO 'Rossiya'." *Novoye Vremya*, April 13.

Economides, Spryos, and Peter Wilson. 2001. *The Economic Factor in International Relations: A Brief Introduction*. London and New York: IB Tauris.

Escribà-Folch, Abel. 2012. "Authoritarian Responses to Foreign Pressure: Spending, Repression, and Sanctions." *Comparative Political Studies* 45 (6): 683–713.

Escribà-Folch, Abel, and Joseph Wright. 2010. "Dealing with Tyranny: International Sanctions and Survival of Authoritarian Rulers." *International Studies Quarterly* 54 (2): 335–359.

EU External Action Service. n.d. *Sanctions Policy*. https://eeas.europa.eu/headquarters/headquarters-homepage_en/423/Sanctions%20policy.

European Investment Bank. 2013. *Small and Medium Entrepreneurship in Russia*. Luxembourg: European Investment Bank.

European Union. 2014. *Fact Sheet: EU Restrictive Measures.* April 29. www.consilium .europa.eu/uedocs/cms_data/docs/pressdata/EN/foraff/135804.pdf.

Fadeyeva, Alina, and Yekaterina Derbilova. 2016. "My dolzhny snova stat' luchshimi po dokhodnosti dlya aktsionerov." *Vedomosti*, July 11.

Falichev, Oleg. 2011. "Den'gi vydeliaiutsia zhdem kachestvennykh izdelii." *Voenno-Promyshlennyy Kur'yer*, October 19.

Faltsman, Vladimir. 2015. "Importozameshchenie v TEK i OPK." *Voprosy Ekonomiki* 1: 116–124.

Farchy, Jack. 2015. "Moscow Snubs Rosneft Funding Plans." *Financial Times*, August 15.

2017. "Gazprom Neft Strives to Go It Alone in Russian Shale." *Financial Times*, January 3.

Farchy, Jack, and Kathrin Hille. 2014. "Moscow Lifts Interest Rate to 17%." *Financial Times*, December 15.

Farkas, Evelyn, interview by Tobin Harshaw. 2017. "Congress Slaps Putin With More Sanctions. Does He Actually Care?" *Bloomberg*, July 29.

Federal State Statistics Service. 2017. *Russia in Figures. 2016.* Moscow: Federal State Statistics Service.

Forbes.ru. 2015a. "Kitayskaya Sinopec kupila 10% 'Sibura'." *Forbes.ru*, December 17.

2015b. "SMI nazvali pokupatelya obligatsiy «Rosnefti» na 400 mlrd rubley." *Forbes.ru*, February 2.

Fortescue, Stephen. 2006. *Russia's Oil Barons and Metal Magnates: Oligarchs and the State in Transition.* Basingstoke: Palgrave Macmillan.

2013. "The Economics of Mineral Resources." In *The Oxford Handbook of the Russian Economy*, by M. Alexeev and S. Weber, 404–425. Oxford: Oxford University Press.

2016. "Russia's "Turn to the East": A Study in Policy Making." *Post-Soviet Affairs* 32 (5): 423–454.

Fortescue, Stephen, and Philip Hanson. 2015. "What Drives Russian Outward Foreign Direct Investment? Some Observations on the Steel Industry." *Post-Communist Economies* 27 (3): 283–305.

Foy, Henry. 2017a. "Rosneft Completes $13bn Takeover of India's Essar Oil." *Financial Times*, June 22.

2017b. "Russian Oil Groups Brave Cold of Western Sanctions to Explore Arctic." *Financial Times*, April 20.

Fried, Daniel. 2016. *State Department Sanctions Policy.* Interview by C-SPAN, January 16.

Frolov, Andrey. 2016. "Svoy vmesto chuzhikh. Importozameshcheniye v OPK Rossii: opyt 2014–2016 godov." *Rossiya v global'noy politike*.

Frye, Timothy. 2017. *Property Rights and Property Wrongs: How Power, Institutions and Norms Shape Economic Conflict in Russia.* Cambridge and New York: Cambridge University Press.

Fungácová, Zuzana, Risto Herrala, and Laurent Weill. 2011. "The Influence of Bank Ownership on Credit Supply: Evidence from the Recent Financial Crisis." *BOFIT Discussion Papers* 34.

Gabuev, Alexander. 2017. *Kak sokhranit' vnimaniye na Kitaye.* July 5. http://carnegie.ru/ 2017/07/05/ru-pub-71431.

Gaddy, Clifford. 1996. *The Price of the Past: Russia's Struggle with the Legacy of a Militarized Economy.* Washington, DC: Brookings Institution Press.

Gaddy, Clifford, and Barry Ickes. 2002. *Russia's Virtual Economy.* Washington, DC: Brookings Institution Press.

———. 2005. "Resource Rents and the Russian Economy." *Eurasian Geography and Economics* 46 (8): 559–583.

———. 2009a. "Putin's Third Way." *The National Interest.*

———. 2009b. "Russia's Declining Oil Production: Managing Price Risk and Rent Addiction." *Eurasian Geography and Economics* 50 (1): 1–13.

———. 2014. *Can Sanctions Stop Putin's Russia?* June 3. www.brookings.edu/articles/can-sanctions-stop-putin/.

Gaidar Institute. 2017, April. *Rossiyskaya ekonomika v 2016 godu: Tendentsii i perspektivy.* Moscow: Gaidar Institute.

Galtung, Johan. 1967. "On the Effects of International Economic Sanctions, with Examples from the Case of Rhodesia." *World Politics* 19 (3): 378–416.

Gans-Morse, Jordan. 2012. "Threats to Property Rights in Russia: From Private Coercion to State Aggression." *Post-Soviet Affairs* 28 (3): 263–295.

Gazeta.ru. 2017. *"Sarmat" zhdet svoyego chasa.* July 3. www.gazeta.ru/army/2017/07/03/10760078.shtml#page4.

Gianella, Christian, and William Tompson. 2007. *Stimulating Innovation in Russia: The Role of Institutions and Policies.* OECD Economic Department Working Papers 539. Paris: OECD.

Glazyev, Sergei. 2015. *Ukrainskaya katastrofa: Ot amerikanskoy agressii k mirovoy voynye?* Moscow: Izborksky Klub.

Gokhberg, Leonid, and Tatiana Kuznetsova. 2011. "S&T and Innovation in Russia: Key Challenges of the Post-Crisis Period." *Journal of East-West Business* 17 (2–3): 73–89.

Golikova, Victoria, Boris Kuznetsov, Maxim Korotkov, and Andrei Govorun. 2017. "Trajectories of Russian Manufacturing Firms' Growth after the Global Financial Crisis of 2008–2009: The Role of Restructuring Efforts and Regional Institutional Environment." *Post-Communist Economies* 29 (2): 139–157.

Golubkova, Katya. 2013. *Russia's Rosneft Agrees to Buy Weatherford's Russian, Venezuelan Assets.* July 14. www.reuters.com/article/rosneft-weatherford-deal-idUSL6N0PO0BN20140713.

———. 2017. *Rosneft Eyes Chinese Gas Market after Beijing Gas Deal.* June 29. http://uk.reuters.com/article/us-russia-rosneft-china-gas-idUKKBN19K253.

Golubkova, Katya, and Olesya Astakhova. 2016. *Russian Oil Majors Raise Output of Hard-to-Recover Crude.* September 26. www.reuters.com/article/us-russia-oil-hard-to-extract-idUSKCN11W1JB.

Gonchar, Ksenia. 2000. *Russia's Defense Industry at the Turn of the Century.* Bonn: Bonn International Center for Conversion.

Gordeev, Vladislav. 2015. *Rogozin nazval datu polnogo importozameshcheniya v oboronke.* December 5. www.rbc.ru/politics/04/12/2015/5660b5679a79473f88734f85.

Government of the Russian Federation, 2014a. Energeticheskaya Strategiya Rossii na period do 2035 goda [Energy Strategy of Russia to 2035]. www.energystrategy.ru/ab_ins/source/ES-2035_09_2015.pdf.

2014b. *Perechen' porucheniy o dopolnitel'nykh merakh po stimulirovaniyu ekonomicheskogo rosta.* May 14. www.kremlin.ru/acts/assignments/orders/23900.

2015a. *Pervoye zasedaniye Pravitel'stvennoy komissii po importozameshcheniyu.* August 11. http://government.ru/news/19246/.

2015b. *Plan pervoocherednykh meropriyatiy po obespecheniyu ustoychivogo razvitiya ekonomiki i sotsial'noy stabil'nosti v 2015 godu. Rasporyazheniye Pravitel'stva RF ot 27 yanvarya 2015 g. N 98-r.* January 27. http://government.ru/docs/16639/.

2016a. *Meeting of the Government Import Substitution Commission.* January 28. http://government.ru/en/news/21577/.

2016b. *Ob utverzhdenii gosudarstvennoy programmy "Razvitiye oboronno-promyshlennogo kompleksa".* May 25. http://government.ru/docs/23173/.

2016c. *Zasedaniye Pravitel'stvennoy komissii po importozameshcheniyu.* May 16. http://government.ru/news/27681/.

2017. *Zasedaniye Pravitel'stvennoy komissii po importozameshcheniyu.* May 16. http://government.ru/news/27681/.

Graham, Loren. 2013. *Lonely Ideas: Can Russia Compete?* Cambridge: MIT Press.

Guriev, Sergei. 2015. *Deglobalizing Russia.* December 16. http://carnegie.ru/2015/12/16/deglobalizing-russia/in6d.

Gurvich, Evsei, and Ilya Prilepskiy. 2015. "The Impact of Financial Sanctions on Russia's Economy." *Russian Journal of Economics,* 1 (4): 359–385.

Gustafson, Thane. 1990. *Crisis amidst Plenty.* Cambridge and New York: Cambridge University Press.

2012. *Wheel of Fortune.* Cambridge: Harvard University Press.

Högselius, Per. 2012. *Red Gas: Russia and the Origins of European Energy Dependence.* Springer.

Hakvåg, Una. 2017. "Russian Defense Spending After 2010: the Interplay of Personal, Domestic, and Foreign Policy Interests." *Post-Soviet Affairs* 33 (6): 496–510.

Hanson, Philip. 2003. *The Rise and Fall of the Soviet Economy: An Economic History of the USSR, 1945–1991.* London: Pearson Education.

2005. "Observations on the Costs of the Yukos Affair to Russia." *Eurasian Geography and Economics* 46 (7): 481–494.

2007. "The Russian Economic Puzzle: Going Forwards, Backwards or Sideways?" *International Affairs* 83 (5): 869–899.

2009. "The Resistible Rise of State Control in the Russian Oil Industry." *Eurasian Geography and Economics* 50 (1): 14–27.

2010. "Russia's Inward and Outward Foreign Direct Investment: Insights into the Economy." *Eurasian Geography and Economics* 51 (5): 632–652.

2014. *Reiderstvo: Asset-Grabbing in Russia.* Russia and Eurasia Programme. London: Chatham House.

Hanson, Philip, and Elizabeth Teague. 2005. "Big Business and the State in Russia." *Europe-Asia Studies* 57 (5): 657–680.

Hedlund, Stefan. 1999. *Russian Path Dependence: A People with a Troubled History.* London and New York: Routledge.

2014. *Putin's Energy Agenda: The Contradictions of Russia's Resource Wealth.* Boulder: Lynne Rienner Publishers.

Henderson, James. 2010. *Non-Gazprom Gas Producers in Russia.* Oxford: Oxford University Press.

2015. *Key Determinants for the Future of Russian Oil Production and Exports.* Oxford: Oxford Institute for Energy Studies.

2017. *Russian Oil Production Outlook to 2020.* Oxford: Oxford Institute for Energy Studies.

Henderson, James, and Alastair Ferguson. 2014. *International Partnership in Russia: Conclusions from the Oil and Gas Industry.* Basingstoke: Palgrave Macmillan.

Henderson, James, and Arild Moe. 2016. "Gazprom's LNG Offensive: a Demonstration of Monopoly Strength or Impetus for Russian Gas Sector Reform?" *Post-Communist Economies* 28 (3): 283–299.

Henderson, James, and Simon Pirani. 2014. *The Russian Gas Matrix: How Markets Are Driving Change.* Oxford: Oxford University Press.

Henderson, James, and Tatiana Mitrova. 2016. *Energy Relations between Russia and China: Playing Chess with the Dragon.* Oxford: Oxford Institute for Energy Studies.

Herbst, Jeffrey. 2000. "Economic Incentives, Natural Resources and Conflict in Africa." *Journal of African Economies* 9 (3): 270–294.

Hewett, Ed, and Victor Winston. 1991. *Milestones in Glasnost and Perestroyka: The Economy.* Washington, DC: Brookings Institution Press.

Hufbauer, Gary Clyde, Jeffrey J. Schott, and Kimberly Elliot. 1985. *Economic Sanctions Reconsidered.* 1st edition. Washington, DC: Peterson Institute for International Economics.

1990. *Economic Sanctions Reconsidered.* 2nd edition. Washington, DC: Peterson Institute for International Economics.

Hufbauer, Gary Clyde, Jeffrey J. Schott, Kimberly Elliot, and Barbara Oegg. 2007. *Economic Sanctions Reconsidered.* 3rd edition. Washington, DC: Peterson Institute for International Economics.

International Institute for Strategic Studies. 2018. *The Military Balance.* London: IISS.

IMF. 2012. Direction of Trade Statistics (DOTS) Database. New York: IMF. www .esds.ac.uk.

2017. *Russian Central Bank: The System Is Stable.* December 5. www.imf.org/en/ News/Articles/2017/12/01/na120517-russian-central-bank-the-system-is-stable.

Interfax. 2014. *Sanctions against Russia Already Affecting Production of Shale Reserves, Could Impact Shelf.* January 10. www.interfax.com/newsinf.asp?id=535345.

2015. "NOVATEK' i 'Fond Shelkovogo Puti' podpisali ramochnoye soglasheniye po 'Yamal SPG'." *Interfax,* September 3.

Istomin, Vsevolod. 2016. *Sputniki sanktsiy Otechestvennyye proizvoditeli uchatsya delat' kosmicheskiye apparaty samostoyatel'no.* March 28. https://vpk-news.ru/articles/ 29967.

Johnson, Juliet. 2000. *A Fistful of Rubles: The Rise and Fall of the Russian Banking Sytem.* Ithaca: Cornell University Press.

Johnson, Juliet, and David Woodruff. 2017. "Currency Crises in Post-Soviet Russia." *The Russian Review* 76: 612–634.

Jones, Lee. 2016. *Societies under Siege.* Oxford: Oxford University Press.

Jones, Lee, and Clara Portela. 2014. *Evaluating the "Success" of International Economic Sanctions: Multiple Goals, Interpretive Methods and Critique.* London: Queen Mary University of London.

Josephson, P. 2000. *Red Atom: Russia's Nuclear Power Program from Stalin to Today.* Pittsburgh, PA: University of Pittsburgh Press.

Karas, Alexei, William Pyle, and Koen Schoors. 2015. "A 'De Soto Effect' in Industry? Evidence from the Russian Federation." *Journal of Law and Economics.* 58 (2): 451–480.

Karavaev, Ivan. 2013. "Osnovnye itogi realizatsii gosudarstvennoi politiki v OPK Rossii v 2012 godu i zadachi na blizhaishuiu perspektivu." In *Federalnyi spravochnik: Oboronno-promyshlennyi kompleks Rossii,* 205–212. Moscow: Federalnyi spravochnik.

Karl, Terry Lynn. 1997. *The Paradox of Plenty: Oil Booms and Petro-States.* Berkeley and Los Angeles: University of California Press.

Kashin, Vassily. 2016. *Industrial Cooperation: Path to Confluence of Russian and Chinese Economies.* Valdai: Vadai Discussion Group.

Keohane, Robert, and Milner, Helen (eds). 1996. *Internationalization and Domestic Politics.* Cambridge and New York: Cambridge University Press.

Khodarenok, Mikhail. 2016. *Strategicheskikh deystviy v okeane bol'she ne planiruyut.* July 31. www.gazeta.ru/army/2016/07/31/9716165.shtml.

——. 2017. *Rossiya i Kitay zapustyat dvigatel'.* June 27. www.gazeta.ru/army/2017/06/16/10724453.shtml.

Kirdina, Svetlana, and Andrey Vernikov. 2013. "Evolution of the Banking System in the Russian Context: An Institutional View." *Journal of Economic Issues* 157 (2): 473–483.

Kirk, Lisbeth. 2015. *France Agrees to Reimburse Russia for Cancelled Mistral Warship Deal.* August 7. https://euobserver.com/news/129849.

Kirshin, Yuri. 1998. "Conventional Arms Transfers during the Soviet Period." In *Russia and the Arms Trade,* by Ian Anthony, 38–57. Stockholm: SIPRI.

Kirshner, Jonathan. 1997. "The Microfoundations of Economic Sanctions." *Security Studies* 6 (3): 32–64.

Kitade, Daisuke. 2016. *Considering the Effects of Japanese Sanctions Against Russia.* Tokyo: Mitsui Global Strategic Studies Institute.

Klein, Margarete. 2012. "Towards a "New Look" of the Russian Armed Forces?: Organizational and Personnel Changes." In *The Russian Armed Forces in Transition,* by Roger McDermott, Bertil Nygren, and Carolina Vendil Pallin, 29–48. London and New York: Routledge.

Kliment'yeva, Lyudmila. 2014. "Minpromtorg: sanktsii YES i SSHA na Rossii poka nikak ne skazyvayutsya." *Vedomosti,* April 8.

Kontorovich, V., and A. Wein. 2009. "What Did Soviet Rulers Maximise?" *Europe-Asia Studies* 61: 1579–1601.

Kornai, Janos. 1992. *The Socialist System: The Political Economy of Communism.* Cambridge: Cambridge University Press.

Korolkov, Alexander. 2016. *Russia Continues to Buy Iveco LMV Armored Cars from Italy.* January 25. www.rbth.com/defence/2016/01/25/russia-continues-to-buy-iveco-lmv-armored-cars-from-italy_562027.

Koshovets, O., and H. Ganichev. 2015. "Eksport rossiiskikh vooruzhenii kak osobyi faktor razvitiya vysokotekhnologichnoi promyshlennosti Rossii." *Problemy prognozirovania* 2: 121–134.

Kotkin, Stephen. 2016. "Russia's Perpetual Geopolitics." *Foreign Affairs* 95 (2): 2–15.

Kozlov, Dmitri. 2017. *Oborudovaniye ne toy sistemy. Minprirody i Minpromtorg sporyat ob importozameshchenii.* July 17. www.kommersant.ru/doc/3359424?utm_source=kommersant&utm_medium=business&utm_campaign=four.

Krause, Keith. 1992. *Arms and the State: Patterns of Military Production and Trade*. Cambridge: Cambridge University Press.

Kremlin.ru. 2014. *Soveshchaniye po ekonomicheskim voprosam*. April 9. http://kremlin .ru/events/president/news/20756.

2017. *Rasshirennoe zasedanie kollegii Ministerstva oborony*. December 11. http:// kremlin.ru/events/president/news/50913.

Kryuchkova, Yevgeniya. 2015. "Promyshlenniye stavki sdelany." *Kommersant*, December 1.

Kuboniwa, Masaaki. 2017. "Can Russia's Military Expansion be Impossible Mission Force for its V-Shaped Growth Recovery under Declining Oil Prices?" *Russian Centre for Research Working Paper Series* 64.

2016. "Estimating GDP and Foreign Rents of the Oil and Gas Sector in the USSR Then and Russia Now." *BOFIT Policy Brief* 10.

Kuboniwa, Masaaki, Shinichiro Tabata, and Nataliya Ustinova. 2005. "How Large Is the Oil and Gas Sector of Russia? A Research Report." *Eurasian Geography and Economics* 46 (1): 68–76.

Kudrin, Alexei, and Evsei Gurvich. 2014. "Novoy modeli rosta dlya rossiyskoy ekonomiki." *Voprosy Ekonomiki* (12): 4–32.

Kudrin, Alexei, and Alexander Knobel'. 2017. "Byudzhetnaya politika kak istochnik ekonomicheskogo rosta." *Voprosy Ekonokiki* (10).

Kudrin, Alexei, and Ilya Sokolov. 2017. "Byudzhetnyye pravila kak instrument sbalansirovannoy byudzhetnoy politiki." *Voprosy Ekonomiki* (11): 5–27.

Kuvshinova, Ol'ga. 2015. "My ne dobilis' samogo vazhnogo." *Vedomosti*, June 22.

Kuznetsov, Boris, Tatiana Dolgopyatova, Victoria Golikova, Ksenia Gonchar, Andrei Yakovlev, and Yevgeny Yasin. 2011. "Russian Manufacturing Revisited: Industrial Enterprises at the Start of the Crisis." *Post-Soviet Affairs* 27 (4): 366–386.

Kuztensov, Vladimir. 2014. *Rosneft Gets Central Bank Help Refinancing $7 Billion Loan*. December 12. www.bloomberg.com/news/articles/2014-12-12/rosneft-s-10-8-billion-refinancing-driven-by-central-bank-cash.

Lavigne, Marie. 1995. *The Economics of Transition: From Socialist Economy to Market Economy*. London: Palgrave Macmillan.

Lavrov, Sergey. 2014. *Vystupleniye Ministra inostrannykh del Rossii S.V.Lavrova na otkrytoy lektsii po aktual'nym voprosam vneshney politiki Rossiyskoy Federatsii*. October 20. www.mid.ru/en/foreign_policy/news/-/asset_publisher/cKNonkJE02Bw/content/id/716270?p_p_id=101_INSTANCE_cKNonkJE02Bw&_101_INSTANCE_cKNonkJE02Bw_languageId=ru_RU.

Lenta.ru. 2015. *Putin podpisal zakon ob amnistii kapitalov*. June 8. https://lenta.ru/news/2015/06/08/amnkap/.

2017. *V ODK rasskazali o tempakh vypuska vertoletnykh dvigateley vmesto ukrainskikh*. July 18. https://lenta.ru/news/2017/07/18/engines/.

Lo, Bobo. 2009. *Axis of Convenience: Moscow, Beijing, and the New Geopolitics*. Washington, DC: Brookings Institution Press.

Lo, Bobo, and Fiona Hill. 2013. "Putin's Pivot: Why Russia Is Looking East." *Foreign Affairs*. www.foreignaffairs.com/articles/russian-federation/2013-07-31/putins-pivot.

Major, Solomon. 2012. "Timing Is Everything: Economic Sanctions, Regime Type and Domestic Instability." *International Interactions* 38 (1): 79–110.

Malle, Silvana. 2017. "Russia and China: Partners or Competitors? Views from Russia." In *Understanding China Today: An Exploration of Politics, Economics, Society, and International Relations*, by Silvio Beretta, Axel Berkofsky, and Lihong Zhang, 45–77. Springer International Publishing.

Malle, Silvana, and Julian Cooper. 2014. "The Pendulum Moves from Europe to Asia. Modernizing Siberia and the Far East. Economic and Security Issues." *Journal of Eurasian Studies* 5 (1): 21–38.

Malmlöf, Tomas. 2016. "A Case Study of Russo-Ukrainian Defense Industrial Cooperation: Russian Dilemmas." *Journal of Slavic Military Studies* 29 (1): 1–22.

Malysheva, Yelena. 2015. "Minpromtorg tayno prodvigayet novyye ogranicheniya na zakupki medizdeliy." *Gazeta.ru*, March 24.

Manturov, Denis. 2017. "Razvitiye vopreki sanktsiyam." *Izvestiya*, August 9.

Mau, Vladimir. 2016. *Krizisy i uroki: Ekonomika Rossii v epokhu turbulentnosti.* Moscow: Gaidar Institute.

———. 2017. *Russia's Economy in an Epoch of Turbulence.* London and New York: Routledge.

Mau, Vladimir, and Irina Starodubrovskaya. 2001. *The Challenge of Revolution: Contemporary Russia in Historical Perspective.* Oxford: Oxford University Press.

Medevdev, Dmitri, Interview with Five Television Channels. 2015a. *In Conversation with Dmitri Medvedev.* December 9.

———. 2015b. *A Meeting on Sectoral Import Substitution Programmes.* April 3. http://government.ru/en/news/17521/.

———. 2015c. *Joint Meeting of Government Commissions on Import Substitution and on the Socioeconomic Development of the Far East and the Baikal region.* December 2015. http://government.ru/en/news/21140/.

———. 2015d. *Prime Minister Dmitri Medvedev's Opening Remarks at the Meeting of the Presidium of the Presidential Council for Economic Modernisation and Innovation-Based Development of Russia.* April 17. http://government.ru/en/news/17709/.

———. 2016a. *Meeting of the Government Import Substitution Commission.* January 26. http://government.ru/en/news/21577/.

———. 2016b. August 20. www.government.ru/en/news/19246.

Mehdiyeva, Nazrin. 2017. *When Sanctions Bite: Global Export Leadership in a Competitive World and Russia's Energy Strategy to 2035.* Russian Studies Review. Rome: NATO Defence College.

Merlevede, Bruno, Koen Schoors, and Bas Van Aarle. 2009. "Russia from Bust to Boom and Back: Oil Price, Dutch Disease and Stabilisation Fund." *Comparative Economic Studies* 51 (2): 213–241.

Ministry for Energy of the Russian Federation. 2016. *Aleksandr Novak prinyal uchastiye v zasedanii Pravitel'stvennoy Komissii po Importozameshcheniyu.* January 26. http://minenergo.gov.ru/node/3982.

Ministry for Industry and Trade of the Russian Federation. 2015. *Prikaz No.645.* March 31. http://prom.pnzreg.ru/files/prom_pnzreg_ru/neftegazovoe(1).pdf.

Ministry of Defence of the Russian Federation. 2016. *Boevoi sostav VMF Rossii do 2018 goda popolniat bolee 50 korablei.* April 18. http://oborona.gov.ru/news/view/9961.

Ministry of Economic Development. 2009. *Kontseptsiya sozdeniya mezhdunarodgovo tsentra v Rossiiskoy Federatsii.* http://economy.gov.ru/minec/activity/sections/finances/creation/conceptmfc.

Ministry of Economic Development of the Russian Federation. 2012. *Kontseptsiya dolgsrochnogo sotsial'no-ekonomicheskogo razvitiya Rossiiskoi Federatsii do 2020.* March. www.economy.gov.ru/wps/portal/e-russia.

2015. *Pravitel'stvennaya komissiya po importozameshcheniyu.* http://economy.gov.ru/minec/activity/sections/importsubstitution/.

Ministry of Energy of the Russian Federation. 2016. *Aleksandr Novak prinyal uchastiye v zasedanii Pravitel'stvennoy Komissii po Importozameshcheniyu.* January 28. http://minenergo.gov.ru/node/3982.

Ministry of Energy. 2009. *Energeticheskaya strategiya Rossii na period do 2030 goda.* Moscow: Ministry of Energy. http://minenergo.gov.ru/node/1026.

2015a. *Energeticheskaya strategiya Rossii na period do 2035 goda.* http://minenergo .gov.ru/node/1920.

2015b. *Minenergo i Minpromtorg pristupili k sozdaniyu avtomatizirovannoy sistemy monitoringa sostoyaniya rynka mashinostroitel'nogo oborudovaniya, tekhnicheskikh ustroystv, komplektuyushchikh i programmnogo obespecheniya, kritichnykh dlya tekhnologicheskikh protsessov organizatsiy TEK Possii, podlezhashchikh importozameshcheniyu.* December 28. http://minenergo.gov.ru/node/3735.

2017. *Importozameshcheniye v TEK.* May 16. https://minenergo.gov.ru/node/7693.

Monaghan, Andrew. 2011. "The Vertikal: Power and Authority in Russia." *International Affairs* 88 (1): 1–16.

2014. *Defibrillating the Vertikal? Putin and Russian Grand Strategy.* Russia and Eurasia Programme. London: Chatham House.

2016. *The New Politics of Russia: Interpreting Change.* Manchester: Manchester University Press.

Mordoshenko, Olga. 2015. "Burovaya ugroza." *Kommersant,* September 17.

Mordyushenko, Olga, and Kirill Melnikov. 2015. "Rosneft' nastrelyayet 10 trillionov." *Kommersant,* May 19.

Moscow Times. 2015. *Obama Says Western Sanctions Have Left Russia's Economy "In Tatters".* January 21. https://themoscowtimes.com/articles/obama-says-western-sanctions-have-left-russias-economy-in-tatters-43069.

Movchan, Andrei. 2017. "Pamyati rossiyskikh bankov: kak perezagruzit' nerabotayushchuyu sistemu." *RBK.ru,* September 18.

Mueller, J. 1970. "Presidential Popularity from Johnson to Truman." *American Political Science Review* 64 (1): 18–34.

Mukhin, Vladimir. 2015. *Sanktsii sryvayut gosprogrammu vooruzheniy.* January 22. www.ng.ru/armies/2015-01-22/2_sanktsii.html.

Nazarova, Galya. 2014. "Russkiy Soft." *Sankt-Peterburgskie Vedomosti,* February 3.

Neftegazavaya Vertikal'. 2015. *Importozameshchenie* (4) (April).

Neftegazovoe Novosti. 2017. *Sberbank vydast "Rosnefti" kredit na 125 mlrd rub.* July 12. http://oilgasfield.ru/news/137013.html.

Nikitin, Anton. 2017. *V Minpromtorge nazvali sroki polnogo importozameshcheniya ukrainskikh komplektuyushchikh.* May 28. https://vz.ru/news/2017/5/28/872150.html.

Nikolsky, Alexei. 2015. "Russian Defense and Dual-Use Technology Programs." *Moscow Defence Brief,* 18–20.

2016a. *Rossiya i Indiya posotrudnichayut na neskol'ko milliardov dollarov.* October 16. www.vedomosti.ru/politics/articles/2016/10/17/661178-rossiya-indiya-posotrudnichayut.

2016b. *Kitay vernulsya v pyaterku krupneyshikh importerov rossiyskogo oruzhiya.* November 2. www.vedomosti.ru/politics/articles/2016/11/02/663309-kitai-krup neishih-importerov.

2017. *U novoy gosprogrammy vooruzheniy budut novyye prioritety.* May 19. www.vedomosti.ru/politics/articles/2017/05/19/690524-novoi-gosprogrammi.

North, Douglass. 1981. *Structure and Change in Economic History.* London and New York: Norton.

1990. *Institutions, Institutional Change and Economic Performance.* Cambridge: Cambridge University Press.

North, Douglass, John Wallis, and Barry Weingast. 2009. *Violence and Social Orders: A Conceptual Framework for Interpreting Recorded Human History.* Cambridge and New York: Cambridge University Press.

North, Douglass, John Wallis, Barry Weingast, and Stephen Webb. 2012. *In the Shadow of Violence: Politics, Economics, and the Problems of Development.* Cambridge and New York: Cambridge University Press.

Nuland, Victoria. 2016. *Testimony Victoria Nuland: Russian Violations of Borders, Treaties, and Human Rights.* June 7. https://ua.usembassy.gov/testimony-vic toria-nuland-russian-violations-borders-treaties-human-rights/.

Office of Foreign Assets Control. 2014. *Changes to the Sectoral Sanctions Identifications Lists Since January 1, 2014.* Washington, DC.

Office of Technology Assessment. 1986. *Technology and Soviet Energy Availability.* Washington, DC: Office of Technology Assessment.

Offshore Energy Today. 2015. *North Atlantic Drilling and Rosneft Give Themselves More Time.* April 17. www.offshoreenergytoday.com/north-atlantic-drilling-ros neft-give-themselves-more-time/.

Oilcapital.ru. 2014. *Rosneft v sluchae okonchatel'nogo vykhoda Exxon iz proekta Kars-kogo morya ne budet iskat' partnera – Sechin.* October 30. www.oilcapital.ru/company/255623.html.

Orlova, Natalya. 2014. "Finansovyye sanktsii protiv Rossii: vliyaniye na ekonomiku i ekonomicheskuyu politiku." *Voprosy Ekonomiki* (12): 54–66.

Orlova, Nataliya, and Sergei Egiev. 2015. "Strukturnye foktory zamyedleniya rosta Rossiyskoy ekonomiki." *Voprosy Ekonomiki* (12): 69–84.

"O strategii." 2017. *O strategii ekonomicheskoi bezopasnosti Rossiiskoi Federatsii na period do 2030.* http://kremlin.ru/acts/bank/41921.

Ostrom, C., and Job, B. 1986. "The President and the Political Use of Force." *American Political Science Review* 80 (2): 541–566.

Overland, Indra, Jakub Godzimirski, Lars Petter Lunden, and Daniel Fjaertoft. 2013. "Rosneft's Offshore Partnerships: The Re-opening of the Russian Petroleum Frontier?" *Polar Record* 140–153.

Oxenstierna, Susanne. 2010. *Russia's Nuclear Energy Expansion.* Stockholm: FOI.

2014. "Nuclear Power in Russia's Energy Policies." In *Russian Energy and Security up to 2030,* by Susanne Oxenstierna, 150–168. London and New York: Routledge.

Papchenkova, Margarita, and Lilia Biryukova. 2014. *"Sergei Glaz'yev znayet, kak ogra-dit' Rossiyu ot sanktsiy" Vedomosti.* April 25.

Pape, Robert. 1997. "Why Economic Sanctions Do Not Work." *International Security* 22 (2): 90–136.

1998. "Why Economic Sanctions Still Do Not Work." *International Security* 23 (1): 66–77.

Pashutinskaya, Elena. 2017. *Inostrantsy vdvoye snizili dolyu vo vneshnem gosdolge Rossii za vremya sanktsiy.* September 3. www.rbc.ru/finances/01/09/2017/59a93f989a7947 0ba6d9d8db?from=main.

Peksen, Dursen, and A. Cooper Drury. 2010. "Coercive or Corrosive: The Negative Impact of Economic Sanctions on Democracy." *International Interactions* 36 (3): 240–264.

Peremitin, Georgiy, and Alina Fadeyeva. 2017. "RFPI i kitayskiy fond proinvestiruyut v Eurasia Drilliing." *RBC.ru,* June 1.

Petlevoy, Vitaliy. 2017. "Raskryta tochnaya summa pokupki kitaytsami doli v 'Rosnefti'." *Vedomosti,* October 16.

Pettersen, Trude. 2015. *New Giant Shipyard to Build Russia's Arctic Tankers and Rigs.* February 25. http://thebarentsobserver.com/industry/2016/02/new-giant-ship yard-build-russias-arctic-tankers-and-rigs.

Pierre, Andrew. 1982. *The Global Politics of Arms Sales.* Washington, DC: Council on Foreign Relations.

Popov, Vladimir. 2014. *Mixed Fortunes: An Economic History of China, Russia, and the West.* Oxford: Oxford University Press.

Popov, Yegor. 2015. "Kommersant." *"Zvezda" oboydetsya bez FNB,* December 4.

Portela, Clara. 2010. *European Union Sanctions and Foreign Policy: When and Why Do They Work?* London and New York: Routledge.

Prime.ru. 2017. *RF s 1 yanvarya poluchayet skidku SWIFT po tarifu na obmen finsoobsh-cheniyami.* October 16. www.1prime.ru/finance/20171016/828021995.html.

Privlov, A., and A. Volkov. 2007. "Rashushdeniye o reyderstve po metode Barona Kyuve." *Ekspert.* May 14. http://expert.ru/expert/2007/18/sobstvennost/

Pukhov, Ruslan, and Colby Howard, eds. 2015. *Brothers Armed: Military Aspects of the Crisis in Ukraine.* Moscow: Centre for Analysis of Strategies and Technologies.

Putin, Vladimir. 2007. *Interview.* June 4. www.spiegel.de/international/world/g-8-inter view-with-vladimir-putin-i-am-a-true-democrat-a-486345-2.html.

2012a. *Biudzhetnoe poslanie Prezidenta RF o biudzhetnoi politike v 2013–2015 godakh.* June 28. www.kremlin.ru/acts/15786.

2012b. *Meeting of the Commission for Military Technology Cooperation with Foreign States.* July 2. http://en.kremlin.ru/events/president/news/15865.

2012c. "Rossiya i menyayushchiysya mir." *Rossiskaya Gazeta,* February 27.

2014a. *Bol'shaya press-konferentsiya Vladimira Putina.* December 18. http://kremlin .ru/events/president/news/47250.

2014b. *Poslaniye Prezidenta Federal'nomu Sobraniyu.* December 4. http://kremlin.ru/ events/president/news/47173.

2015. *Prezident RF Vladimir Putin obratilsya k federal'nomu sobraniyu s yezhegod-nym poslaniyem.* December 3. http://minenergo.gov.ru/node/3507.

RANEPA. 2012. "Posledstviya slaboy konkurentsii: kolichestvennyye otsenki i vy- vody dlya politiki." *Ekonomicheskaya Politika* 5–53.

RBK.ru. 2014. *Zapadnyye kompanii nashli sposob oboyti sanktsii dlya raboty v Arktike.* December 29. https://www.rbc.ru/business/29/12/2014/549d81419a794786d446225f.

2015. "SMI uznali o nedovol'stve FSB sdelkoy Schlumberger i Eurasia Drilling." *RBK. ru,* August 25.

Recknagel, Charles. 2012. *Explainer: How Does a SWIFT Ban Hurt Iran?* March 16. www.rferl.org/a/explainer_how_does_swift_ban_hurt_iran/24518153.html.

Renz, Bettina. 2014. "Russian Military Capabilities after 20 Years of Reform." *Survival: Global Politics and Strategy* 56 (3): 61–84.

Renz, Bettina, and Rod Thornton. 2012. "Russian Military Modernization: Cause, Course, and Consequences." *Problems of Post-Communism* 59 (1): 44–54.

RFE/RL. 2017. *Russia Steps Up Efforts to Cut Reliance on U.S. Dollar, Payments System.* August 8. www.rferl.org/a/russia-steps-up-efforts-cut-reliance-us-dollar-visa-pay ments-system-mastercard/28664423.html.

RIA Novosti. 2013. *Rogozin: FSVTS segodnya yavlyayetsya vtorym vneshnepoliticheskim vedomstvom.* December 11. https://ria.ru/defense_safety/20131211/983472868 .html.

——— 2014. *Putin: kontakty s KNR po linii minoborony - vazhnyy faktor bezopasnosti.* May 20. https://ria.ru/defense_safety/20140520/1008512315.html.

——— 2015a. *Dvorkovich: sredstva FNB, vozmozhno, vydelyat' na verf 'Zvezda'.* April 3. http://ria.ru/economy/20150403/1056442172.html#ixzz41f6Acbvc.

——— 2015b. *Medvedev nastaivayet na stroitel'stve trekh ocheredey zavoda 'Zvezda.* December 18. http://ria.ru/economy/20151218/1344234557.html#ixzz41f7zFadj.

——— 2015c. *Minenergo opredelilo tseli po importozameshcheniyu v neftegazovoy otrasli.* March 11. http://ria.ru/economy/20150311/1051917023.html.

——— 2015d. *Minenergo opredelilo tseli po importozameshcheniyu v neftegazovoy otrasli.* March 11. http://ria.ru/economy/20150311/1051917023.html.

——— 2016a. *Fregaty 22350 pervymi poluchat rossiyskiye dvigateli vmesto Ukrainskikh.* December 29. https://ria.ru/arms/20161229/1484869981.html.

——— 2016b. *Kitay nameren priobresti shirokuyu lineyku rossiyskikh vertoletov.* November 2. https://ria.ru/defense_safety/20161102/1480513970.html.

——— 2016c. *ODK gotova sozdat' dvigatel' dlya rossiysko-kitayskogo vertoleta.* November 1. https://ria.ru/defense_safety/20161101/1480435782.html.

——— 2016d. *Pervoye sudno na "Zvezde" budet postroyeno v 2019 godu.* September 1.

——— 2016e. *Postavki Su-35 v Kitay poka ne nachalis', rabota po kontraktu prodolzhayetsya.* November 19. https://ria.ru/defense_safety/20161119/1481705114.html.

——— 2016f. *Postavki Su-35 v Kitay poka ne nachalis', rabota po kontraktu prodolzhayetsya.* November 19. https://ria.ru/defense_safety/20161119/1481705114.html.

——— 2016g. *Rossiya dolzhna byt' nezavisima v oboronnoy promyshlennosti, zayavil Putin.* December 5. https://ria.ru/defense_safety/20161205/1482894814.html.

——— 2016h. *Rossiya "v samom aktivnom rezhime" vedet peregovory s Indoneziyey po Su-35.* November 2. https://ria.ru/defense_safety/20161102/1480519618.html.

——— 2016i. *Rossiya "v samom aktivnom rezhime" vedet peregovory s Indoneziyey po Su-35.* November 2. https://ria.ru/defense_safety/20161102/1480519618.html.

——— 2016j. *V FSVTS rasskazali o sotrudnichestve s Frantsiyey.* October 18. https://ria.ru/ defense_safety/20161018/1479485262.html.

——— 2017a. *Rosoboroneksport: sanktsii ne sorvali ni odin dogovor na eksport oruzhiya.* July 18. https://ria.ru/defense_safety/20170718/1498676743.html.

——— 2017b. *Rossiyskiye kompanii adaptirovalis' k sanktsiyam, zayavil Manturov.* October 27. https://ria.ru/economy/20171027/1507648328.html.

——— 2017c. *Shoygu: uglubleniye vzaimodeystviya s Kitayem yavlyayetsya prioritetom dlya Rossii.* December 8. https://ria.ru/defense_safety/20171208/1510493761.html.

Robinson, Neil. 1999. "The Global Economy, Reform and Crisis in Russia." *Review of International Political Economy* 6 (4): 531–564.

2001. "The Myth of Equilibrium: Winner Power, Fiscal Crisis and Russian Economic Reform." *Communist and Post-Communist Studies* 34 (4): 423–446.

Rochlitz, Michael. 2013. "Corporate Raiding and the Role of the State in Russia." *Post-Soviet Affairs* 30 (2–3): 89–114.

Roffey, Roger. 2013. "Russian Science and Technology Is Still Having Problems: Implications for Defense Research." *Journal of Slavic Military Studies* 26 (2): 162–188.

Rosbalt.ru. 2015. *Rogozin obeshchayet preodolet' zavisimost' OPK ot ukrainskikh obraztsov k 2018 godu.* July 1. www.rosbalt.ru/main/2015/07/01/1414358.html.

Rosgeo. 2015. *Rosgeologia to Implement Measures towards Improving Operational Efficiency.* February 23. http://rosgeo.com/en/content/rosgeologia-implement-measures-towards-improving-operational-efficiency.

Rosneft. 2014. *Rosneft, Seadrill and North Atlantic Drilling Expand Cooperation.* May 24. www.rosneft.com/news/pressrelease/240520143.html.

2015. *Rosneft Closes the Transaction for the Acquisition of a Russian Oilfield Service Company from Trican Well Service Ltd.* August 20. www.rosneft.com/news/press release/20082015.html.

Rostec.ru. 2017. *Sergey Chemezov: My zavershim importozameshcheniye po komplektuyushchim k 2020 godu.* July 19. http://rostec.ru/news/4520711.

Rotnem, Thomas E. 2018. "Putin's Arctic Strategy." *Problems of Post-Communism* 65 (1): 1–17.

Rowe, David. 2001. *Manipulating the Market: Understanding Economic Sanctions, Institutional Change, and the Political Unity of White Rhodesia.* Ann Arbor: University of Michigan Press.

Rozhdestvenskaya, Yana. 2017. "Yevropeyskiye neftyaniki stradayut ot sanktsiy men'she, chem amerikanskiye." *Kommersant,* June 25.

RT. 2014. *Russia to Redirect Trade Elsewhere in Case of EU-US Sanctions.* March 19. www.rt.com/business/russia-eu-us-sanctions-742/.

Russoft. 2013. *10th Annual Survey of the Russian Software Developing Industry and Software Exports.* Moscow: Russoft Association.

Rutland, Peter. 1985. *The Myth of the Plan: Lessons of Soviet Planning Experience.* London: Hutchinson and Co.

Sakwa, Richard. 2009. *The Quality of Freedom: Putin, Khodorkovsky and the Yukos Affair.* Oxford and New York: Oxford University Press.

2014. *Putin and the Oligarch: The Khodorkovsky-Yukos Affair.* London and New York: IB Tauris.

Sanchez-Andres, Antonio. 1998. "Privatisation, Decentralisation and Production Adjustment in the Russian Defence Industry." *Europe-Asia Studies* 50 (2): 241–255.

2000. "Restructuring the Defence Industry and Arms Production in Russia." *Europe-Asia Studies* 52 (5): 897–914.

Security Council of the Russian Federation. 2015. *Strategiya natsional'noi bezopasnosti Rossiiskoi Federatsii do 2020 goda.* http://kremlin.ru/acts/bank/40391.

Shadrina, Tat'yana. 2016. *Pravitel'stvo opredelilo trebovaniya dlya navigatorov.* June 26. https://rg.ru/2017/06/26/pravitelstvo-opredelilo-trebovaniia-dlia-navigatorov.html.

Sharafutdinova, Gulnaz, and Gregory Kisunko. 2014. *Governors and Governing Institutions: a Comparative Study of State-Business Relations in Russia's Regions.* World Bank Policy Research Working Paper, World Bank.

Sharkovskiy, Aleksandr. 2016. "Gosoboronzakaz stimuliruet promyshlennost." *Nezavisimoe Voennoe Obozrenie,* April 22.

Sherfinski, David. 2014. "McCain: 'Russia Is a Gas Station Masquerading as a Country'." *Washington Post,* March 14.

Sherr, James. 2013. *Hard Diplomacy and Soft Coercion.* London: Royal Institute for International Affairs.

Shestopal, Ol'ga. 2015a. "'TsB zaimetsya bol'shim biznesom'." *Kommersant,* July 20.
———. 2015b. "Mir udarit bankam po karmanam." *Kommersant,* November 17.

Shlapentokh, Vladimir, and Anna Aruntunyan. 2013. *Freedom, Represssion, and Private Property in Russia.* Cambridge and New York: Cambridge University Press.

Shliefer, Andrey, and Daniel Treisman. 2000. *Without a Map: Political Tactics and Economic Reform in Russia.* Cambridge: MIT Press.

Shlykov, Vitaly. 1995. "Economic Readjustment within the Russian Defense-Industrial Complex." *Security Dialogue* 26 (1): 19–34.
———. 2004. "The Economics of Defense in Russia and the Legacy of Structural Militarization." In *The Russian Military: Power and Policy,* by Steven Miller and Dmitri Trenin, 157–182. Cambridge: MIT Press.

Skocpol, Theda. 1979. *States and Social Revolutions: A comparative Analysis of France, Russia and China.* Cambridge and New York: Cambridge University Press.

Smith, A. 1996. "The Success and Use of Economic Sanctions." *International Interactions* 21 (3): 229–245.

Soldatkin, Vladimir. 2016. *Russia Eyes Unified Payment Systems with China: PM.* November 4. www.reuters.com/article/us-russia-china-payments-sanctions/russia-eyes-unified-payment-systems-with-china-pm-idUSKBN12Z1RU?il=0.

Soldatkin, Vladimir, and Olesya Astakhova. 2016. *Russia's Yamal LNG Gets Round Sanctions with $12 bln Chinese Loan Deal.* April 29. http://uk.reuters.com/article/russia-china-yamal-idUKL5N17W2G8.

Solnick, Steven. 1998. *Stealing from the State: Control and Collapse in Soviet Institutions.* Cambridge, MA: Harvard University Press.

Soyustov, Andrey. 2015. *Dvizhki-2: letayushchiy "pylesos", chemodany deneg i Serdyukov.* December 22. https://riafan.ru/491620-dvizhki-2-letayushij-pylesos-chemodany-deneg-i-serdyukov.

Starinskaya, Galina. 2015a. "Rosneft" pokupayet rossiyskiy biznes kanadskoy Trican." *Vedomosti,* August 16.
———. 2015b. "Oborudovaniye nuzhno proizvodit' v Rossii." *Vedomosti,* September 23.

Stockholm International Peace Research Institute. 2016. *SIPRI Military Expenditure Database.* www.sipri.org/research/armaments/milex/milex_database.

Streltsov, Dmitri. 2015. *Russian-Japanese Relations: A Systemic Crisis or a New Opportunity?* Moscow: Russian International Affairs Council.

Stuenkel, Oliver. 2016. *Post Western World.* London and New York: Polity.

Sutela, Pekka. 2012. *The Political Economy of Putin's Russia.* London and New York: Routledge.

Szakonyi, David. 2017. "Foreign Direct Investment into Russia Since the Annexation of Crimea." *Russian Analytical Digest* (Centre for Security Studies, Zurich).

TASS. 2014. *Ukraine's Poroshenko Stops Military Cooperation with Russia.* June 17. http://tass.com/world/736363.

2015a. "Dvorkovich: limity na vydeleniye sredstv FNB blizki k ischerpaniyu." *Tass. ru,* April 3.

2015b. *Rogozin: rossiyskaya "oboronka" k 2018 godu preodoleyet zavisimost' ot postavok s Ukrainy.* July 1. http://tass.ru/armiya-i-opk/2085106.

2016a. *"Rosneft'" i ONGC podpisali dogovor kupli-prodazhi 11% aktsiy "Vankornefti".* September 14. http://tass.ru/ekonomika/3621437.

2016b. *Dolya vooruzheniy v rossiyskom eksporte sostavlyayet 4.2%.* November 2. http://tass.ru/armiya-i-opk/3755729.

2016c. *Russia Will Supply First Four Su-35 Fighters to China by End of 2016 – Source.* February 19. http://tass.com/defense/857813.

2016d. *V Kitaye vidyat neobkhodimost' razvivat' sotrudnichestvo s VMF Rossii.* November 22. https://ria.ru/defense_safety/20161104/1480684197.html.

2016e. *VMF Rossii v 2018 godu poluchit ot "Severnoy verfi" srazu tri korveta.* September 3. http://tass.ru/armiya-i-opk/3590179.

2017a. *OSK dostroit dlya Indii dva fregata proyekta 11356, zalozhennyye dlya VMF RF.* August 23. http://tass.ru/armiya-i-opk/4500131.

2017b. *Schlumberger dostigla soglasheniya o priobretenii boleye poloviny aktsiy rossiyskoy EDC.* July 21. http://tass.ru/ekonomika/4429350.

Taylor, Brendan. 2010. *Sanctions as Grand Strategy.* London: IISS/Routledge.

Taylor, Brian. 2011. *State Building in Putin's Russia: Policing and Coercion after Communism.* Cambridge and New York: Cambridge University Press.

Teksler, Aleksey. 2015. *Remarks by Deputy Minister for Energy.* October 2. http://minenergo.gov.ru/node/1367.

Tetryakov, P. 2014. "'Sistema' dolzhna vernut' gosudarstvu ostavshiyesya u neye aktsii 'Bashnefti'." *Vedomosti,* December 11.

The White House Office of the Press Secretary. 2014a. *Obama White House Archives.* May 2. https://obamawhitehouse.archives.gov/the-press-office/2014/05/02/remarks-president-obama-and-german-chancellor-merkel-joint-press-confere.

2014b. *Executive Order 13360 – Blocking Property of Certain Persons Contributing to the Situation in Ukraine.* March 6.

2014c. *Executive Order 13661 – Blocking Property of Additional Persons Contributing to the Situation in Ukraine.* March 18.

2014d. *Executive Order 13662 – Blocking Property of Additional Persons Contributing to the Situation in Ukraine.* March 20.

Thomson, Elspeth, and Nobuhiro Horii. 2009. "China's Energy Security: Challenges and Priorities." *Eurasian Geography and Economics* 50 (6): 643–664.

Tilly, Charles. 1992. *Coercion, Capital, and European States, AD 990–1990.* Oxford: Blackwell.

Tomiuc, Eugen. 2016. "Nuland: No Deadline for Ukraine Vote, Sanctions to Stay Until Minsk Fulfilled." *Radio Free Europe Radio Liberty,* April 27.

Tompson, William. 2004. "Banking Reform in Russia: Problems and Prospects." *OECD Economics Working Paper No. 410* (OECD).

2005. "Putting Yukos in Perspective." *Post-Soviet Affairs* 21 (2): 159–181.

Topalov, Aleksei. 2014. *ExxonMobil vygnali s Sakhalina.* August 15. www.gazeta.ru/business/2014/05/15/6034441.shtml.

Topalov, Alexei, and Rustyem Falchev. 2014. *Putin prodiktoval Kitayu tsenu.* May 21. www.gazeta.ru/business/2014/05/21/6042329.shtml.

Treisman, Daniel. 2010. *The Return: Russia's Journey from Gorbachev to Medvedev.* New York: Simon and Schuster.

Trenin, Dmitri. 2016. "The Revival of Russia's Military." *Foreign Affairs* 95 (2): 32–38.

———. 2017. "Russia Has Grand Designs for the International Order." *Moscow Times,* October 26.

Ulyukaev, Alexei. 2009. *Sovremennaya denezhno-kreditnaya politika: Problemy i perspektivy.* Moscow: Delo.

Umnoye proizvodstvo. 2014. *Programmu importozameshcheniya otsenili v 50 mlrd. rubley.* August 12. www.umpro.ru/index.php?page_id=2.

United Nations Comtrade. 2017. *Commodity Trade Statistics Database.* United Nations Statistics Division. http://comtrade.un.org/.

United Nations Office on Drugs and Crime. 2013. *Global Study on Homicide.* Vienna: United Nations.

US Treasury. 2014a. "Executive Order 13685 – Blocking Property of Certain Persons and Prohibiting Certain Transactions With Respect to the Crimea Region of Ukraine." December 19.

———. 2014b. *Treasury Sanctions Russian Officials, Members of the Russian Leadership's Inner Circle, and an Entity for Involvement in the Situation in Ukraine.* March 20. www.treasury.gov/press-center/press-releases/Pages/jl23331.aspx.

van Bergeijk, Peter. 2009. *Economic Diplomacy and the Geography of International Trade.* Aldershot: Edward Elgar.

Vaseykina, Inna. 2014. *Glava VTB: Otklyucheniye Rossii ot mezhdunarodnoy platezh-noy sistemy SWIFT - eto voyna.* December 4. www.mk.ru/economics/2014/12/04/glava-vtb-otklyuchenie-rossii-ot-mezhdunarodnoy-platezhnoy-sistemy-swift-eto-voyna.html.

Vedomosti. 2016. *Putin: OPK dolzhen narashchivat' proizvodstvo grazhdanskoy pro-duktsii.* December 1.

Vernikov, Andrei. 2012. "The Impact of State-Controlled Banks on the Russian Banking Sector." *Eurasian Geography and Economics* 53 (2): 250–266.

———. 2013. "'Natsional'nye chempiony' v strukture rossiiskogo rynka bankovskikh uslug'." *Voprosy Ekonomiki* (3): 94–108.

———. 2017. "Measuring Institutional Change: The Case of the Russian Banking Industry." *Journal of Institutional Studies* 9 (2): 119–136.

Vesti.ru. 2017. *TSB gotov zashchitit' finansovuyu sistemu RF ot sanktsiy.* November 16. www.vestifinance.ru/articles/93878.

Vlasova, Anastasiya. 2017. *V MID RF reshili povremenit' s otkazom ot dollara.* August 23. www.mk.ru/economics/2017/08/23/v-mid-rf-reshili-povremenit-s-otkazom-ot-dollara.html.

Volkov, Vadim. 2002. *Violent Entrepreneurs: The Use of Force in the Making of Russian Capitalism.* Ithaca: Cornell University Press.

von Soest, Christian, and Michael Wahman. 2015. "Are Democratic Sanctions Really Counterproductive?" *Democratization* 22 (6): 957–980.

Voronov, Vladimir. 2016. *Importozamechenye dlya Rogozina*. January 10. www.svoboda
.org/content/article/27477140.html.

Voyenno-promyshlennyy kur'yer. 2015. *V Kolomne razrabotan dvigatel', kotoryi zamenit importnye analogi na korabliakh VMF RF*. June 19. http://vpk.name/news/
134224_v_kolomne_razrabotan_dvigatel_kotoryii_zamenit_importnyie_analogi_
na_korablyah_vmf_rf.html.

VPK.ru. 2013. *Primernyi kolichestvennyi sostav VVS RF k 2020 godu*. March 12. http://
vpk.name/news/85870_primernyii_kolichestvennyii_sostav_vvs_rf_k_2020_godu
.htm.

——— 2014. *Razrabotchik fregatov proekta 11356 rassmatrivaet dva varianta zameny
ukrainskikh dvigatelei*. October 16. http://vpk.name/news/119510_razrabotchik_
fregatov_proekta_11356_rassmatrivaet_dva_varianta_zamenyi_ukrainskih_dvigatelei
.html.

——— 2015. *V Kolomne razrabotan dvigatel', kotoryi zamenit importnye analogi na korabliakh VMF RF*. June 19. http://vpk.name/news/134224_v_kolomne_razrabotan_
dvigatel_kotoryii_zamenit_importnyie_analogi_na_korablyah_vmf_rf.html.

VPK-news.ru. 2015. *Boleye 800 obraztsov oruzhiya i tekhniki iz Ukrainy, stran NATO i
YES budet zameshcheno*. July 16. https://vpk-news.ru/news/26152.

——— 2016. *Korvet 'Gremiashchii' gotoviat k montazhu glavnykh dvigatelei*. February 17.
http://vpk-news.ru/news/29265.

VTB Capital Research. 2013. Research note.

Vzglyad. 2015. *Rossiya reshila na 95% izbavit'sya ot zavisimosti ot ukrainskikh detaley
dlya OPK*. June 25. https://vz.ru/news/2014/6/24/692503.html.

——— 2017. *MID: Rossiya aktiviziruyet rabotu po sokrashcheniyu zavisimosti ot dollara*.
August 7. https://vz.ru/news/2017/8/7/881770.html.

Wegren, Stephen, Alexander Nikulin, and Irina Trotsuk. 2018. *Food Policy and Food
Security: Putting Food on the Russian Table*. Lanham: Lexington Books.

——— 2017. "The Russian Variant of Food Security." *Problems of Post-Communism* 64 (1):
47–62.

Wegren, Stephen, Frode Nilssen, and Elvestad, Christel. 2016. "The Impact of Russian
Food Security Policy on the Performance of the Food System." *Eurasian Geography and Economics* 57 (6): 671–699.

Weiss, Andrew, and Richard Nephew. 2016. *The Role of Sanctions in U.S.–Russian
Relations*. New York: Carnegie.

Wintour, Patrick. 2014. *Cameron Warns Putin as Russian President Lashes Sanctions*.
Guardian. November 25.

Witte, Griff, and Karen DeYoung. 2014. "Obama Announces Expanded Sanctions
against Russia as EU Aligns." *Washington Post*, July 29.

World Bank. 2017. *Development Indicators*. http://wdi.worldbank.org/table/WV.1.

Yakovlev, Andrei. 2014. "Russian Modernization: Between the Need for New Players
and the Fear of Losing Control of Rent Sources." *Journal of Eurasian Studies* 5 (1):
10–20.

Yakovlev, Andrei, Anton Sobolev, and Anton Kazun. 2014. "Means of Production
versus Means of Coercion: Can Russian Business Limit the Violence of a Predatory
State?" *Post-Soviet Affairs*, 30 (2–3): 171–194.

Yaramenko, Yuri. 1981. *Strukturnye izmeneniya v sotsialisticheskoi ekonomike*.
Moscow: Mysl.

Yedovina, Tatiyana, and Aleksei Shapovalov. 2015. "Gossovet sobral plody importoza-meshcheniya." *Kommersant*, November 26.

Yurgens, Igor. 2014. "The West vs. Russia: The Unintended Consequences of Targeted Sanctions." *The National Interest*, October 4.

Zamaraev, Boris, Anna Kiiutsevskaia, Angela Nazarova, and Evgeniy Sukhanov. 2013. "Zamedlenie e'konomicheskogo rosta v Rossii." *Voprosy Ekonomiki* (8): 4–34.

Zatsepin, Vasily. 2012. "The Economics of Russian Defense Policy: In Search for the Roots of Inefficiency." In *The Russian Armed Forces in Transition: Economic, Geopolitical, and Institutional Uncertainties*, by Roger McDermott, Bertil Nygren, and Carolina Vendil Pallin, 115–133. London and New York: Routledge.

2016. *The Specifics of the New State Program for the Development of the Military-Industrial Complex.* https://papers.ssrn.com/Sol3/papers.cfm?abstract_id=2841178.

Zhernov, Sergei. 2015. "Rossiyskiy antikrizis upirayetsya v importozameshcheniye." *Nezavisimaya Gazeta*, March 29.

Zubkov, Igor. 2017. *Karta "Mira".* November 7. https://rg.ru/2017/11/07/kartoj-mir-s-2018-goda-mozhno-budet-rasplachivatsia-po-telefonu.html.

Index